Edco Drama for Schools

William Shakespeare's

Othello

for Leaving Certificate

with annotations, analysis and commentary by
Patrick Murray

GW00547069

Edco

The Educational Company of Ireland

First published 2013

The Educational Company of Ireland
Ballymount Road
Walkinstown
Dublin 12

www.edco.ie

A member of the Smurfit Kappa Group plc

ISBN: 978-1-84536-554-7

The paper used in this book comes from Managed Forests in Northern Europe For every tree felled, at least one new tree is planted

Editor: Jennifer Armstrong

Proofreader: Eleanor Ashe

Design, layout and cover: Liz White Designs

Cover photography: Johan Persson/ArenaPAL/Topfoto

Photograph acknowledgements: Pages iv, 6, 13, 16, 41, 47, 67, 69, 94, 103, 107, 122, 138, 155, 158, 171, 189, 194, 195, 196, 199, 201, 202, 203, 204, 206, 210, 214, 219, 220, 234, 236: Arena PAL/Topfoto.

Pages 5, 23, 41, 58, 62, 76, 77, 82, 84, 110, 121, 149, 151, 158, 159, 168, 173, 188, 191, 198, 211, 216: photos by Karl Hugh, courtesy of the Utah Shakespeare Festival, 2008.

Pages 30, 97, 208, 218: photos by Karl Hugh, courtesy of the Utah Shakespeare Festival, 2002.

Page 39: SNAP/Rex Features.

Page 41: Simone Becchetti/iStockPhoto.

Pages 42, 76: Johan Persson, courtesy of the Crucible Theatre, Sheffield.

Pages 57, 76: Maisna/Shutterstock.

Pages 76, 121, 158, 188: Phant/Shutterstock.

Page 221: Nejron Photo/Shutterstock.

Page 209: Donald Cooper/Rex Features.

07J20

Preface

ALL MODERN STUDENTS OF Shakespeare's plays struggle with the difference between his language, particularly his diction, and present-day English. Some of the words in *Othello* are no longer in common use and some have different meanings from those they had when the play was written over four hundred years ago. On top of that, the syntax, or ordering of words, can be complex, even puzzling.

In response, this edition of *Othello* seeks to enlighten the reader by providing useful explanatory notes in the margins of the text, summaries for each scene and detailed commentary on the play. These features will ensure that students fully understand the text.

To appreciate *Othello*, we must think about what is happening to and within the characters, as revealed by their actions, dialogue, soliloquies and asides. The questions at the end of each scene and the activities at the end of each Act stimulate such thinking. They are designed to suit both Ordinary and Higher Level students. Detailed accounts of the characters are provided at the back of the book.

It is also important to be aware of the kind of world in which *Othello* was written (early seventeenth-century England) and the kind of world in which the play is set (sixteenth-century Venice and Cyprus). This book therefore includes information on the historical background to the action, and on the type of theatre and audience for which Shakespeare wrote.

All the major areas prescribed for study in the Leaving Certificate syllabus in relation to *Othello* are extensively covered. These include literary genre (i.e. tragedy), themes, imagery, general vision and viewpoint, roles of hero and villain, character change and development, and relationships between characters.

Colour photographs from various theatre and film productions of *Othello* are displayed throughout the book. These images remind students that they are reading a play and provide a chance to consider different casting and staging decisions.

To assist with revision and exam preparation, the book identifies the key moments in the play and highlights useful quotations. It also sets out the different stages in 'Iago's plot'. A final section is devoted to typical exam questions, accompanied by some tips and sample answers.

The approach taken to *Othello* in this edition will help students to:

- develop an appreciation of Shakespeare's use of language

- acquire a sound knowledge of the meaning of the text

- understand the workings of the plot

- recognise the play's tragic elements, themes, imagery and use of irony

- study the characters, their motives and their interactions with each other

- learn about the social, cultural and intellectual background to the play

- remember that *Othello* was written for performance rather than reading

- learn about the early seventeenth-century stage and Shakespeare's audience

- consider how the play might be performed and produced today.

Podcasts and additional revision material are available at **www.edco.ie/othello**

Teachers can access the *Othello* e-book and podcasts at **www.edcodigital.ie**

Contents

Introduction

About William Shakespeare

LITTLE IS KNOWN FOR certain about William Shakespeare. His father, John, moved to Stratford-upon-Avon in Warwickshire in the 1550s, practised a variety of trades, achieved prosperity, owned property and became a leading citizen of the town, which then had a population of about 1,000. William Shakespeare was christened in the parish church in Stratford on 26 April 1564.

It seems likely that Shakespeare went to the local grammar school until he was aged sixteen. However, the attendance records of the school have not been preserved. At that time a grammar school education focused on the study of the Latin language, its grammar and its literature, and rhetoric, the art of public speaking. Such training is evident in Shakespeare's plays.

In 1582 Shakespeare married Anne Hathaway. She was twenty-six years of age; he was eighteen. They had three children: Susanna and twins, Judith and Hamnet. Hamnet died in 1596, aged eleven. No record of Anne exists between the baptism of her children and the drafting of her husband's will in 1616, when he left her his second-best bed.

By the 1590s Shakespeare was an established actor and a promising dramatist, based in London. We do not know how he became a man of the theatre or when he left Stratford.

By 1595 he was a shareholder in an acting company. Two years later he was able to buy New Place, the second largest property in Stratford. He retired to Stratford in 1611, and died there in 1616.

Shakespeare combined his supreme creative ability with an impressive business sense. He wrote at least thirty-seven plays, including five tragic masterpieces: *Hamlet*, *Othello*, *King Lear*, *Macbeth* and *Anthony and Cleopatra*. He also wrote poetry and he contributed thousands of new words and phrases to the English language.

Records show him acquiring considerable property and shrewdly protecting his legal interests. He also purchased farmland and an interest in tithes, which guaranteed a substantial income. When debts owing to him remained unpaid, he was quick to sue the defaulters, even in petty cases.

About *Othello*

SHAKESPEARE DID NOT OVERSEE the printing of those editions of his plays published during his lifetime. Much of his work was still in manuscript form when he died, and remained so until two of his friends and colleagues published his plays in 1623 in an edition now known as the First Folio.

Othello was probably written between 1601 and 1604. It has been preserved in two separate printed versions: a Quarto, published in 1622, and the First Folio of 1623, which has about 160 lines not found in the earlier text.

It is likely that *Othello* was first performed at the Globe theatre in London. Its first recorded performance, however, was at the court of King James I on All Saints' Day (1 November) 1604, in the presence of the king and queen.

It proved immensely popular and was revived more often than any other tragedy until the theatres were closed in 1649.

The roles of Othello and Iago excited the imaginations of Shakespeare's contemporaries, particularly as Iago displays all the wicked characteristics that the seventeenth-century audience might have expected to find in Othello. Where they featured in plays before *Othello*, Moors were presented as diabolical characters.

About Shakespeare's theatre

THE THEATRES THAT HOSTED most of the early performances of *Othello* were public ones, such as the Globe theatre. Shakespeare was a shareholder in the Globe, which was situated close to the River Thames in Southwark, London. It opened in 1599.

A Dutch traveller called Johannes de Witt made a drawing around 1596 of London's Swan theatre. A copy of de Witt's drawing is shown here. It is the only surviving sketch of the interior of the kind of playhouse in which Shakespeare's plays were first performed. The Swan was quite a large theatre and de Witt estimated that it could hold 3,000 spectators.

The drawing, labelled in Latin, shows a round, open-air playhouse. The main feature is the large stage (*proscaenium*) with its overhead canopy known as 'the heavens'. The stage extends into an open yard, described as level ground without sand (*planities sine arena*).

For the price of a penny, spectators (called 'groundlings') stood in the yard looking up at the actors. There were also three tiers of galleries, where, for an extra penny or two, people could sit and avail of some shelter under the roof (*tectum*).

The wealthiest members of the audience wanted to see and also to be seen and therefore availed of a private box in a gallery above the stage. This gallery was part of the tiring-house (*mimorum ades*) building at the back of the stage. It housed a dressing area where actors changed their costumes or attire (hence the term 'tiring-house') and stored props.

The tiring-house was topped by a storage loft and a flagpole. A banner was hoisted to indicate that a play would be performed that afternoon. Different flags may have been used for different types of play, for example comedy or tragedy. The man shown outside the loft in the drawing appears to be sounding a trumpet.

Actors entered and exited the stage through two sets of large doors in the tiring-house façade. There was no painted scenery to indicate where the action was taking place. The audience members suspended their disbelief and understood the stage to be any place required by the action.

Women were not permitted to take part in dramatic performances and therefore female characters were played by boy-actors. A contemporary report of one performance indicated that the boy playing Desdemona moved the audience to tears.

Dramatists used language, costumes and props to set the scene. For example, the first scene of *Othello* is at night, but the performances in the playhouse took place in daylight. To overcome this, Shakespeare includes references to snoring citizens, officers of the night, etc. He also has the characters carry torches and Brabantio is wearing a nightgown.

Sometimes Shakespeare drew attention to the permanent structure of the theatre. For example, the underside of 'the heavens' was painted to represent the sky and the heavenly

Sketch of the interior of the Swan Theatre, by Johannes de Witt,
as copied by Aernout van Buchel, c. 1596.

KEY

1 Playhouse flag	**5** Tiring-house	**9** Entrance to lower gallery
2 Storage loft	**6** Stage doors	**10** Stage
3 The heavens	**7** Upper gallery	**11** Hell (under stage)
4 Gallery over stage	**8** Middle gallery	**12** Yard

bodies. In Act 3, Scene 3 Othello kneels and swears 'by yond marble heaven' as he looks upward (line 467). Iago then calls on the 'ever-burning lights above' as well as the 'elements that clip us round about' to witness his loyalty to Othello (lines 470, 471) – the 'lights' were painted on the canopy and the 'elements' were in the sky visible above the roofless theatre.

Audience members were trained listeners, and much better equipped than modern audiences to cope with Shakespeare's blank (unrhymed) verse and complex word order. For example, the majority enjoyed listening to and learning from very long church sermons. Such sermons featured magnificent passages of rhetoric, subtle argument and splendid imagery.

OTHELLO

Dramatis personae

OTHELLO a Moorish general in the military service of Venice

DESDEMONA his wife

CASSIO his lieutenant or deputy

IAGO his ensign or flagbearer

EMILIA Iago's wife

BIANCA a courtesan

RODERIGO a foolish gentleman

DUKE of Venice

BRABANTIO a Venetian senator, Desdemona's father

LODOVICO
GRATIANO } two noble Venetians, Brabantio's relatives

MONTANO governor of Cyprus

SENATORS of Venice

GENTLEMEN of Cyprus

SAILORS

CLOWN servant to Othello

OFFICERS

MESSENGER

HERALD

MUSICIANS

ATTENDANTS

ACT 1 ✟ Scene 1

Plot summary

IAGO, THE VILLAIN OF the play, and Roderigo, one of Iago's victims, are outside the house of a Venetian senator named Brabantio. It is late at night and Brabantio's daughter, Desdemona, has just eloped with Othello, a Moorish general in the service of Venice. Iago persuades Roderigo to wake Brabantio and tell him the news. At first Brabantio thinks Roderigo has come to woo Desdemona, and makes it clear that he does not approve of him. When he discovers the real purpose of the visit, he checks his house, finds Desdemona missing and goes off to seek help in tracing her. Meanwhile, Iago steals away to join Othello, to whom he will pretend to be loyal.

What is the reason of this terrible summons?
What is the matter there?

BRABANTIO, Act 1, Scene 1, 82–3

Venice. A street.

Enter RODERIGO and IAGO.

RODERIGO

Tush! never tell me; I take it much unkindly

That thou, Iago, who hast had my purse

As if the strings were thine, shouldst know of this.

IAGO

'Sblood, but you will not hear me,

If ever I did dream of such a matter,   5

Abhor me.

RODERIGO

Thou told'st me thou didst hold him in thy hate.

IAGO

Despise me if I do not. Three great ones of the city,

In personal suit to make me his lieutenant,

Off-capp'd to him, and, by the faith of man,   10

I know my price: I am worth no worse a place.

But he, as loving his own pride and purposes,

Evades them with a bombast circumstance,

Horribly stuff'd with epithets of war,

And in conclusion   15

Nonsuits my mediators. For 'Certes,' says he,

'I have already chose my officer.'

And what was he?

Forsooth, a great arithmetician,

One Michael Cassio, a Florentine,   20

A fellow almost damn'd in a fair wife,

That never set a squadron in the field,

Nor the division of a battle knows,

More than a spinster, unless the bookish theoric

Wherein the toga'd consuls can propose   25

As masterly as he. Mere prattle without practice

Is all his soldiership. But he, sir, had the election.

And I, of whom his eyes had seen the proof,

At Rhodes, at Cyprus and on other grounds,

Christian and heathen, must be be-lee'd and calm'd   30

By debitor and creditor. This counter-caster,

He in good time must his lieutenant be.

And I, God bless the mark, his worship's ancient.

1–3 These lines make sense if 'this' (line 3) refers to Othello's secret marriage. Roderigo rebukes Iago, to whom he has been extremely generous with his money, for not sharing this knowledge with him

4 *'Sblood:* by God's blood (an oath)

7 *him:* Othello

8 *great ... city:* influential citizens

9 *In ... lieutenant:* in their efforts to get Othello to make me [Iago] his lieutenant

10 *Off-capp'd:* often flattered; suggests the doffing of a cap as a token of respect

11 *worth ... place:* at least worthy of this position (as Othello's lieutenant)

12–14 *But ... war:* but Othello, full of his own importance, answers them in high-flown language, full of military terms, and ignores their pleas

16 *Nonsuits:* turns down
Certes: certainly

19 *Forsooth:* in truth
great arithmetician: Iago intends this as a term of abuse, implying that Cassio's military knowledge is purely theoretical

20 *Florentine:* native of Florence

21 *A fellow ... wife:* Iago suggests that a man who marries a pretty wife is damned, since he will be subject to jealousy and suspicion. However, Cassio is not married and 'wife' in Shakespeare can sometimes mean 'woman', in which case Iago may be suggesting that Cassio's fondness for pretty women will lead to his undoing

22–4 *That never ... theoric:* Cassio knows no more about devising a battle plan than a woman does, unless one is prepared to equate military expertise with knowledge derived merely from books. He is an armchair soldier; his knowledge is abstract rather than practical

25 *toga'd:* wearing togas (in the manner of Ancient Roman rulers during peacetime)

27 *had the election:* got the job

30–1 *be-lee'd ... creditor:* have the wind taken out of my sails (i.e. have my progress stopped) by an accountant

31 *counter-caster:* bookkeeper

33 *ancient:* a corruption of 'ensign' – standard-bearer (a lower rank of commissioned officer)

RODERIGO

By heaven, I rather would have been his hangman.

IAGO

35 Why, there's no remedy. 'Tis the curse of service:

Preferment goes by letter and affection,

And not by old gradation where each second

Stood heir to the first. Now, sir, be judge yourself,

Whether I in any just term am affin'd

40 To love the Moor.

RODERIGO

                I would not follow him then.

IAGO

O, sir, content you.

I follow him to serve my turn upon him.

We cannot be all masters, nor all masters

Cannot be truly follow'd. You shall mark

45 Many a duteous and knee-crooking knave

That, doting on his own obsequious bondage,

Wears out his time, much like his master's ass,

For nought but provender; and when he's old, cashier'd.

Whip me such honest knaves! Others there are

50 Who, trimm'd in forms and visages of duty,

Keep yet their hearts attending on themselves,

And throwing but shows of service on their lords

Do well thrive by 'em, and when they have lin'd their coats

Do themselves homage. These fellows have some soul;

55 And such a one do I profess myself. — For, sir,

It is as sure as you are Roderigo,

Were I the Moor, I would not be Iago.

In following him, I follow but myself.

Heaven is my judge, not I for love and duty,

60 But seeming so for my peculiar end.

For when my outward action doth demonstrate

The native act and figure of my heart

In complement extern, 'tis not long after

But I will wear my heart upon my sleeve

65 For daws to peck at. I am not what I am.

RODERIGO

What a full fortune does the thicklips owe

If he can carry't thus!

36–8 *Preferment ... first:* promotion depends on influence and favouritism, rather than on seniority. This is hypocritical as Iago has already admitted to using influential friends to try to assure his promotion

39 *affin'd:* bound, obliged

40 *the Moor:* Othello. 'Moor' refers to the mixed Berber and Arab people of north-west Africa. In Shakespeare's time this term may also have been used for a person from sub-Saharan Africa

42 *serve ... him:* use him for my own purposes

45–55 Iago contrasts two kinds of servant. The first, whom he despises, shows exaggerated respect and obedience to his master, gets nothing but his keep in return and is cast aside when he is no longer useful. The second, such as himself, puts on a convincing show of duty to his master, but keeps his own interests uppermost and profits considerably as a result

46 *obsequious bondage:* fawning, cringing slavery

48 *provender:* food
cashier'd: dismissed from service

49 *Whip ... knaves:* such honesty, in Iago's view, is deserving of a whipping

50 *trimm'd in forms:* putting on an impressive outward show
visages: masks

53 *lin'd their coats:* lined their pockets

57 *Were ... Iago:* a cryptic remark, perhaps meaning: If I were Othello, I would not have anything to do with Iago; or: If I were a general, I would not behave like a subordinate

58–60 *In following ... end:* I only appear to be a loyal and loving follower of Othello. I am really serving him for my own purposes

60 *peculiar:* own

61–5 *when ... peck at:* when my outward behaviour reflects the movements and intentions of my heart, it will not be long before I expose my thoughts and feelings to everyone and so become vulnerable to predatory persons

63 *complement extern:* outward show

65 *I am not what I am:* Iago means either that if he exposed his real self he would cease to be Iago, or that he is not what he seems

66–7 *What ... thus:* Othello is a lucky man if he can get away with it [marrying Desdemona] like this

IAGO

                  Call up her father,
Rouse him, make after him, poison his delight,
Proclaim him in the street, incense her kinsmen,
And though he in a fertile climate dwell,   70
Plague him with flies. Though that his joy be joy,
Yet throw such changes of vexation on't
As it may lose some colour.

RODERIGO

Here is her father's house. I'll call aloud.

IAGO

Do, with like timorous accent and dire yell   75
As when, by night and negligence, the fire
Is spied in populous cities.

RODERIGO

What ho! Brabantio, Signior Brabantio, ho!

IAGO

Awake, what ho, Brabantio! Thieves, thieves, thieves!
Look to your house, your daughter and your bags.   80
Thieves, thieves!

BRABANTIO at a window.

BRABANTIO

What is the reason of this terrible summons?
What is the matter there?

RODERIGO

Signior, is all your family within?

IAGO

Are your doors lock'd?

BRABANTIO

                Why, wherefore ask you this?   85

IAGO

Zounds, sir, you are robbed! For shame, put on your gown!
Your heart is burst, you have lost half your soul.
Even now, now, very now, an old black ram
Is tupping your white ewe. Arise, arise!
Awake the snorting citizens with the bell,   90
Or else the devil will make a grandsire of you.
Arise, I say.

---

67 *her father:* Desdemona's father, Brabantio

69 *incense her kinsmen:* enrage or exasperate her relatives

70–1 *though ... flies:* turn his good fortune to torment

71–3 *his joy ... colour:* his happiness is now genuine, yet we must do something to blight it

75–7 *Do ... cities:* call aloud, in the same fearful tones as would be used by someone calling attention to a fire in a densely populated city at night

80 *bags:* money bags

window: Shakespeare probably made use of the private gallery overlooking the stage to show that Brabantio has been woken from his sleep and is looking out a bedroom window to see what is going on

85 *Why:* this is a word of exclamation
wherefore ... this: for what reason do you ask me this question?

86 *Zounds:* by God's wounds (an oath)
gown: coat; senator's robes

89 *tupping:* covering

90 *snorting:* snoring

91 *devil ... of you:* the devil was thought of as black, so Iago thinks of Othello as a devil who will make Desdemona bear him a child and so make Brabantio a grandfather

BRABANTIO
What, have you lost your wits?

RODERIGO
Most reverend signior, do you know my voice?

BRABANTIO
Not I. What are you?

RODERIGO
95   My name is Roderigo.

BRABANTIO
           The worser welcome!
I have charg'd thee not to haunt about my doors.
In honest plainness thou hast heard me say
My daughter is not for thee; and now in madness,
Being full of supper and distempering draughts,
100   Upon malicious bravery, dost thou come
To start my quiet.

RODERIGO
Sir, sir, sir, …

BRABANTIO
         But thou must needs be sure,
My spirit and my place have in them power
To make this bitter to thee.

RODERIGO
            Patience, good sir.

BRABANTIO
105   What tell'st thou me of robbing? This is Venice,
My house is not a grange.

RODERIGO
          Most grave Brabantio,
In simple and pure soul I come to you.

IAGO
Zounds, sir, you are one of those that will not serve
God if the devil bid you. Because we come to do you
110   service, you think we are ruffians. You'll have your
daughter cover'd with a Barbary horse, you'll have
your nephews neigh to you, you'll have coursers for
cousins, and gennets for germans.

BRABANTIO
What profane wretch art thou?

---

99 *distempering draughts:* drink that has excited you

101 *start my quiet:* startle me from my rest

106 *a grange:* a remote house that is vulnerable to robbery

108–13 Iago switches from speaking blank verse (i.e. unrhymed iambic pentameter) to using everyday prose here, perhaps to conceal his identity
110 *service:* a favour
111 *Barbary horse:* Arab horse
112 *nephews:* grandsons
     coursers: swift horses
113 *gennets for germans:* small Spanish horses for blood relatives
114 *profane:* filthy, foul-mouthed

IAGO

I am one, sir, come to tell you your daughter and the   115
Moor are now making the beast with two backs.

BRABANTIO

Thou art a villain.

IAGO

You are a senator.

BRABANTIO

This thou shalt answer. I know thee, Roderigo.

RODERIGO

Sir, I will answer anything. But, I beseech you,   120
If't be your pleasure and most wise consent
(As partly I find it is) that your fair daughter,
At this odd-even and dull watch o' the night,
Transported with no worse nor better guard
But with a knave of common hire, a gondolier,   125
To the gross clasps of a lascivious Moor —
If this be known to you and your allowance,
We then have done you bold and saucy wrongs.
But if you know not this, my manners tell me
We have your wrong rebuke. Do not believe   130
That from the sense of all civility
I thus would play and trifle with your reverence.
Your daughter (if you have not given her leave,
I say again) hath made a gross revolt,
Tying her duty, beauty, wit and fortunes,   135
In an extravagant and wheeling stranger
Of here and everywhere. Straight satisfy yourself.
If she be in her chamber, or your house,
Let loose on me the justice of the state
For thus deluding you.

BRABANTIO

                Strike on the tinder, ho!   140
Give me a taper, call up all my people.
This accident is not unlike my dream;
Belief of it oppresses me already.
Light, I say, light!

Exit above.

---

116 *making ... backs:* one of Iago's many degraded images of human love; lovers are seen as no better than animals

121–8 *If't ... wrongs:* if, as I partly suspect, you approve of the fact that your daughter has been conveyed, between midnight and one o'clock ('odd-even') in the dead of night by a common gondolier to the arms of a lustful Moor, then we have treated you in an insolent way

125 *a knave ... gondolier:* a modern Roderigo might say that Othello brought her off in a taxi, rather than in his own car

127 *your allowance:* permitted by you

129–30 *my manners ... rebuke:* my sense of propriety tells me that you have rebuked us without just cause

131 *from ... civility:* neglecting civilised forms of behaviour

135 *wit:* intellect

136 *extravagant and wheeling:* vagrant, erratic

137 *Straight:* straightaway

140–1 *Strike ... taper:* strike a light there! Give me a candle

142 *accident:* happening

Exit above: Brabantio closes the window (or curtain) in the private gallery, disappearing from the audience's sight

IAGO

                                    Farewell, for I must leave you.

145 It seems not meet nor wholesome to my place

To be produc'd, as if I stay I shall,

Against the Moor, for I do know the state,

However this may gall him with some check,

Cannot with safety cast him, for he's embark'd,

150 With such loud reason, to the Cyprus wars,

Which even now stands in act, that, for their souls,

Another of his fathom they have not

To lead their business. In which regard,

Though I do hate him as I do hell's pains,

155 Yet for necessity of present life

I must show out a flag and sign of love,

Which is indeed but sign. That you shall surely find him,

Lead to the Sagitary the raised search,

And there will I be with him. So farewell.

Exit.

Enter BRABANTIO, in his night-gown, and ATTENDANTS with torches.

BRABANTIO

160 It is too true an evil. Gone she is;

And what's to come of my despised time

Is naught but bitterness. Now, Roderigo,

Where didst thou see her? — Oh unhappy girl! —

With the Moor, say'st thou? — Who would be a father? —

165 How didst thou know 'twas she? — O she deceives me

Past thought! — What said she to you? — Get more tapers,

Raise all my kindred. — Are they married, think you?

RODERIGO

Truly, I think they are.

BRABANTIO

O heaven, how got she out? O treason of the blood!

170 Fathers from hence, trust not your daughters' minds

By what you see them act. Is there not charms

By which the property of youth and maidhood

May be abus'd? Have you not read, Roderigo,

Of some such thing?

145–7 *It seems ... Moor:* in view of the position I hold, I do not think it appropriate that I should appear as a witness against Othello

147–9 *state ... cast him:* Venice, although it may hurt or annoy him with a reprimand, cannot, for its own safety, get rid of him

150 *loud reason:* strong backing of all reasonable judges

151 *stands in act:* are in full swing (the wars)

152 *fathom:* ability

153 *lead their business:* take charge of their military affairs

156 *show out a flag:* give a token

157–8 *That you ... search:* to be sure of finding him, lead the search party you have raised to the Sagitary Inn

159 *And ... him:* the details are reminiscent of the betrayal of Christ by Judas

Costumes and props are used here to remind the audience that it is night time

161 *despised time:* Brabantio is thinking of his future, when everybody will despise him because of Desdemona's elopement

166 *Past thought:* beyond belief

167 *Raise ... kindred:* call all my relatives

170 *from hence:* from now on

171 *charms:* magic spells

172 *property:* nature

173 *abus'd:* deceived

O that you had her!

BRABANTIO, Act 1, Scene 1, 176

RODERIGO

I have, sir.   175

BRABANTIO

Call up my brother. O that you had her!

Some one way, some another. Do you know

Where we may apprehend her and the Moor?

176 *O ... her:* compare Brabantio's flat rejection of Roderigo minutes earlier (line 98)

RODERIGO

I think I can discover him, if you please

To get good guard and go along with me.   180

179 *discover:* uncover

BRABANTIO

Pray lead me on. At every house I'll call,

I may command at most. Get weapons, ho!

And raise some special officers of night.

On, good Roderigo, I'll deserve your pains.

Exeunt.

182 *command at most:* demand with authority at most of the houses I call to

183 *officers of night:* officers specifically assigned to night duties

184 *deserve your pains:* reward you for your trouble

Exeunt: all characters leave the stage

Key points

This scene conveys much necessary information about the principal characters and their relationships.

- We learn that the foolish, deluded Roderigo has been making his money freely available to Iago so that the latter will help him to win the love of Desdemona. It is clear that Roderigo is no match for Iago in cunning and skill.

- We see that Iago has a talent for getting out of awkward situations. For example, Roderigo is understandably angry with Iago for not fulfilling his part of their bargain (lines 1–3), but Iago quickly turns the conversation by launching a vigorous verbal offensive against Othello, who has not yet been identified by name.

- We get a fairly full, but (as we will later discover) largely inaccurate, picture of Othello. Most of what we hear about him in this scene is unflattering: he is said to be unduly proud, to use inflated language and to stuff his speech with warlike terms.

- Iago accuses Othello of favouritism and poor judgement in appointing Cassio (rather than Iago) as his deputy. Iago considers himself better qualified for this senior military post. He claims that he has greater practical experience of war, whereas Cassio's knowledge of military affairs is derived from books.

- It is important to note that Iago's grievance about his failure to be promoted provides him with a motive for avenging himself on the man who failed to promote him (Othello) and the man who was promoted (Cassio).

- Iago's hatred of Othello can seem irrational, as when he presents him as 'an old black ram' (line 88).

- It is clear that there is some good in Othello. He has a mind of his own; he rejected the pleadings of three leading Venetians in support of Iago, instead appointing his choice, Cassio. Also, the Venetians cannot safely do without Othello's military experience and leadership, since they have nobody else of his depth of talent (lines 152–3) to lead them in the Cyprus wars.

- Brabantio emerges from this scene without credit. He quickly accepts Roderigo's sordid and distorted version of his daughter's relationship with Othello without looking for further evidence (line 160). Othello will behave in a similar fashion later, when he is confronted by Iago's charges against Cassio and Desdemona.

- The scene establishes an atmosphere of conflict and confusion, intrigue and deception.

- The real significance of the scene is its presentation of Iago's character. He is a trouble maker. His words and actions reveal his depraved mind, his fiendish ingenuity, his simmering hatred and his hypocrisy. For example: 'Though I do hate him … I must show out a flag and sign of love, which is indeed but sign' (lines 154–7).

- When challenged by Roderigo about Desdemona's elopement and marriage to Othello, Iago has to admit total ignorance of the event (lines 5–6). In other words, Iago is not in Othello's confidence. Worse still, from his point of view, a rival soldier, Cassio, obviously enjoys Othello's favour.

Useful quotes

> *I know my price: I am worth no worse a place.*
> *But he, as loving his own pride and purposes,*
> *Evades them with a bombast circumstance*
>
> (Iago, lines 11–13)

> *One Michael Cassio, a Florentine,*
> *A fellow almost damn'd in a fair wife,*
> *That never set a squadron in the field,*
> *Nor the division of a battle knows*
>
> (Iago, lines 20–3)

> *I follow him to serve my turn upon him.*
>
> (Iago, line 42)

> *What a full fortune does the thicklips owe*
> *If he can carry't thus!*
>
> (Roderigo, lines 66–7)

> *Another of his fathom they have not*
> *To lead their business.*
>
> (Iago, lines 152–3)

Questions ?

1 Describe the setting of this scene.

2 What did you learn from this scene about the relationship between Iago and Roderigo? Why, for example, does this relationship exist? Do these two characters need each other?

3 Look closely at the language used about Desdemona and Othello in this scene. What type of language is it?

4 Why are Iago and Roderigo discontented? What do you think might make them happy?

5 In what way is the news broken to Brabantio? What effect does this have on him?

6 On the evidence of this scene, what impression did you form of Brabantio?

7 Do you think that everything Iago says can be believed? Give reasons in support of your answer, based on this scene.

8 What does this scene tell you about Iago's opinion of himself?

9 Othello and Cassio have not yet appeared in person. Based on what you have heard about them so far, what do you expect them to be like when they act and speak for themselves?

10 Why does Iago leave the scene before the end? What does his exit tell us about him?

11 Discuss Iago's role in this scene. For example, you might consider how he manages events to his own advantage.

12 Imagine you are either Iago or Roderigo. Compose a diary entry giving your thoughts on the events recorded in this scene.

ACT 1 † Scene 2

Plot summary

IAGO APPEARS IN A different guise, as Othello's friend, pretending readiness to defend his master's honour. We know, but Othello does not, that Iago's account of what Brabantio actually said about Othello is far from the truth. Cassio arrives with an urgent summons from the Venetian Senate concerning the impending war with the Turks. Othello is confronted by Brabantio, Roderigo and their followers. Othello meets Brabantio's abusive threats with calm self-assurance. Since both men are required on urgent state business, the conflict between them is prevented from developing.

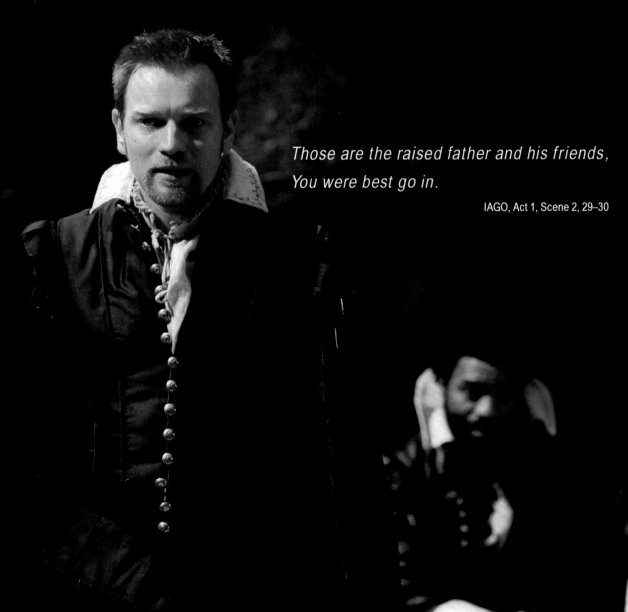

Those are the raised father and his friends,
You were best go in.

IAGO, Act 1, Scene 2, 29–30

Venice. Another street.

Enter OTHELLO, IAGO, and ATTENDANTS with torches.

IAGO

Though in the trade of war I have slain men,

Yet do I hold it very stuff of conscience

To do no contriv'd murder. I lack iniquity

Sometimes to do me service. Nine or ten times

I had thought to have yerk'd him here, under the ribs.   5

OTHELLO

'Tis better as it is.

IAGO

           Nay, but he prated,

And spoke such scurvy and provoking terms

Against your honour,

That with the little godliness I have

I did full hard forbear him. But I pray you, sir,   10

Are you fast married? For be sure of this,

That the magnifico is much belov'd,

And hath in his effect a voice potential

As double as the duke's; he will divorce you,

Or put upon you what restraint and grievance   15

That law (with all his might to enforce it on)

Will give him cable.

OTHELLO

           Let him do his spite.

My services, which I have done the signiory,

Shall out-tongue his complaints. 'Tis yet to know —

Which, when I know that boasting is an honour,   20

I shall provulgate — I fetch my life and being

From men of royal siege, and my demerits

May speak unbonneted to as proud a fortune

As this that I have reach'd. For know, Iago,

But that I love the gentle Desdemona,   25

I would not my unhoused free condition

Put into circumscription and confine

For the sea's worth. But look what lights come yond?

---

2   *very stuff of conscience:* the essence of a good person's practice

3   *contriv'd:* planned

3–4   *I lack … service:* I am sometimes not wicked enough to further my ends

5   *yerk'd him:* stabbed him (Brabantio)

6   Othello's simple, quiet reply is totally unlike the inflated mode of speech Iago earlier attributed to him

6   *prated:* prattled, babbled

7   *spoke … terms:* used such low, insulting and provocative expressions

10   *I did … him:* it was with difficulty that I spared him

11   *fast:* definitely

12   *the magnifico:* one of the chief men of Venice, here referring to Brabantio

13–14   *And hath … duke's:* he has as powerful an influence as that of the Duke of Venice. Various explanations have been offered for the phrase 'as double as', including: that double means large or extensive; and that Shakespeare imagined that the Duke of Venice had a casting vote, and therefore a double vote in a tie, meaning that Brabantio is as powerful as if he, too, had two votes

15–17   *put … cable:* impose the controls and harsh penalties on you that his considerable power will give him scope for

18–19   *My services … complaints:* my service to the governing body of Venice ('signiory') will carry greater weight than his accusations

21   *provulgate:* inform the common people of the facts

21–2   *I fetch … siege:* I am descended from kings ('siege' means throne)

22–4   *my demerits … reach'd:* my merits (or worth) quite entitle me to the exalted position I now enjoy

23   *unbonneted:* in all modesty

26   *unhoused free condition:* free and unconfined state of life (i.e. his status as a bachelor)

27   *Put … confine:* set boundaries or limits to

28   *the sea's worth:* all the treasure in the sea

29 *raised:* compare the spelling here with the use of an apostrophe in line 43 ('rais'd'). This is an example of how Shakespeare adapted words to maintain the rhythm of blank verse. The word should be spoken as two syllables here – raisèd – and as one syllable in line 43

31 *parts:* qualities, abilities
perfect soul: fully prepared soul

33 *Janus:* the two-faced Roman god; an appropriate deity for Iago to swear by

37 *haste post-haste:* speediest possible

38 *matter:* business

39 *divine:* guess or deduce

40 *heat:* urgency

41 *sequent:* one after another

43 *consuls:* senators

44 *hotly:* urgently

46 *sent … quests:* sent three different searches or search-parties about [or all over] the city

49 *makes he:* is he doing

IAGO
Those are the raised father and his friends,
30   You were best go in.

OTHELLO
                  Not I. I must be found.
My parts, my title and my perfect soul
Shall manifest me rightly. Is it they?

IAGO
By Janus, I think no.

Enter CASSIO, and OFFICERS with torches.

OTHELLO
The servants of the duke, and my lieutenant.
35   The goodness of the night upon you, friends!
What is the news?

CASSIO
              The duke does greet you, general,
And he requires your haste post-haste appearance,
Even on the instant.

OTHELLO
             What is the matter, think you?

CASSIO
Something from Cyprus, as I may divine.
40   It is a business of some heat. The galleys
Have sent a dozen sequent messengers
This very night, at one another's heels,
And many of the consuls, rais'd and met,
Are at the duke's already. You have been hotly call'd for,
45   When, being not at your lodging to be found,
The senate sent about three several quests
To search you out.

OTHELLO
          'Tis well I am found by you.
I will but spend a word here in the house
And go with you.

Exit.

CASSIO
          Ancient, what makes he here?

IAGO

Faith, he to-night hath boarded a land carrack.

If it prove lawful prize, he's made for ever.

50

CASSIO

I do not understand.

IAGO

He's married.

CASSIO

To who?

IAGO

Marry, to …

Enter OTHELLO.

Come, captain, will you go?

OTHELLO

Ha' with you.

CASSIO

Here comes another troop to seek for you.

Enter BRABANTIO, RODERIGO, and others, with torches and weapons.

IAGO

It is Brabantio, general, be advis'd

He comes to bad intent.

55

OTHELLO

Holla, stand there!

RODERIGO

Signior, it is the Moor.

BRABANTIO

Down with him, thief!

They draw on both sides.

IAGO

You, Roderigo, come sir, I am for you.

OTHELLO

Keep up your bright swords, for the dew will rust 'em;

Good signior, you shall more command with years

60

Than with your weapons.

---

50 *land carrack:* treasure ship, i.e. Desdemona

51 *If … prize:* if he is allowed to keep her

52 *To who:* as we discover in Act 3, Scene 3, Cassio was involved in Othello's courtship of Desdemona and therefore he may be assuming ignorance here to avoid betraying Othello's confidence

53 *Marry:* by the Virgin Mary (an oath)

53 *Ha' with you:* I'll go along with you

draw: take out their swords, ready to fight

58 *I am for you:* I will fight for you (Iago does not want his generous benefactor to come to harm)

59 *Keep … rust 'em:* put your shiny swords back in their scabbards; if they are to become rusty, it will be from the damp night air (i.e. not from blood or fighting)

60–1 *signior … weapons:* sir, your seniority will win more respect than your weapons will

BRABANTIO

O thou foul thief, where hast thou stow'd my daughter?

Damn'd as thou art, thou hast enchanted her.

For I'll refer me to all things of sense,

65   If she in chains of magic were not bound,

Whether a maid, so tender, fair and happy,

So opposite to marriage, that she shunn'd

The wealthy curled darlings of our nation,

Would ever have (to incur a general mock)

70   Run from her guardage to the sooty bosom

Of such a thing as thou, to fear, not to delight?

Judge me the world if 'tis not gross in sense

That thou hast practis'd on her with foul charms,

Abus'd her delicate youth with drugs or minerals

75   That weakens motion. I'll have't disputed on.

'Tis probable, and palpable to thinking.

I therefore apprehend and do attach thee

For an abuser of the world, a practiser

Of arts inhibited and out of warrant.

80   Lay hold upon him; if he do resist,

Subdue him at his peril.

OTHELLO

          Hold your hands,

Both you of my inclining, and the rest.

Were it my cue to fight, I should have known it

Without a prompter. Whither will you that I go

85   To answer this your charge?

BRABANTIO

          To prison, till fit time

Of law, and course of direct session,

Call thee to answer.

OTHELLO

        What if I do obey?

How may the duke be therewith satisfied,

Whose messengers are here about my side

90   Upon some present business of the state

To bear me to him?

OFFICER

        'Tis true, most worthy signior.

The duke's in council, and your noble self,

I am sure, is sent for.

---

62 *stow'd:* hidden

64 *I'll refer ... sense:* I appeal to those among you of normal intelligence

67 *opposite:* hostile

69 *incur ... mock:* undergo public ridicule

70 *her guardage:* my guardianship over her

71 *such ... delight:* Brabantio is calling Othello a thing to cause terror, not delight

72 *gross in sense:* obvious to the senses

75 *weakens motion:* deadens or dulls reactions
disputed on: argued, debated, dealt with

76 *'Tis ... thinking:* it can be proved, and would occur to anybody

77 *attach:* arrest

78 *abuser of the world:* person who corrupts society

79 *inhibited ... warrant:* forbidden and illegal

82 *Both ... rest:* both you who would support me, and those who are not on my side

84 *Whither:* to which place

86 *course ... session:* the normal legal process

90 *present:* urgent

BRABANTIO

How? The duke in council?

In this time of the night? Bring him away.

Mine's not an idle cause. The duke himself, 95

Or any of my brothers of the state,

Cannot but feel this wrong as 'twere their own.

For if such actions may have passage free,

Bond-slaves and pagans shall our statesmen be.

Exeunt.

95 *idle cause:* trivial, insignificant grievance

98 *may have passage free:* are allowed to go unpunished

99 *Bond-slaves and pagans:* Brabantio is making a slighting reference to Othello's origins, thereby showing his characteristic prejudice. Othello, however, is not a pagan

Key points

This scene throws considerable light on the character of Othello. Scene 1 prepared us for a boastful, vain, pompous and somewhat disreputable officer, who has run away at night with a senator's daughter. This picture of him gradually disintegrates.

- Othello's very first words, 'Tis better as it is' (line 6), carry a wealth of significance. Their restrained simplicity is in total contrast to the bombastic style Iago earlier attributed to him.

- Othello is a model of confidence. He loves Desdemona and is prepared to answer for his actions in any forum. He is secure in his position and in the rightness of all he has done.

- Given that Iago undermined Othello's honour in the opening scene, his role as its defender in this scene is an example of the irony he generates throughout the play. This scene serves as a warning about Iago's credibility. It helps us to realise that we are not to believe what he says (except in soliloquy) without testing his statements against other evidence.

- Othello's air of authority, quiet dignity and courteous behaviour are impressive. It is also to his credit that he finds needless violence repugnant. In contrast, Brabantio appears devoid of manners and good breeding and becomes almost hysterical with passion.

- Othello puts Brabantio in his place very firmly: 'Good signior, you shall more command with years than with your weapons' (lines 60–1). His response to Brabantio's insulting question, 'O thou foul thief, where hast thou stow'd my daughter?' (line 62), is beautifully controlled and reasonable. He will not be provoked.

- Othello stands apart from all those around him. He is a noble, romantic figure, commanding respect. He appears to have deep reserves of dignity and self-control.

Useful quotes

> But that I love the gentle Desdemona,
> I would not my unhoused free condition
> Put into circumscription and confine
> For the sea's worth.
>
> (Othello, lines 25–8)

> Keep up your bright swords, for the dew will rust 'em;
> Good signior, you shall more command with years
> Than with your weapons.
>
> (Othello, lines 59–61)

> Judge me the world if 'tis not gross in sense
> That thou hast practis'd on her with foul charms,
> Abus'd her delicate youth with drugs or minerals
>
> (Brabantio, lines 72–4)

Questions ?

1 How does the Othello we meet in this scene differ from the Othello described by Iago and Roderigo in the opening scene?

2 Are your first impressions of Othello favourable?

3 How does Othello view himself? How do we know?

4 Describe the relationship between Othello and Iago in this scene.

5 What is the importance of the Turkish threat to Cyprus? How does it affect Othello's position?

6 Give your opinion of Brabantio's attitudes as they emerge in this scene. Can you find anything to say in favour of Brabantio?

7 What props would be needed for this scene? What atmosphere do they create?

My noble father,
I do perceive here a divided duty

DESDEMONA, Act 1, Scene 3, 180–1

ACT 1 ✝ Scene 3

Plot summary

THE DUKE AND SENATORS consider the Turkish threat and discuss military action. These urgent matters are set aside when Othello, Brabantio and their followers arrive and the meeting turns into a tribunal of enquiry into Othello's conduct. The highlight of the scene is Othello's defence of what he has done. Desdemona also gives her account, which supports Othello's and indicates that the initiative for the marriage was as much hers as his. The Duke is convinced by what the lovers have said, and tries to persuade Brabantio to accept the marriage with good grace. Brabantio refuses to give his blessing, and instead issues a solemn warning to Othello not to take Desdemona's fidelity for granted. Othello is ordered by the Duke to go to Cyprus. Desdemona requests that she accompany Othello and is entrusted to the care of Iago for the journey.

The scene ends with an exposition of Iago's plans. He will maintain his hold over Roderigo (and his money) by keeping alive Roderigo's hopes of winning Desdemona. He will make Othello jealous by suggesting that Cassio is overly familiar with Desdemona.

Venice. A council chamber.

DUKE and SENATORS, sitting at a table with lights.
ATTENDANTS.

DUKE
There is no composition in these news
That gives them credit.

FIRST SENATOR
                 Indeed they are disproportion'd.
My letters say a hundred and seven galleys.

DUKE
And mine, a hundred and forty.

SECOND SENATOR
                    And mine, two hundred.

5 But though they jump not on a just account
(As in these cases, where the aim reports,
'Tis oft with difference), yet do they all confirm
A Turkish fleet, and bearing up to Cyprus.

DUKE
Nay, it is possible enough to judgement.

10 I do not so secure me in the error,
But the main article I do approve
In fearful sense.

SAILOR *[within]*
            What ho, what ho, what ho!

OFFICER
A messenger from the galleys.

Enter a SAILOR.

DUKE
                 Now, what's the business?

SAILOR
The Turkish preparation makes for Rhodes,
15 So was I bid report here, to the state,
By Signior Angelo.

DUKE
How say you by this change?

FIRST SENATOR

                     This cannot be,

By no assay of reason — 'tis a pageant

To keep us in false gaze. When we consider

The importancy of Cyprus to the Turk,   20

And let ourselves again but understand

That as it more concerns the Turk than Rhodes,

So may he with more facile question bear it,

For that it stands not in such warlike brace,

But altogether lacks the abilities   25

That Rhodes is dress'd in. If we make thought of this,

We must not think the Turk is so unskilful

To leave that latest which concerns him first,

Neglecting an attempt of ease and gain

To wake and wage a danger profitless.   30

DUKE

Nay, in all confidence, he's not for Rhodes.

OFFICER

Here is more news.

Enter a MESSENGER.

MESSENGER

The Ottomites, reverend and gracious,

Steering with due course toward the isle of Rhodes,

Have there injointed them with an after fleet …   35

FIRST SENATOR

Ay, so I thought. How many, as you guess?

MESSENGER

Of thirty sail, and now they do re-stem

Their backward course, bearing with frank appearance

Their purposes toward Cyprus. Signior Montano,

Your trusty and most valiant servitor,   40

With his free duty recommends you thus,

And prays you to believe him.

DUKE

'Tis certain then for Cyprus.

Marcus Luccicos, is not he in town?

---

18 *By … reason:* by any reasonable standard of judgement

19 *To keep … gaze:* designed to deceive us

22 *it more … Rhodes:* Cyprus is of greater interest and importance to the Turks than Rhodes is

23 *So may … bear it:* the Turks can capture Cyprus much more easily than they can capture Rhodes

24–6 *For … dress'd in:* Cyprus is not ready for war or in the good state of defensive preparation that Rhodes is endowed with

28 *latest:* last

29–30 *Neglecting … profitless:* not attacking a place that would fall easily to them, while at the same time risking defeat against a stronger enemy

31 *Nay … Rhodes:* indeed, I am sure the Turks are not heading for Rhodes

33 *Ottomites:* Turks
reverend and gracious: this refers to the Duke, not to the Turks

35 *injointed them:* joined up
after fleet: the fleet following the first one

37 *re-stem:* steer again

38–9 *bearing … Cyprus:* heading very obviously towards Cyprus

41 *With … recommends:* with boundless respect informs

44 *Marcus Luccicos:* possibly a Cypriot who might have useful local knowledge

FIRST SENATOR

45 He's now in Florence.

DUKE

Write from us to him post post-haste, dispatch!

FIRST SENATOR

Here comes Brabantio and the valiant Moor.

Enter BRABANTIO, OTHELLO, CASSIO, IAGO, RODERIGO, and OFFICERS.

DUKE

Valiant Othello, we must straight employ you

Against the general enemy Ottoman.

50 *[to Brabantio]* I did not see you. Welcome, gentle signior,

We lack'd your counsel and your help to-night.

BRABANTIO

So did I yours. Good your grace, pardon me.

Neither my place nor aught I heard of business

Hath rais'd me from my bed, nor doth the general care

55 Take hold on me, for my particular grief

Is of so flood-gate and o'erbearing nature

That it engluts and swallows other sorrows,

And it is still itself.

DUKE

Why, what's the matter?

BRABANTIO

My daughter! O my daughter!

ALL

Dead?

BRABANTIO

Ay, to me.

60 She is abus'd, stol'n from me and corrupted

By spells and medicines bought of mountebanks.

For nature so preposterously to err,

Being not deficient, blind or lame of sense,

Sans witchcraft could not.

DUKE

65 Whoe'er he be that in this foul proceeding

Hath thus beguil'd your daughter of herself,

And you of her, the bloody book of law

---

46 *Write ... post-haste:* the Duke is directing that Marcus Luccicos be written to immediately
dispatch: make haste

49 *Ottoman:* Turk

53 *place:* official position
aught: anything

54 *general care:* problems confronting the state

55–7 *my particular ... sorrows:* my personal grief is so overwhelming that it absorbs all other sorrows

61 *mountebanks:* travelling dealers in illegal medicines, quacks

62–4 *For ... could not:* since Desdemona has full use of her senses, her nature could not make so absurd an error as this without ('sans') being subjected to witchcraft

65–70 *Whoe'er ... action:* whoever it is that in this disgraceful way has deprived your daughter of her judgement and robbed you of your daughter, you will have the strictest justice against him, even if your action is against my own son

You shall yourself read in the bitter letter
After your own sense, though our proper son
Stood in your action.

BRABANTIO
      Humbly I thank your grace. 70
Here is the man, this Moor, whom now it seems
Your special mandate for the state-affairs
Hath hither brought.

ALL
     We are very sorry for't.

DUKE
[to Othello] What in your own part can you say to this?

BRABANTIO
Nothing, but this is so. 75

OTHELLO
Most potent, grave and reverend signiors,
My very noble and approv'd good masters:
That I have ta'en away this old man's daughter,
It is most true. True, I have married her.
The very head and front of my offending 80
Hath this extent, no more. Rude am I in my speech,
And little blessed with the soft phrase of peace,
For since these arms of mine had seven years' pith
Till now some nine moons wasted, they have us'd
Their dearest action in the tented field, 85
And little of this great world can I speak
More than pertains to feats of broil and battle,
And therefore little shall I grace my cause
In speaking for myself. Yet, by your gracious patience,
I will a round unvarnish'd tale deliver, 90
Of my whole course of love, what drugs, what charms,
What conjuration and what mighty magic,
For such proceeding I am charged withal,
I won his daughter …

BRABANTIO
     A maiden never bold,
Of spirit so still and quiet that her motion 95
Blush'd at herself. And she, in spite of nature,

72 *mandate:* commission

80–1 *The very … more:* this is the height or full extent of my offence
81 *Rude:* plain
82 *little … peace:* I have little grace or eloquence of speech
83 *pith:* strength
84 *wasted:* past. Othello is saying that he had been in continuous warlike activity until nine months ago
85 *dearest:* most important, most significant
tented field: battlefield
87 *broil:* turmoil, violence

90 *round unvarnish'd tale:* plain, blunt story

92 *conjuration:* magic spell
93 *withal:* with

95–6 *her motion … herself:* Brabantio thinks of Desdemona as so unobtrusive and unassuming that her ordinary movements caused her to blush

97 *credit:* reputation

99–103 *It is … should be:* anybody who claims that so perfect a creature as Desdemona would act in so unnatural a way [as to elope with Othello] must have poor ('maim'd') judgement, and therefore the only logical conclusion is that hellish stratagems are responsible for her actions

105 *dram … effect:* dose (of the 'mixtures powerful') deriving its effect from magic spells

106 *wrought:* worked

106–9 *To vouch … him:* your assertions do not amount to proof; without more certain and objective testimony, the accusations you bring against him are shaky and flimsy; they are untested, commonplace suspicions and hypotheses

111 *indirect … courses:* wrong, unjust and devious procedures

113–14 *Or came … affordeth:* or did she agree to marry you as a result of your pleading, and the kind of fair discussion ('question') that one gets between two free people?

115 *Sagitary:* presumably the inn where Othello and Desdemona are staying

117 *foul:* false, dishonest

121 This line is addressed to Iago

123 *I do … blood:* Othello is a Christian and is ready to confess his serious sins

Of years, of country, credit, everything,

To fall in love with what she fear'd to look on?

It is a judgement maim'd and most imperfect

100 That will confess perfection so would err

Against all rules of nature, and must be driven

To find out practices of cunning hell

Why this should be. I therefore vouch again,

That with some mixtures powerful o'er the blood,

105 Or with some dram conjured to this effect,

He wrought upon her.

DUKE
                To vouch this is no proof,

Without more certain and more overt test.

These are thin habits, and poor likelihoods

Of modern seemings, you prefer against him.

FIRST SENATOR

110 But, Othello, speak.

Did you by indirect and forced courses

Subdue and poison this young maid's affections?

Or came it by request and such fair question

As soul to soul affordeth?

OTHELLO
                I do beseech you,

115 Send for the lady to the Sagitary

And let her speak of me before her father.

If you do find me foul in her report,

The trust, the office, I do hold of you,

Not only take away, but let your sentence

120 Even fall upon my life.

DUKE
                Fetch Desdemona hither.

OTHELLO

Ancient, conduct them, you best know the place.

Exeunt ATTENDANTS and IAGO.

And till she come, as faithful as to heaven

I do confess the vices of my blood,

So justly to your grave ears I'll present

125 How I did thrive in this fair lady's love,

And she in mine.

DUKE
Say it, Othello.

OTHELLO
Her father lov'd me, oft invited me,
Still question'd me the story of my life,
From year to year, the battles, sieges, fortunes,   130
That I have pass'd.
I ran it through, even from my boyish days,
To the very moment that he bade me tell it.
Wherein I spake of most disastrous chances;
Of moving accidents by flood and field;   135
Of hair-breadth 'scapes i' th' imminent deadly breach;
Of being taken by the insolent foe
And sold to slavery, and my redemption thence;
And with it all my travels' history;
Wherein of antres vast and deserts idle,   140
Rough quarries, rocks and hills, whose heads
          touch heaven,
It was my hint to speak. Such was the process.
And of the cannibals that each other eat,
The Anthropophagi, and men whose heads
Grew beneath their shoulders. These things to hear   145
Would Desdemona seriously incline,
But still the house-affairs would draw her thence,
And ever as she could with haste dispatch,
She'ld come again and with a greedy ear
Devour up my discourse, which I observing,   150
Took once a pliant hour, and found good means
To draw from her a prayer of earnest heart
That I would all my pilgrimage dilate,
Whereof by parcels she had something heard,
But not intentively. I did consent,   155
And often did beguile her of her tears,
When I did speak of some distressful stroke
That my youth suffer'd. My story being done,
She gave me for my pains a world of sighs.
She swore i' faith 'twas strange, 'twas passing strange;   160
'Twas pitiful, 'twas wondrous pitiful.

---

129 *Still question'd me:* always asked me about

132 *ran it through:* told the story of it

134 *chances:* happenings, events

135 *moving ... field:* exciting adventures on water and land
136 *imminent:* threatening

138 *my redemption thence:* my being set free from there (i.e. from slavery through the payment of a ransom)

140 *antres ... idle:* huge caves and empty deserts

142 *hint:* opportunity
process: story

144 *Anthropophagi:* cannibals. Shakespeare is drawing on contemporary travellers' tales

146 *seriously incline:* greatly desire

149 *She'ld come again:* she would come back

151 *pliant:* favourable

153 *all ... dilate:* narrate at length the story of my life

154–5 *Whereof ... intentively:* she had heard separate parts of his story, but not a continuous narrative

156 *did beguile ... tears:* drew tears from her

157 *distressful stroke:* hurtful blow

160 *passing:* very

161 *wondrous:* exceedingly

I think this tale would win my daughter, too.

DUKE OF VENICE, Act 1, Scene 3, 171

She wish'd she had not heard it, yet she wish'd

That heaven had made her such a man. She thank'd me

And bade me, if I had a friend that loved her,

I should but teach him how to tell my story   165

And that would woo her. Upon this hint I spake.

She loved me for the dangers I had pass'd,

And I loved her that she did pity them.

This only is the witchcraft I have us'd.

Here comes the lady. Let her witness it.   170

Enter DESDEMONA, IAGO, and ATTENDANTS.

DUKE

I think this tale would win my daughter, too.

Good Brabantio,

Take up this mangled matter at the best;

Men do their broken weapons rather use

Than their bare hands.

BRABANTIO

              I pray you hear her speak.   175

If she confess that she was half the wooer,

Destruction on my head if my bad blame

Light on the man! Come hither, gentle mistress:

Do you perceive in all this noble company

Where most you owe obedience?

DESDEMONA

              My noble father,   180

I do perceive here a divided duty:

To you I am bound for life and education,

My life and education both do learn me

How to respect you: you are lord of all my duty,

I am hitherto your daughter; but here's my husband,   185

And so much duty as my mother show'd

To you, preferring you before her father,

So much I challenge that I may profess

Due to the Moor my lord.

BRABANTIO

              God bu'y, I ha' done.

Please it your grace, on to the state-affairs.   190

I had rather to adopt a child than get it.

Come hither, Moor,

162–3 *yet ... man:* the most likely meaning here is that Desdemona is wishing that she was a man as brave as Othello. An alternative is that Desdemona is wishing that heaven had made such a man as Othello for her; however, this does not accord well with the impression already given of Desdemona's reserved, bashful manner

173 *Take ... best:* make the best of a bad job

180 *obedience:* women were considered inferior to men and were required to be obedient to their father, and later, if they married, to their husband

183 *learn:* teach

184 *lord ... duty:* Desdemona cannot mean that she regards her father as her lord and master. The duty in question is the duty a good daughter owes to her father. She made it clear a few lines earlier that her duty must now be divided between Othello and her father

189 *God bu'y:* God be with you

193–5 *I here ... from thee:* I am willingly giving you what I would willingly deprive you of if you didn't have it already

197–8 *For thy ... 'em:* if I had other children, I would become a tyrant and keep them in chains, now that you have eloped

199–209 *Let ... grief:* let me adopt your own pompous style, and offer a maxim ('sentence') to act as a guide that may help to give you a more favourable view of these lovers. Four related maxims (propositions expressing some general truth or laying down principles of conduct) complete the Duke's speech. His point is that we should not grieve over losses that we cannot recover or restore

202–3 *When ... depended:* when we have looked forward in hope, only to find our hopes dashed, our sorrows should cease because they are futile

204–5 *To mourn ... on:* the surest way to bring new problems on our heads is to lament over wrongs that cannot be righted

206–7 *What ... makes:* when fortune deprives us of something we value, patience comes to our aid by enabling us to bear our loss with indifference

209 *He ... grief:* the man who spends his time in pointless grief over his losses robs himself of his peace of mind

210–15 Brabantio offers his own maxims to contradict the Duke's and to illustrate how useful, or useless, a maxim can be in reconciling him to his loss

210–11 *let ... smile:* let the Turks rob us of Cyprus; as long as we can smile at our loss, we shall not really have lost at all

212–15 *He bears ... borrow:* it is relatively easy for a person to listen to consoling maxims if the predicament to which they refer is not his; the man to be pitied is the one who suffers grief and who must have the patience to bear it

216–17 *These ... equivocal:* maxims are ambiguous; they can offer either comfort or pain

218–19 *I never ... ear:* I have never heard of a heart bruised by grief being relieved ('pierced' means lanced) by mere words

222 *fortitude:* strength

223–4 *substitute ... sufficiency:* deputy acknowledged as fit for his job

224–5 *yet ... on you:* the majority view, which ultimately decides on what is to be done, is that we are safer with you in charge

226–8 *be content ... expedition:* be prepared to forgo the glory of your fortunate union with Desdemona in favour of this rough and violent enterprise

226 *slubber:* sully, smear over

I here do give thee that with all my heart
Which, but thou hast already, with all my heart
195 I would keep from thee. For your sake, jewel,
I am glad at soul I have no other child,
For thy escape would teach me tyranny,
To hang clogs on 'em. I have done, my lord.

DUKE
Let me speak like yourself, and lay a sentence
200 Which, as a grise or step, may help these lovers
Into your favour.
When remedies are past, the griefs are ended
By seeing the worst which late on hopes depended.
To mourn a mischief that is past and gone
205 Is the next way to draw more mischief on.
What cannot be preserv'd when fortune takes,
Patience her injury a mockery makes.
The robb'd that smiles steals something from the thief;
He robs himself that spends a bootless grief.

BRABANTIO
210 So let the Turk of Cyprus us beguile,
We lose it not so long as we can smile.
He bears the sentence well that nothing bears
But the free comfort which from thence he hears,
But he bears both the sentence and the sorrow
215 That, to pay grief, must of poor patience borrow.
These sentences to sugar, or to gall,
Being strong on both sides, are equivocal.
But words are words; I never yet did hear
That the bruised heart was pierced through the ear.
220 Beseech you now, to the affairs of state.

DUKE
The Turk with most mighty preparation makes for Cyprus. Othello, the fortitude of the place is best known to you, and though we have there a substitute of most allowed sufficiency, yet opinion, a sovereign
225 mistress of effects, throws a more safer voice on you. You must therefore be content to slubber the gloss of your new fortunes with this more stubborn and boisterous expedition.

OTHELLO

The tyrant custom, most grave senators,

Hath made the flinty and steel couch of war   230

My thrice-driven bed of down. I do agnize

A natural and prompt alacrity

I find in hardness, and would undertake

This present war against the Ottomites.

Most humbly therefore, bending to your state,   235

I crave fit disposition for my wife,

Due reference of place and exhibition,

With such accommodation and besort

As levels with her breeding.

DUKE

                              If you please,

Be't at her father's.

BRABANTIO

                        I'll not have it so.   240

OTHELLO

Nor I.

DESDEMONA

          Nor I. I would not there reside,

To put my father in impatient thoughts

By being in his eye. Most gracious duke,

To my unfolding lend a gracious ear

And let me find a charter in your voice,   245

And if my simpleness …

DUKE

What would you? Speak.

DESDEMONA

That I did love the Moor to live with him,

My downright violence and scorn of fortunes

May trumpet to the world. My heart's subdued   250

Even to the utmost pleasure of my lord.

I saw Othello's visage in his mind,

And to his honours and his valiant parts

Did I my soul and fortunes consecrate;

So that, dear lords, if I be left behind,   255

A moth of peace, and he go to the war,

The rites for which I love him are bereft me,

229–34 *The tyrant … Ottomites:* Othello tells the senators that force of habit has made battle conditions agreeable to him; he accepts the spartan life of the warrior with enthusiasm, which is why he is ready to serve against the Turks

231 *thrice-driven bed of down:* the softest of feather beds
agnize: acknowledge

232 *alacrity:* eagerness

236 *fit disposition:* suitable arrangements

237 *exhibition:* funds

238 *besort:* company

239 *levels … breeding:* suits or is appropriate to a person of her birth

240 *Be't:* let it be

244 *To my … ear:* listen favourably to my explanation

245 *find … voice:* hear you grant me permission

248–59 *That I … absence:* my bold action and contempt for fortune provide impressive public evidence that I love Othello enough to want to live with him. I am entirely his; I have dedicated all that I am and have to his honour and valour. If I am left behind to languish in peace while he is at war, I shall be deprived of my rights as a wife, and find his absence a burden

And I a heavy interim shall support

By his dear absence. Let me go with him.

OTHELLO

260   Your voices, lords, beseech you, let her will

Have a free way. I therefore beg it not

To please the palate of my appetite,

Nor to comply with heat, the young effects

In me defunct, and proper satisfaction,

265   But to be free and bounteous to her mind.

And heaven defend your good souls that you think

I will your serious and great business scant

For she is with me. No, when light-winged toys

And feather'd Cupid foils with wanton dullness

270   My speculative and active instruments,

That my disports corrupt and taint my business,

Let housewives make a skillet of my helm,

And all indign and base adversities

Make head against my reputation!

DUKE

275   Be it as you shall privately determine,

Either for her stay or going. Th'affair cries haste,

And speed must answer; you must hence to-night.

DESDEMONA

To-night, my Lord?

DUKE

               This night.

OTHELLO

                    With all my heart.

DUKE

At ten i' the morning here we'll meet again.

280   Othello, leave some officer behind

And he shall our commission bring to you,

With such things else of quality and respect

As doth import you.

OTHELLO

              Please your grace, my ancient,

A man he is of honesty and trust,

261–74 *I therefore ... reputation:* I am not asking this favour in order to gratify my sexual appetites, which are anyway not those of a young man, but to share her conversation. May heaven forgive you if you think I will neglect your affairs of state because she is with me. When the pleasures of love impair or subjugate my spiritual and bodily faculties, so that my pastimes prevent me from performing my public duties properly, let me become an object of ridicule

264 *defunct:* put aside, laid aside

268 *light-winged toys:* airy trifles

269 *wanton dullness:* listlessness or lethargy of body or mind, due to over-indulgence

271 *disports:* pleasures

272 *make ... helm:* make a saucepan of my helmet

273–4 *indign ... reputation:* shameful and low accusations from enemies damage my good name

277 *hence:* go from here

278 Shakespeare mostly wrote in blank verse, i.e. unrhymed iambic pentameters. Each line has five stressed syllables and five unstressed syllables. Here, the line is divided between three speakers, suggesting fast-moving dialogue. Shakespeare used blank verse flexibly to create variations in rhythm and pace

282–3 *With such ... you:* with further details of your rank and status

283 *import:* concern

284 *honesty:* this is the first of many uses of this word by Othello in relation to Iago; the attribution of honesty to Iago is one of the major ironies of the play. Dramatic irony occurs when the audience knows more about a character's situation than the character does

To his conveyance I assign my wife,   285

With what else needful your good grace shall think

To be sent after me.

DUKE

                Let it be so.

Good night to every one. And, noble signior,

If virtue no delighted beauty lack,

Your son-in-law is far more fair than black.   290

FIRST SENATOR

Adieu, brave Moor, use Desdemona well.

BRABANTIO

Look to her, Moor, if thou hast eyes to see,

She has deceived her father, and may thee.

Exeunt DUKE, CASSIO, SENATORS, and OFFICERS.

OTHELLO

My life upon her faith. Honest Iago,

My Desdemona must I leave to thee;   295

I prithee let thy wife attend on her,

And bring her after in the best advantage.

Come, Desdemona, I have but an hour

Of love, of worldly matters, and direction,

To spend with thee. We must obey the time.   300

Exeunt OTHELLO and DESDEMONA.

RODERIGO

Iago!

IAGO

What sayest thou, noble heart?

RODERIGO

What will I do, think'st thou?

IAGO

Why, go to bed and sleep.

RODERIGO

I will incontinently drown myself.   305

IAGO

Well, if thou dost, I shall never love thee after. Why,

thou silly gentleman?

---

285 *conveyance:* guardianship

289–90 *If virtue … black:* if virtue possesses every delightful quality, then Othello, being the epitome of virtue, belies his outward appearance. In Shakespeare's time fairness was thought of as beautiful and blackness as ugly

294 *My … Iago:* here is the central theme of the play, epitomised in seven simple words laden with dramatic irony. There is irony in Othello's expressing his total trust in Desdemona's faith while at the same time expressing his absolute faith in Iago's honesty. He does not know the true accuracy of his words. Both terms of Othello's wager ironically come true: she is faithful, and Othello pays with his life for doubting her

296 *I prithee:* please

297 *in … advantage:* at the most suitable opportunity

300 *obey the time:* adjust to the situation

305 *incontinently:* immediately

[handwritten annotation: She deceived her father so she might deceive him]

OTHELLO **35**

309–10 *then ... physician:* if death will take us out of our misery, then we have every right to wish for death

314 *Ere:* before

315 *guinea-hen:* any woman. Iago does not see women, or indeed men, in a very flattering light

318 *fond:* infatuated

319 *fig:* worthless thing

322 *set hyssop:* plant hyssop (a herb)

323 *gender:* kind
distract: vary

324–5 *manur'd with industry:* cultivated through hard work
325 *corrigible authority:* the ability to correct or control
326–9 *If ... conclusions:* if our rational faculties did not counterbalance our sensual instincts, then our baser passions would encourage us to the most preposterous experiments

330–1 *our raging ... lusts:* our fierce impulses, our compelling desires, our unbridled lusts

332 *sect or scion:* cutting or shoot (terms from horticulture). Love is, for Iago, merely an offshoot of base desires ('a lust of the blood' as he describes it in his next speech)

337 *knit to thy deserving:* dedicated to earning your good will
perdurable: everlasting
338 *stead:* help

RODERIGO

It is silliness to live, when to live is a torment; and then we have a prescription to die, when death is our
310 physician.

IAGO

O villainous! I ha' look'd upon the world for four times seven years, and since I could distinguish between a benefit and an injury, I never found a man that knew how to love himself. Ere I would say I would drown
315 myself for the love of a guinea-hen, I would change my humanity with a baboon.

RODERIGO

What should I do? I confess it is my shame to be so fond, but it is not in my virtue to amend it.

IAGO

Virtue? A fig! 'Tis in ourselves that we are thus, or
320 thus. Our bodies are our gardens, to the which our wills are gardeners: so that if we will plant nettles, or sow lettuce, set hyssop and weed up thyme, supply it with one gender of herbs or distract it with many, either to have it sterile with idleness or manur'd with
325 industry, why, the power, and corrigible authority of this, lies in our wills. If the balance of our lives had not one scale of reason to poise another of sensuality, the blood and baseness of our natures would conduct us to most preposterous conclusions. But we have
330 reason to cool our raging motions, our carnal stings, our unbitted lusts; whereof I take this that you call love to be a sect or scion.

RODERIGO

It cannot be.

IAGO

It is merely a lust of the blood and a permission of the
335 will. Come, be a man! Drown thyself? Drown cats and blind puppies! I profess me thy friend, and I confess me knit to thy deserving with cables of perdurable toughness. I could never better stead thee than now. Put money in thy purse; follow these wars;

defeat thy favour with an usurp'd beard. I say, put money in thy purse. It cannot be that Desdemona should long continue her love unto the Moor — put money in thy purse — nor he to her; it was a violent commencement, and thou shalt see an answerable sequestration: put but money in thy purse. These Moors are changeable in their wills — fill thy purse with money. The food that to him now is as luscious as locusts, shall be to him shortly as acerb as the coloquintida. When she is sated with his body, she will find the error of her choice; she must have change, she must. Therefore put money in thy purse. If thou wilt needs damn thyself, do it a more delicate way than drowning: make all the money thou canst. If sanctimony and a frail vow betwixt an erring barbarian and a super-subtle Venetian be not too hard for my wits, and all the tribe of hell, thou shalt enjoy her. Therefore make money. A pox o' drowning, 'tis clean out of the way; seek thou rather to be hang'd in compassing thy joy than to be drown'd and go without her.

RODERIGO

Wilt thou be fast to my hopes if I depend on the issue?

IAGO

Thou art sure of me — go, make money — I have told thee often, and I tell thee again, and again, I hate the Moor. My cause is hearted, thine hath no less reason. Let us be communicative in our revenge against him: if thou canst cuckold him, thou doest thyself a pleasure, me a sport. There are many events in the womb of time which will be delivered. Traverse, go, provide thy money! We will have more of this to-morrow. Adieu.

RODERIGO

Where shall we meet i' the morning?

IAGO

At my lodging.

RODERIGO

I'll be with thee betimes.

---

340 *defeat ... beard:* change your appearance for the worse with a false beard

343–5 *it was ... sequestration:* their love began with a violent suddenness, and it will end in a correspondingly violent separation

349 *acerb:* bitter
coloquintida: apple with a sour taste
sated: satisfied to the full

354–6 *sanctimony ... Venetian:* a holy rite [the marriage service] and a weak vow [Iago's description of the marriage vow] between a vagrant savage and an excessively refined Venetian

358 *'tis ... way:* you are on the wrong track (if you are thinking of drowning yourself)

358–60 *seek ... without her:* it would be better for you to risk hanging in trying to have Desdemona for yourself, than to drown yourself thinking she is beyond your reach

361 *Wilt ... issue:* will you firmly support my hope [of winning Desdemona], as I depend upon this outcome?

364 *hearted:* deeply felt. Iago is ready to pursue his cause (his vendetta against Othello for not promoting him) with vigour and enthusiasm

365 *be communicative:* work together, exchanging ideas

366 *cuckold him:* make his wife unfaithful to him

368 *Traverse:* an order to march

373 *betimes:* early

IAGO

Go to, farewell. Do you hear, Roderigo?

RODERIGO

375   What say you?

IAGO

No more of drowning, do you hear?

RODERIGO

I am chang'd.

IAGO

Go to, farewell! Put money enough in your purse.

Exit RODERIGO.

Thus do I ever make my fool my purse.

380   For I mine own gain'd knowledge should profane,

If I would time expend with such a snipe,

But for my sport and profit. I hate the Moor,

And it is thought abroad that 'twixt my sheets

He's done my office; I know not if't be true,

385   Yet I, for mere suspicion in that kind,

Will do, as if for surety — he holds me well,

The better shall my purpose work on him.

Cassio's a proper man; let me see now,

To get his place and to plume up my will

390   In double knavery. How? How? Let's see.

After some time, to abuse Othello's ear

That he is too familiar with his wife —

He has a person and a smooth dispose,

To be suspected, fram'd to make women false.

395   The Moor is of a free and open nature

That thinks men honest that but seem to be so

And will as tenderly be led by the nose …

As asses are.

I have't. It is engendered. Hell and night

400   Must bring this monstrous birth to the world's light.

Exit.

---

379 *Thus … purse:* I always make use of fools like Roderigo for my own profit

380–2 *For … profit:* if I were to waste my time on such a dupe [Roderigo] without deriving amusement and gain from the exercise, I would be degrading my acquired wisdom

383–4 *And … office:* opinion has it that Othello has had sexual intercourse with my wife [Emilia]. This may be dismissed as an instance of what Coleridge called 'the motive-hunting of a motiveless malignity'. But while it is difficult to believe that anything so discreditable is 'thought abroad' about Othello, it is true that Iago has been sufficiently concerned about an imagined intrigue between Othello and Emilia to challenge her on the point (see Act 4, Scene 2, line 149)

385–6 *I … surety:* I will treat this sort of suspicion as if it were an established fact

386 *holds me well:* thinks well of me

388 *proper:* handsome, accomplished

389 *plume … will:* heighten my sense of power or superiority

393 *dispose:* manner

379–400 This is an example of a soliloquy, which is a speech spoken by a character to himself or herself. The character is usually alone on stage. It is as though he or she is thinking out loud. This gives the audience a chance to understand the character's inner thoughts and feelings

Key points

This scene marks the end of the preliminary action. Shakespeare has laid the groundwork for the main details of character and intrigue that will lead to the tragic climax.

- This is a most impressive scene in the theatre. Othello's account of the wooing of Desdemona is a magnificent display of his worth. It can hold an audience enthralled, as it does the Duke, whose comment on it amounts to a complete justification of Othello: 'I think this tale would win my daughter, too' (line 171).

- Othello's great and moving speeches are not delivered in pompous or self-glorifying tones. He speaks quietly, solemnly and sincerely. He is sure of his position, but free from false pride.

- The Turkish threat to Cyprus, and hence to Venice, adds further lustre to Othello's character, since it brings into prominence his unrivalled reputation as a soldier and saviour of the state.

- Iago describes Othello as a man 'of honesty and trust' (line 284), with a 'free and open nature' (line 397). Iago will later use these positive traits to manipulate Othello.

- Desdemona asserts herself in an engaging and positive manner. She counters her father's wilder outbursts with a courteous firmness. She defends her marriage and tactfully explains her view of the father–daughter relationship.

- Iago comes into his own at the close of the scene. We are both fascinated and appalled as his schemes begin to unfold. In the soliloquy that rounds off the scene, Iago's attention is fixed on taking Cassio's place. He is not yet primarily concerned with getting revenge on Othello.

- We have the sense that Iago does not have a definite course of action in mind. He may be hoping that circumstances will work in his favour.

- Iago sneers at the fragile bond between Othello, the 'erring barbarian' (line 355) as he calls him, and the refined Desdemona. However, we see that Othello, far from being a 'barbarian', is as polished and courtly as any Venetian. Iago's principal role in the play will be to turn Othello into a barbarian, as he gradually provokes him to a jealous rage.

Useful quotes

> A maiden never bold,
> Of spirit so still and quiet that her motion
> Blush'd at herself. And she, in spite of nature,
> Of years, of country, credit, everything,
> To fall in love with what she fear'd to look on?
>
> (Brabantio, lines 94–8)

> She loved me for the dangers I had pass'd,
> And I loved her that she did pity them.
> This only is the witchcraft I have us'd.
>
> (Othello, lines 167–9)

> Look to her, Moor, if thou hast eyes to see,
> She has deceived her father, and may thee.
>
> (Brabantio, lines 292–3)

> My life upon her faith. Honest Iago,
> My Desdemona must I leave to thee;
> I prithee let thy wife attend on her,
> And bring her after in the best advantage.
>
> (Othello, lines 294–7)

> The Moor is of a free and open nature
> That thinks men honest that but seem to be so
> And will as tenderly be led by the nose …
> As asses are.
>
> (Iago, lines 395–8)

? Questions

1 What is the general opinion of Othello as revealed in this scene?

2 How does Othello acquit himself at his trial before the Duke and the senators?

3 What features of Othello's character are most prominently displayed in this scene?

4 What do we learn about Desdemona from her speeches in the Council Chamber?

5 Does Desdemona's behaviour in this scene coincide with her father's opinion of her?

6 In this scene, what do we learn of Othello's attitude to Desdemona and of her attitude to him?

7 What impression do you get of the Duke of Venice from this scene?

8 If you were choosing an actor to play the Duke in a stage or film version of *Othello,* what characteristics or features would you look for?

9 What does the Iago–Roderigo dialogue reveal about these two characters and their relationship?

10 What do we learn about Iago's motives and plans from his soliloquy at the close of the scene?

11 On the evidence of this soliloquy, how would you describe Iago? What colour(s) and shape(s) would you associate with this character?

12 What themes are beginning to emerge in the play? Give reasons for your suggestions.

ACT 1 ⚔ Key moments

Scene 1

- Othello's elopement with Desdemona is reported.
- Iago and Roderigo disclose their grievances against Othello.
- Iago reveals his resentment of Cassio.
- Roderigo succeeds, with Iago's help, in provoking Brabantio to have Othello and Desdemona arrested.

Scene 2

- Iago pretends to be loyal to Othello.
- Othello is seen to be a noble, dignified, fearless man, descended from kings.
- Othello has a central leadership role in the Venetians' war with the Turks.

Scene 3

- Othello makes two impressive speeches defending his actions and wins the Duke's approval.
- Desdemona supports Othello's version of events and declares her love for him.
- Othello swears his faith in Desdemona.
- Iago reveals his sinister plan to make Othello believe that Desdemona and Cassio are lovers.

ACT 1 ⚔ Speaking and listening

1 In pairs, discuss how you would stage the first part of the opening scene (lines 1 to 85). Consider issues such as stage design, lighting, sound effects, props, make-up and costumes. How would you handle Brabantio's appearance at line 82? Where would Iago and Roderigo be positioned on stage when they speak lines 84 and 85?

2 In groups of five, assign the roles of Desdemona, Brabantio, Roderigo, Othello and the Duke. The other four characters take turns to tell Desdemona how they feel about her marriage and to question her on the events surrounding her early meetings with Othello, their elopement and whether his race had any effect on her or her father.

ACT 2 ✝ Scene 1

Plot summary

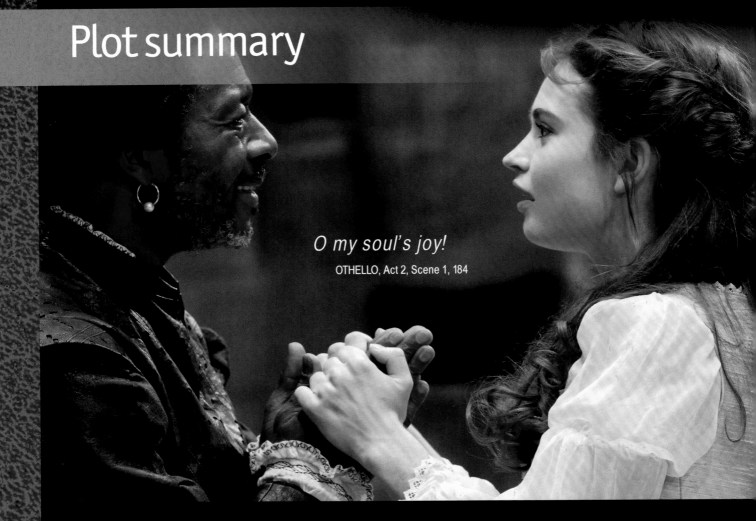

O my soul's joy!

OTHELLO, Act 2, Scene 1, 184

MONTANO, GOVERNOR OF CYPRUS, awaits the arrival of the Venetian ships. There is a storm at sea but the play's chief characters arrive safely. First comes Cassio, who reports Othello's marriage and recites Desdemona's qualities with much enthusiasm. When Desdemona arrives, with Iago, Cassio gives her a courteous welcome. She then engages in banter with Iago about the characteristics of women. Iago reflects that he will soon turn Cassio's and Desdemona's innocent behaviour to his own dark purposes. Eventually Othello arrives with the news that the fierce storm has dispersed the Turkish fleet and thus removed the danger to Venice. His joy at this outcome and his happy reunion with Desdemona are movingly expressed. The serene picture is darkened by Iago's cynical commentary to Roderigo on the Othello–Desdemona relationship. He suggests that Desdemona will inevitably be unfaithful to her husband, and that she is already in love with Cassio. Iago intends to use Roderigo's jealousy as a weapon to

Setting: Venice is the location of all three scenes in Act 1. In Act 2 the action moves to Cyprus, where it remains for the rest of the play. Venice and Cyprus had a specific set of significances for Shakespeare's early audiences. Venice was a sophisticated city and a major economic power, with Cyprus as its wilder colony. Venice was seen as the defender of Western Christendom against the advance of the infidel Turks, and its survival depended on the success of its armed forces. It was also a city notorious for its permissive attitude to marital infidelity – an aspect Iago fully exploits later in the play.

Cyprus. A sea-port.

Enter MONTANO, governor of Cyprus, with two other GENTLEMEN.

MONTANO

What from the cape can you discern at sea?

FIRST GENTLEMAN

Nothing at all. It is a high-wrought flood,

I cannot 'twixt the heaven and the main

Descry a sail.

MONTANO

Methinks the wind hath spoke aloud at land.   5

A fuller blast ne'er shook our battlements.

If it ha' ruffian'd so upon the sea,

What ribs of oak, when the huge mountains melt,

Can hold the mortise? What shall we hear of this?

SECOND GENTLEMAN

A segregation of the Turkish fleet.   10

For do but stand upon the banning shore,

The chiding billow seems to pelt the clouds,

The wind-shak'd surge, with high and monstrous main,

Seems to cast water on the burning bear,

And quench the guards of the ever-fixed pole.   15

I never did like molestation view

On the enchafed flood.

MONTANO

If that the Turkish fleet

Be not enshelter'd and embay'd, they are drown'd.

It is impossible they bear it out.

Enter a THIRD GENTLEMAN.

2 *high-wrought flood:* sea driven skywards

3 *'twixt:* between
   main: sea

4 *Descry:* catch sight of

7–9 *If … mortise:* if the wind has been as fierce at sea as it has been on land, what can save the ships from breaking up

9 *mortise:* cavity into which the end of some other part of a framework is fitted so as to form a joint

10 *segregation:* dispersal, scattering

11–12 *For … clouds:* anyone standing on the shore will see that the fierce winds are blowing the waters of the ocean skywards. The storm is a foretaste of what is to happen in Othello's soul

14–15 *Seems … pole:* the bear is the constellation known as the Little Bear, the guards are two stars in that constellation, and the pole is the Pole Star

16–17 *I never … flood:* I have never seen the sea so disturbed and angry ('enchafed')

19 *bear it out:* should survive

THIRD GENTLEMAN

20 News, lords, your wars are done:

The desperate tempest hath so bang'd the Turk

That their designment halts. Another ship, of Venice,

Hath seen a grievous wrack and sufferance

On most part of their fleet.

MONTANO

25 How, is this true?

THIRD GENTLEMAN

               The ship is here put in,

A Veronesa. Michael Cassio,

Lieutenant to the warlike Moor Othello,

Is come ashore. The Moor himself at sea,

And is in full commission here for Cyprus.

MONTANO

30 I am glad on't, 'tis a worthy governor.

THIRD GENTLEMAN

But this same Cassio, though he speak of comfort

Touching the Turkish loss, yet he looks sadly

And prays the Moor be safe, for they were parted

With foul and violent tempest.

MONTANO

               Pray heavens he be,

35 For I have serv'd him and the man commands

Like a full soldier. Let's to the seaside, ho!

As well to see the vessel that's come in

As to throw out our eyes for brave Othello,

Even till we make the main and the aerial blue

40 An indistinct regard.

THIRD GENTLEMAN

               Come, let's do so.

For every minute is expectancy

Of more arrivance.

Enter CASSIO.

CASSIO

Thanks, you the valiant of this warlike isle,

That so approve the Moor, and let the heavens

45 Give him defence against the elements,

For I have lost him on a dangerous sea.

Glossary / notes (left margin):

22 *designment:* plan, intention

23 *wrack and sufferance:* shipwreck and damage

25 Shakespeare uses the character Montano to give information to the audience through his commentary and questions

26 *Veronesa:* probably a type of ship, such as a cutter, rather than a geographical term

29 *in full commission:* with full authority

32 *sadly:* grave, serious

39–40 *Even ... regard:* till our straining eyes confuse sea and sky at the horizon

41–2 *For ... arrivance:* since we are expecting new arrivals every minute

44 *approve:* honour, esteem

46 *For ... sea:* this is a moving irony, since Cassio is soon to lose Othello's friendship on the much more dangerous sea of Othello's passion

MONTANO
Is he well shipp'd?

CASSIO
His bark is stoutly timber'd, and his pilot
Of very expert and approv'd allowance,
Therefore my hopes, not surfeited to death,   50
Stand in bold cure.

VOICES [within]
           A sail, a sail, a sail!
Enter a MESSENGER.

CASSIO
What noise?

MESSENGER
The town is empty, on the brow o' the sea
Stand ranks of people, and they cry, 'A sail!'

CASSIO
My hopes do shape him for the governor.   55
A shot.

SECOND GENTLEMEN
They do discharge their shot of courtesy,
Our friends at least.

CASSIO
           I pray you sir, go forth,
And give us truth who 'tis that is arriv'd.

SECOND GENTLEMAN
I shall.

Exit.

MONTANO
But, good lieutenant, is your general wiv'd?   60

CASSIO
Most fortunately, he hath achiev'd a maid
That paragons description and wild fame;
One that excels the quirks of blazoning pens,
And in th'essential vesture of creation
Does tire the ingener.
Enter a SECOND GENTLEMAN.
           Now, who has put in?   65

SECOND GENTLEMAN
'Tis one Iago, ancient to the general.

---

48 *bark:* ship, vessel

49 *Of … allowance:* recognised with good reason as an expert

50–1 *my hopes … cure:* my hopes for his safety are reasonably based and healthy, and at the same time not so great as to be in danger of disappointment

55 *My … governor:* I hope he is the governor (Othello)

A shot: Shakespeare's Globe theatre had its own cannon in the loft above the tiring-house. In 1613 the theatre burnt down when sparks from the cannon set fire to the thatched roof

56–7 *They … least:* they are firing a salvo of welcome, which at any rate indicates the approach of friends

60 *wiv'd:* married

61–2 *Most … fame:* he has been most fortunate in winning a maid whose qualities are beyond description and the most extravagant praise

63 *One … pens:* one whose merits are such that even the elaborate and imaginative comparisons ('quirks') of fanciful authors cannot do them justice
    blazoning: setting forth the merits of

64–5 *th'essential … ingener:* the human nature she was given by her creator challenges and exhausts the most ingenious imagination to depict it adequately

67 *happy speed:* good fortune as well as quickness of movement

69 *gutter'd:* fretted and jagged (i.e. dangerous to ships)
congregated: compacted

70 *Traitors … keel:* the rocks and sands are treacherous underwater enemies to the inoffensive keel of a boat
clog: impede

71–3 *As having … Desdemona:* the storm and the submerged hazards, having an awareness of beauty, cease to function in their usual deadly way, and allow the lovely Desdemona to pass unharmed. There is clear anticipation here of the more deadly activities of Iago: the raging storm of Othello's jealousy, to be released by Iago, will not spare Desdemona, or Othello

76 *footing:* landing

77 *se'nnight's:* week's (seven nights)
Jove: king of the gods (Roman)

79 *tall:* brave

81 *extincted:* dulled

84 *let … knees:* kneel to her

87 *Enwheel:* encircle

92–3 *The great … fellowship:* the storm has parted Othello and Cassio; soon their friendship is to be parted more drastically by the fury released in Othello through the efforts of Iago

CASSIO
He has had most favourable and happy speed.

Tempests themselves, high seas and howling winds,

The gutter'd rocks and congregated sands,

70   Traitors ensteep'd to clog the guiltless keel,

As having sense of beauty do omit

Their common natures, letting go safely by

The divine Desdemona.

MONTANO
                              What is she?

CASSIO
She that I spoke of, our great captain's captain,

75   Left in the conduct of the bold Iago,

Whose footing here anticipates our thoughts

A se'nnight's speed. Great Jove, Othello guard,

And swell his sail with thine own powerful breath

That he may bless this bay with his tall ship

80   And swiftly come to Desdemona's arms,

Give renew'd fire to our extincted spirits,

And bring all Cyprus comfort …

Enter DESDEMONA, IAGO, EMILIA, RODERIGO, and ATTENDANTS.

                              O, behold,

The riches of the ship is come ashore!

Ye men of Cyprus, let her have your knees.

85   Hail to thee, lady, and the grace of heaven,

Before, behind thee, and on every hand,

Enwheel thee round!

DESDEMONA
                              I thank you, valiant Cassio.

What tidings can you tell me of my Lord?

CASSIO
He is not yet arriv'd, nor know I aught

90   But that he's well and will be shortly here.

DESDEMONA
O, but I fear. How lost you company?

CASSIO
The great contention of the sea and skies

Parted our fellowship.

Hail to thee, lady, and the grace of heaven,
Before, behind thee, and on every hand,
Enwheel thee round!

CASSIO, Act 2, Scene 1, 85–7

VOICES *[within]*

        A sail, a sail!

CASSIO

                But, hark! A sail.

A shot.

SECOND GENTLEMAN

They give their greeting to the citadel,

This likewise is a friend.

CASSIO

            See for the news.   95

Exit GENTLEMAN.

Good ancient, you are welcome. Welcome, mistress.

Let it not gall your patience, good Iago,

That I extend my manners; 'tis my breeding

That gives me this bold show of courtesy.

Kisses her.

94 *citadel:* fortress

96 Cassio speaks first to Iago, and then to Emilia

97–9 *Let … courtesy:* do not be irritated if I greet your wife familiarly [by kissing her], it is my training in refined manners that makes it natural for me to indulge in this liberal show of sociability. The Florentines, of whom Cassio is one, were noted for their excellent manners

100–2 *would she ... enough:* you would have enough kisses if she kissed you as much as she scolds me

104–7 *for when ... thinking:* she still persists in scolding me even when I desire ('list') to sleep. In your ladyship's presence I declare that she holds her tongue and makes her very silence a means of scolding me

109 *pictures ... doors:* models of virtue in public

110 *Bells:* noisy individuals

111 *in your injuries:* when you injure others

112 *Players ... housewifery:* not taking your work as housekeepers very seriously
  housewives: wantons

113 *fie upon thee:* shame on you

114 *a Turk:* an infidel

117 *What ... of me:* Desdemona's flippant talk with Iago for almost the next fifty lines has attracted unfavourable comment. Her enquiry whether someone has gone to the harbour to seek after Othello is made only in passing. One would expect the Desdemona we have so far come to know to go to meet Othello, rather than to challenge Iago to display his verbal dexterity

119 *critical:* a satirist
120 *assay:* try

IAGO

100 Sir, would she give you so much of her lips

As of her tongue she oft bestow'd on me,

You would have enough.

DESDEMONA

Alas, she has no speech!

IAGO

I know, too much.

I find it, I; for when I ha' list to sleep —

105 Marry, before your ladyship, I grant,

She puts her tongue a little in her heart,

And chides with thinking.

EMILIA

You ha' little cause to say so.

IAGO

Come on, come on, you are pictures out o' doors;

110 Bells in your parlours; wild-cats in your kitchens;

Saints in your injuries; devils being offended;

Players in your housewifery; and housewives in your beds.

DESDEMONA

O, fie upon thee, slanderer!

IAGO

Nay, it is true, or else I am a Turk.

115 You rise to play, and go to bed to work.

EMILIA

You shall not write my praise.

IAGO

No, let me not.

DESDEMONA

What would thou write of me, if thou shouldst praise me?

IAGO

O gentle lady, do not put me to't,

For I am nothing if not critical.

DESDEMONA

120 Come on, assay. There's one gone to the harbour?

IAGO

Ay, madam.

DESDEMONA

I am not merry, but I do beguile

The thing I am, by seeming otherwise:

Come, how would thou praise me?

IAGO

I am about it, but indeed my invention   125

Comes from my pate as birdlime does from frieze,

It plucks out brain and all; but my Muse labours,

And thus she is deliver'd.

If she be fair and wise, fairness and wit;

The one's for use, the other using it.   130

DESDEMONA

Well prais'd! How if she be black and witty?

IAGO

If she be black, and thereto have a wit,

She'll find a white, that shall her blackness hit.

DESDEMONA

Worse and worse.

EMILIA

How if fair and foolish?   135

IAGO

She never yet was foolish that was fair,

For even her folly help'd her to an heir.

DESDEMONA

These are old fond paradoxes to make fools laugh i'

the alehouse; and what miserable praise has thou for

her that's foul and foolish?   140

IAGO

There's none so foul and foolish thereunto,

But does foul pranks which fair and wise ones do.

DESDEMONA

O heavy ignorance. Thou praisest the worst best.

But what praise couldst thou bestow on a deserving

woman indeed? One that in the authority of her   145

merits did justly put on the vouch of very malice

itself?

122–3 *I am … otherwise*: in spite of appearances, I am not in a cheerful mood. Desdemona suggests that she is engaging in humorous banter to divert her attention from her anxiety about Othello

125–6 *my invention … frieze*: my inventiveness (or imaginative power) is stuck in my head ('pate') like birdlime (a sticky substance used to snare birds) on coarse cloth ('frieze')

127 *Muse*: poetic faculty

129 *fair*: of a light complexion, blonde. Shakespeare's contemporaries admired this kind of woman *wit*: intelligence, quickness of understanding

130 *The one's … it*: her intelligence can make use of her looks

131 *black*: of a dark complexion, brunette

132–3 *If … hit*: if she is black and also intelligent she will find a fair partner who will hit it off with her

136–7 *She … heir*: fair (beautiful) women can turn their folly to good account by making it the means of giving them an heir. 'Folly' here means both foolishness and loose behaviour

138 *fond paradoxes*: silly opinions that contradict the general opinion

141 *thereunto*: in addition

142 *But … do*: the fair and wise are capable of the same mischievous deeds as the ugly and foolish

145–7 *One … itself*: a woman of such outstanding virtue that even malice (or malicious people) would be obliged to pay tribute to her

IAGO
She that was ever fair and never proud;
Had tongue at will and yet was never loud;
150 Never lack'd gold and yet went never gay;
Fled from her wish and yet said 'Now I may';
She that, being anger'd, her revenge being nigh,
Bade her wrong stay and her displeasure fly;
She that in wisdom never was so frail
155 To change the cod's head for the salmon's tail;
She that could think and ne'er disclose her mind,
See suitors following and not look behind;
She was a wight, if ever such wight were …

DESDEMONA
To do what?

IAGO
160 To suckle fools and chronicle small beer.

DESDEMONA
O most lame and impotent conclusion. Do not learn of him, Emilia, though he be thy husband. How say you, Cassio? Is he not a most profane and liberal counsellor?

CASSIO
165 He speaks home, madam. You may relish him more in the soldier than in the scholar.

IAGO *[aside]*
He takes her by the palm. Ay, well said, whisper: as little a web as this will ensnare as great a fly as Cassio. Ay, smile upon her, do. I will catch you in your own 170 courtesies. You say true, 'tis indeed. If such tricks as these strip you out of your lieutenantry, it had been better you had not kiss'd your three fingers so oft, which now again you are most apt to play the sir in. Good; well kiss'd, and excellent courtesy. 'Tis so 175 indeed. Yet again, your fingers at your lips? Would they were clyster-pipes for your sake … *[trumpets within]*

[aloud] The Moor! I know his trumpet.

CASSIO

'Tis truly so.

DESDEMONA

Let's meet him and receive him.   180

Enter OTHELLO and ATTENDANTS.

CASSIO

Lo, where he comes!

OTHELLO

O my fair warrior!

DESDEMONA

           My dear Othello!

OTHELLO

It gives me wonder great as my content

To see you here before me. O my soul's joy!

If after every tempest come such calms,   185

May the winds blow till they have waken'd death,

And let the labouring bark climb hills of seas,

Olympus-high, and duck again as low

As hell's from heaven! If it were now to die,

'Twere now to be most happy, for I fear   190

My soul hath her content so absolute

That not another comfort like to this

Succeeds in unknown fate.

DESDEMONA

              The heavens forbid

But that our loves and comforts should increase,

Even as our days do grow.

OTHELLO

              Amen to that, sweet powers!   195

I cannot speak enough of this content.

It stops me here. It is too much of joy.

And this *[they kiss]*, and this, the greatest discords be

That e'er our hearts shall make!

IAGO *[aside]*

                O, you are well tun'd now,

But I'll set down the pegs that make this music   200

As honest as I am.

---

185   This is a poignant irony as another, altogether more terrible, tempest will soon overwhelm Othello and Desdemona; it will be unleashed by Iago, who is standing by as Othello speaks

189   *hell's:* hell is

191–3   *My … fate:* I am now so absolutely happy that I cannot imagine the future holding anything like the same degree of happiness for me. This is one of the play's most moving ironies. As he speaks, Othello can have no conception of the horrors the future holds for him

198   *And this, and this:* the kisses he is giving her

199–201   *O … I am:* the relationship between Othello and Desdemona is now harmonious; Iago will turn this harmony to discord ('set down the pegs' means to slacken the strings of a musical instrument to produce a discord), while always appearing honest

OTHELLO

Come, let us to the castle.

News, friends, our wars are done, the Turks are drown'd.

How do my old acquaintance of this isle?

Honey, you shall be well desir'd in Cyprus;

205   I have found great love amongst them. O my sweet,

I prattle out of fashion and I dote

In mine own comforts. I prithee, good Iago,

Go to the bay and disembark my coffers.

Bring thou the master to the citadel;

210   He is a good one, and his worthiness

Does challenge much respect. Come, Desdemona,

Once more well met at Cyprus.

Exeunt all but IAGO and RODERIGO.

IAGO

Do thou meet me presently at the harbour. Come hither. If thou be'st valiant — as they say base men

215 being in love have then a nobility in their natures more than is native to them — list me. The lieutenant to-night watches on the court of guard. First, I will tell thee this: Desdemona is directly in love with him.

RODERIGO

With him? Why, 'tis not possible!

IAGO

220 Lay thy finger thus, and let thy soul be instructed. Mark me, with what violence she first lov'd the Moor, but for bragging and telling her fantastical lies; and will she love him still for prating? Let not thy discreet heart think it. Her eye must be fed, and what delight

225 shall she have to look on the devil? When the blood is made dull with the act of sport, there should be again to inflame it, and give satiety a fresh appetite, loveliness in favour, sympathy in years, manners and beauties; all which the Moor is defective in.

230 Now, for want of these requir'd conveniences, her delicate tenderness will find itself abus'd, begin to heave the gorge, disrelish and abhor the Moor. Very nature will instruct her in it and compel her to some second choice. Now, sir, this granted (as

235 it is a most pregnant and unforc'd position), who stands so eminently in the degree of this fortune

---

204   *well desir'd:* much loved

206   *out of fashion:* at random, beside the point

208   *coffers:* luggage
209   *master:* navigator or sailing-master of the warship

211   *challenge:* demand, claim

213   *presently:* in Shakespeare this almost always means immediately but here it is used in its modern sense of after a while

216   *native to them:* normally part of their natures
     list me: listen to what I say
217   *court of guard:* guardhouse
218   *directly:* without doubt, plainly

Desdemona in love with Cassio

220   *Lay thy finger thus:* Iago puts his finger to his lips as he says this, indicating that Roderigo should be quiet
222   *but for bragging:* for nothing else but boasting

225   *the devil:* an allusion to Othello's colour; blackness and darkness are key terms in the diabolic imagery of the play

228   *loveliness in favour:* beautiful appearance
     sympathy in years: similarity of age

230   *requir'd conveniences:* necessary advantages
231–2   *find ... Moor:* consider itself defrauded, begin to vomit and find Othello disgusting and repulsive
233–4   *Very ... choice:* her natural instincts will prompt her in that direction, and urge her to choose somebody else
234–7   *this granted ... does:* if what I have said be admitted (and it is based on very cogent and reasonable arguments), Cassio is the obvious choice as Othello's successor (in Desdemona's favours)

as Cassio does? — a knave very voluble, no farther conscionable than in putting on the mere form of civil and humane seeming for the better compassing of his salt and hidden affections; a subtle slippery knave, a finder out of occasions, that has an eye can stamp and counterfeit the true advantages never present themselves. Besides the knave is handsome, young and hath all those requisites in him that folly and green minds look after. A pestilent complete knave, and the woman has found him already.

RODERIGO

I cannot believe that in her, she's full of most blessed condition.

IAGO

Blessed fig's-end! The wine she drinks is made of grapes. If she had been blessed, she would never have lov'd the Moor. Didst thou not see her paddle with the palm of his hand?

RODERIGO

Yes, but that was but courtesy.

IAGO

Lechery, by this hand; an index and prologue to the history of lust and foul thoughts. They met so near with their lips that their breaths embrac'd together. When these mutualities so marshal the way, hard at hand comes the main exercise, the incorporate conclusion. But, sir, be you rul'd by me, I have brought you from Venice. Watch you to-night for your command, I'll lay't upon you. Cassio knows you not; I'll not be far from you. Do you find some occasion to anger Cassio, either by speaking too loud, or tainting his discipline, or from what other cause you please, which the time shall more favourably minister.

RODERIGO

Well.

IAGO

Sir, he is rash, and very sudden in choler, and haply with his truncheon may strike at you. Provoke him that he may, for even out of that will I cause these of Cyprus to mutiny, whose qualification shall come into no true trust again but by the displanting of

240

245

250

255

260

265

270

237 *voluble:* talkative, perhaps also smooth in manner

237–40 *no farther ... affections:* his conscience influences his behaviour only to the extent that it prompts him to assume a polite and civilised exterior in order to further all the more effectively his lecherous and loose desires

240 *subtle:* here it probably means smoothly treacherous

241 *occasions:* opportunities

242 *stamp and counterfeit:* improvise and invent

245 *green:* immature, inexperienced

246 *has found him:* has him in mind for herself

248 *condition:* character, outlook

249–50 *The wine ... grapes:* she is a human being, not a saint

251–2 *paddle with:* stroke, fondle

254 *index and prologue:* a table of contents and an introduction (i.e. a foreshadowing)

257 *mutualities so marshal:* mutual tokens of affection pave

258–9 *incorporate conclusion:* carnal conclusion, final bodily union

260–1 *Watch ... upon you:* be ready for me to give you your instructions tonight

262 *Do you find:* make sure you find

263 *tainting:* discrediting

265 *which ... minister:* for which time will provide you with a more favourable opportunity

267 *sudden in choler:* quick to anger
haply: perhaps

270–2 *whose qualification ... Cassio:* the mutinous Cypriots will be appeased only when Cassio has been removed from his post

Cassio. So shall you have a shorter journey to your desires by the means I shall then have to prefer them, and the impediment most profitably remov'd,
275 without the which there were no expectation of our prosperity.

RODERIGO

I will do this, if I can bring it to any opportunity.

IAGO

I warrant thee, meet me by and by at the citadel. I must fetch his necessaries ashore. Farewell.

RODERIGO

280 Adieu.

Exit.

IAGO

That Cassio loves her, I do well believe it.

That she loves him, 'tis apt and of great credit.

The Moor, howbe't that I endure him not,

Is of a constant, noble, loving nature,

285 And I dare think he'll prove to Desdemona

A most dear husband. Now, I do love her too,

Not out of absolute lust (though peradventure

I stand accountant for as great a sin),

But partly led to diet my revenge

290 For that I do suspect the lusty Moor

Hath leap'd into my seat, the thought whereof

Doth like a poisonous mineral gnaw my inwards,

And nothing can nor shall content my soul

Till I am even with him, wife for wife;

295 Or failing so, yet that I put the Moor

At least into a jealousy so strong

That judgement cannot cure, which thing to do,

If this poor trash of Venice, whom I trace

For his quick hunting, stand the putting on,

300 I'll have our Michael Cassio on the hip,

Abuse him to the Moor in the rank garb

(For I fear Cassio with my night-cap too),

Make the Moor thank me, love me and reward me

For making him egregiously an ass

305 And practising upon his peace and quiet,

Even to madness. 'Tis here, but yet confused.

Knavery's plain face is never seen, till us'd.

Exit.

Handwritten annotations: 2nd Soliliquay; he thinks; Othello is having an affair

---

273 *prefer:* advance; promote

275–6 *were ... prosperity:* would be no hope that our schemes will succeed (unless the 'impediment' or obstacle, Cassio, is removed)

277 *bring ... opportunity:* manage it (Roderigo is not so sure)

279 *his necessaries:* Othello's luggage

282 *apt ... credit:* natural and very easy to believe

283 *howbe't ... not:* although I cannot stand him

287 *Not ... lust:* not entirely out of lust
peradventure: perhaps

288 *accountant for:* accountable for, guilty of

289 *diet:* feed

291 *Hath ... seat:* has taken my place (with Emilia). See Act 1, Scene 3, lines 383–4 and Act 4, Scene 2, line 149 for similar ideas on Iago's part

298–9 *poor trash ... hunting:* the contemptible Roderigo, whom I set on the trace (or on the track) because of his eagerness to pursue Desdemona

299 *stand the putting on:* is up to the demands of the hunt

300 *on the hip:* a term from wrestling meaning that one is ready to give an opponent the decisive throw. Iago means that he will have Cassio where he wants him

301 *Abuse:* slander
the rank garb: a coarse and filthy manner

302 Iago is now suggesting a possible affair between Cassio and Emilia

304 *making ... ass:* making him an outstanding or remarkable fool

305–6 *practising ... madness:* plotting to destroy his peace of mind, even to the point of insanity

306–7 *'Tis here ... us'd:* Iago is still somewhat unsure about the exact course his schemes will take, although he knows he will be able to make effective use of whatever opportunity arises

Key points

The storm has more than one function in this scene. Its most basic purpose is to dispose of the political and military themes of the play by scattering the Turkish fleet, thus ending the threat to the security of Venice. This leaves Shakespeare free to focus full attention on the domestic theme.

- A second function of the storm is to create suspense: the safe arrival of the main characters remains for some time in question. Othello's arrival is awaited with particular anxiety, which highlights the general admiration for his person and achievements. Montano and Cassio echo each other's hopes for his safety.

- Othello's delay allows us to sense the depth of Desdemona's feelings for her husband. In this regard we might ask whether Shakespeare should have portrayed this love more effectively. As she waits for Othello's arrival, Desdemona engages in trivial banter with Iago. One might have expected her to go to the harbour to check whether Othello's vessel was in sight; instead she merely interrupts her chat with Iago to ask whether someone else has gone.

- There is the further oddity that Desdemona seems able to accommodate herself with surprising ease to Iago's vulgar and insinuating line of talk. Her defence of her conduct may, however, be taken as sincere: 'I am not merry, but I do beguile the thing I am, by seeming otherwise' (lines 122–3).

- The imagery associated with the storm and the troubled sea suggests menace, destructiveness and treachery. The chaos in the world of nature is a foretaste of what is soon to happen in Othello's soul. Othello and Desdemona survive the storm at sea unharmed, but a storm of passionate jealousy will soon overwhelm Othello and destroy Desdemona.

- There are some subtle anticipations of these later events. For example, the First Gentleman talks of the 'high-wrought flood' caused by the storm (line 2), and Othello later speaks of himself as 'wrought' by jealous passion (Act 5, Scene 2, line 346).

- The storm imagery also gives rise to some notable ironies. Cassio has 'lost' Othello 'on a dangerous sea' (line 46). 'The great contention of the sea and skies,' he declares, 'parted our fellowship' (lines 92–3). He does not know that they are soon to be parted in a more extreme way through the efforts of Iago: first when Cassio is dismissed from service, and then by the fury of passion released in Othello.

- There is irony in Othello's words to Desdemona: 'If after every tempest come such calms … fate' (lines 185–93). The couple are experiencing, although they do not know it, the calm before the next storm. The only calm that either of them will ever know again will be the repose of death, ironically anticipated in Othello's: 'May the winds blow till they have waken'd death' (line 186).

- Iago continues to develop his plot to destroy Othello and Cassio. He persuades Roderigo that Desdemona loves Cassio. He will use Roderigo's jealousy to bring down Cassio.

Useful quotes

> and let the heavens
> Give him defence against the elements,
> For I have lost him on a dangerous sea.
>
> (Cassio, lines 44–6)

> The gutter'd rocks and congregated sands,
> Traitors ensteep'd to clog the guiltless keel,
> As having sense of beauty do omit
> Their common natures, letting go safely by
> The divine Desdemona.
>
> (Cassio, lines 69–73)

> If it were now to die,
> 'Twere now to be most happy, for I fear
> My soul hath her content so absolute
> That not another comfort like to this
> Succeeds in unknown fate.
>
> (Othello, lines 189–93)

> That Cassio loves her, I do well believe it.
> That she loves him, 'tis apt and of great credit.
> The Moor, howbe't that I endure him not,
> Is of a constant, noble, loving nature,
> And I dare think he'll prove to Desdemona
> A most dear husband.
>
> (Iago, lines 281–6)

> For that I do suspect the lusty Moor
> Hath leap'd into my seat, the thought whereof
> Doth like a poisonous mineral gnaw my inwards
>
> (Iago, lines 290–2)

? Questions

1 How does Shakespeare create the atmosphere of a storm in this scene?

2 The setting of the play has changed. How do we know this?

3 What impression do you form of Cassio in this scene?

4 What do we learn about Desdemona on the evidence of her conversation with Iago?

5 In what ways is our knowledge of Iago's character deepened by his speeches in this scene?

6 Describe Othello's mood and state of mind at this point in the play.

7 How does Iago use Roderigo in this scene?

8 What are Iago's plans at this stage?

9 Imagine you are Cassio. Write a diary entry on the events of this scene, conveying the excitement caused by the storm, and giving your views on Othello and Desdemona.

10 'At the root of all irony is a contrast between what is said, implied, suggested or believed and what is actually the case, or what is about to be the case.' Using this definition, mention some examples of irony in this scene. (See also Themes: Tragic irony, p. 211.)

ACT 2 ✛ Scene 2

Plot summary

O THELLO'S HERALD ANNOUNCES FESTIVITIES to celebrate the end of the military threat and the marriage of Desdemona and Othello.

Cyprus. A street. / *Spokes person*

Enter Othello's HERALD with a proclamation; people following.

HERALD

It is Othello's pleasure, our <u>noble and valiant general</u>, that, upon certain tidings now arrived importing the mere perdition of the Turkish fleet, every man put himself into triumph: some to dance, some to make bonfires, each man to what sport and revels his addiction leads him. For besides these beneficial news, it is the celebration of his nuptial. *Marrige* So much was his pleasure should be proclaimed. All offices are open, and there is full liberty of feasting from this present hour of five till the bell hath told eleven. Heaven bless the isle of Cyprus, and our <u>noble general, Othello</u>!

Exit.

5

10

2–3 *importing the mere perdition:* concerning the complete and utter destruction

4 *put himself into triumph:* get ready to celebrate

6 *addiction:* inclination

7 *nuptial:* wedding

7–8 *So much ... proclaimed:* it was his desire that this much should be publicly announced

8 *offices:* kitchens, pantries and other places where food is kept

Plot summary

OTHELLO HOPES CASSIO WILL keep the victory celebrations under control. Cassio wants to take up his duties at once, but Iago persuades him to celebrate a little. Cassio is soon drunk. Iago 'confides' to Montano that Cassio's soldierly qualities are unfortunately impaired by his drinking habits. Roderigo provokes the drunken Cassio, and they fight. Iago tells Roderigo to cry out that a riot is in progress. An angry Othello interrupts the rowdy scene. Iago exposes Cassio's fault, while at the same time pretending to excuse it. Othello dismisses Cassio from his post. Iago advises Cassio to ask Desdemona to plead his case with Othello. Cassio departs in hope, convinced, like everybody else, of Iago's honesty.

Some wine, boys!

IAGO, Act 2, Scene 3, 69

Cyprus. The citadel.

Enter OTHELLO, DESDEMONA, CASSIO, and ATTENDANTS.

OTHELLO

Good Michael, look you to the guard to-night:
Let's teach ourselves that honourable stop
Not to outsport discretion.

CASSIO

Iago hath direction what to do,
But notwithstanding with my personal eye   5
Will I look to it.

OTHELLO

              Iago is most honest.
Michael, good night, to-morrow with your earliest
Let me have speech with you. Come, my dear love,
The purchase made, the fruits are to ensue;
That profit's yet to come 'twixt me and you.   10
Good night.

Exeunt OTHELLO and DESDEMONA.

Enter IAGO.

CASSIO

Welcome, Iago. We must to the watch.

IAGO

Not this hour, lieutenant, 'tis not yet ten o'clock.
Our general cast us thus early for the love of his
Desdemona, who let us not therefore blame: he hath   15
not yet made wanton the night with her, and she is
sport for Jove.

CASSIO

She is a most exquisite lady.

IAGO

And I'll warrant her full of game.

CASSIO

Indeed she's a most fresh and delicate creature.   20

IAGO

What an eye she has! Methinks it sounds a parley of
provocation.

2–3 *Let's ... discretion:* let us practise an honourable self-control, so that we do not go beyond proper limits in our revels

5 *notwithstanding:* in spite of this

6 *honest:* honesty is a recurring theme in Othello's speeches about Iago and one of the iterated ironies of the play
7 *with your earliest:* as early as possible
8–10 These lines are addressed to Desdemona
9 The marriage has not yet been consummated

12 *We must:* we must go

13 *Not this hour:* not for another hour
14 *cast:* dismissed

17 *sport for Jove:* a fit mate for Jove, king of the Roman gods

19 *full of game:* sexually responsive

21 *parley:* here it means prelude, introduction

CASSIO

An inviting eye, and yet methinks right modest.

IAGO

And when she speaks, 'tis an alarm to love.

CASSIO

25 She is indeed perfection.

IAGO

Well, happiness to their sheets! — Come, lieutenant, I have a stoup of wine and here without are a brace of Cyprus gallants that would fain have a measure to the health of black Othello.

CASSIO

30 Not to-night, good Iago. I have very poor and unhappy brains for drinking. I could well wish courtesy would invent some other custom of entertainment.

IAGO

O, they are our friends. But one cup! I'll drink for you.

CASSIO

35 I ha' drunk but one cup to-night, and that was craftily qualified too, and, behold what innovation it makes here. I am unfortunate in the infirmity and dare not task my weakness with any more.

IAGO

What, man, 'tis a night of revels, the gallants desire
40 it.

CASSIO

Where are they?

IAGO

Here at the door. I pray you call them in.

CASSIO

I'll do't, but it dislikes me.

Exit.

IAGO

If I can fasten but one cup upon him,
45 With that which he hath drunk to-night already,
He'll be as full of quarrel and offence

---

23 *right:* entirely. Cassio is countering Iago's suggestions about Desdemona

24 *an alarm:* a signal

27 *stoup:* tankard holding four pints
27–8 *without ... measure:* outside are a couple of Cypriot men of fashion who would willingly drink

36 *qualified:* diluted
36–7 *behold ... here:* notice what a disturbance or agitation it causes here (Cassio is pointing to his head)
38 *task:* put a strain on

43 *it dislikes me:* I dislike it

Iago's
third soliloquy →

46 *offence:* readiness to be easily offended

As my young mistress' dog. Now, my sick fool Roderigo,

Whom love has turn'd almost the wrong side out,

To Desdemona hath to-night carous'd

Potations pottle-deep, and he's to watch. 50

Three lads of Cyprus, noble swelling spirits,

That hold their honours in a wary distance,

The very elements of this warlike isle,

Have I to-night fluster'd with flowing cups,

And they watch too. Now, 'mongst this flock of drunkards 55

I am to put our Cassio in some action

That may offend the isle.

Enter MONTANO, CASSIO, and others.

But here they come.

If consequence do but approve my dream,

My boat sails freely, both with wind and stream.

CASSIO

'Fore God they have given me a rouse already. 60

MONTANO

Good faith, a little one, not past a pint,

As I am a soldier.

IAGO

Some wine, ho!

[*sings*]   *And let me the cannikin clink, clink,*

And let me the cannikin clink, clink, 65

A soldier's a man,

A life's but a span,

Why then let a soldier drink.

Some wine, boys!

CASSIO

'Fore God, an excellent song. 70

IAGO

I learn'd it in England, where indeed they are most potent in potting: your Dane, your German and your swag-bellied Hollander — drink, ho! — are nothing to your English.

CASSIO

Is your Englishman so expert in his drinking? 75

---

47 *my young mistress' dog:* any young lady's dog; this does not mean Iago's mistress's dog

49–50 *carous'd ... pottle-deep:* drank at length to the bottom of the tankard. He has drained a full tankard in honour of Desdemona tonight

50 *watch:* be on guard

51 *swelling spirits:* proud, assertive, arrogant fellows

52 *That ... distance:* who are very keen on maintaining their honour and so, presumably, are touchy enough to take offence easily

53 *very ... isle:* typical representatives of the Cypriot population

54 *fluster'd ... cups:* excited with liberal quantities of drink

55 *they watch too:* they are also on guard

58–9 *If ... stream:* if only the events to come confirm my plans (or hopes), then everything will run smoothly for me

60 *rouse:* drink

64 *cannikin:* small can or drinking-vessel

67 *but a span:* short

72 *potting:* tippling, drinking

73 *swag-bellied:* big-bellied

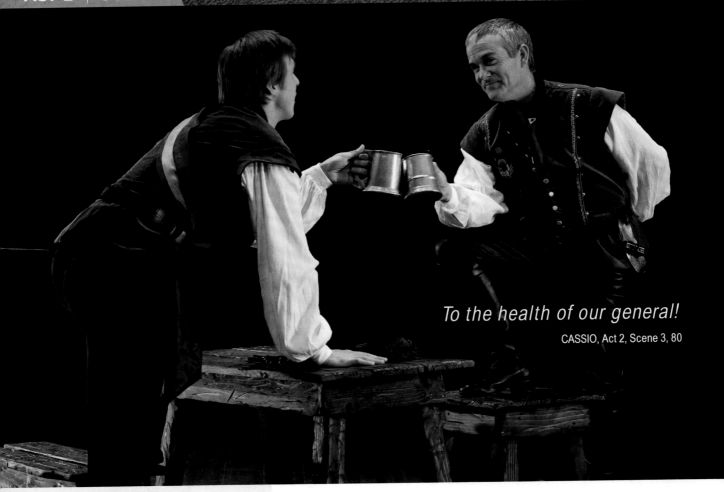

To the health of our general!

CASSIO, Act 2, Scene 3, 80

76–9 *he drinks ... fill'd:* he can easily out-drink Danes, Germans ('Almain') and Dutchmen ('Hollander')

IAGO

Why, he drinks you with facility your Dane dead drunk; he sweats not to overthrow your Almain; he gives your Hollander a vomit ere the next pottle can be fill'd.

CASSIO

80 To the health of our general!

MONTANO

81 *do you justice:* drink as much as you do

I am for it, lieutenant, and I'll do you justice.

IAGO

O sweet England!

[*sings*] *King Stephen was a worthy peer,*
His breeches cost him but a crown;
85 *He held them sixpence all too dear,*
With that he call'd the tailor lown,

86 *lown:* a lout

87 *wight:* person

He was a wight of high renown,
And thou art but of low degree,
'Tis pride that pulls the country down,

90 *take ... thee:* wrap your old cloak around yourself

90 *Then take thine auld cloak about thee.*
Some wine, ho!

CASSIO

'Fore God this is a more exquisite song than the other.

IAGO

Will you hear't again?

CASSIO

No, for I hold him to be unworthy of his place that does those things. Well, God's above all, and there be souls that must be saved, and there be souls must not be saved.

IAGO

It is true, good lieutenant.

CASSIO

For mine own part, no offence to the general, nor any man of quality, I hope to be saved.

IAGO

And so do I, lieutenant.

CASSIO

Ay, but by your leave, not before me. The lieutenant is to be saved before the ancient. Let's ha' no more of this; let's to our affairs. God forgive us our sins! Gentlemen, let's look to our business. Do not think, gentlemen, I am drunk. This is my ancient, this is my right hand and this is my left hand. I am not drunk now. I can stand well enough and speak well enough.

ALL

Excellent well.

CASSIO

Very well then, you must not think that I am drunk.

Exit.

MONTANO

To the platform, masters. Come, let's set the watch.

IAGO

You see this fellow that is gone before,
He is a soldier fit to stand by Caesar

95

100

105

110

113

115

92 Cassio is losing his judgement

103–4 *lieutenant ... ancient:* Cassio's pride in his rank emerges in his drunken ramblings

113 *platform:* gun-platform
set the watch: mount the guard

115 *stand by Caesar:* be Caesar's collaborator

116	*give direction:* issue orders
116–18	*And ... th'other:* his vice [drunkenness] perfectly counteracts or counterbalances his virtue, just as day and night balance each other at the equinox

And give direction. And do but see his vice,

'Tis to his virtue a just equinox,

The one as long as th'other. 'Tis pity of him.

I fear the trust Othello puts him in, ✳

120	*On ... infirmity:* some time or other when he is drunk

120 On some odd time of his infirmity,

Will shake this island.

MONTANO

But is he often thus?

IAGO

'Tis evermore the prologue to his sleep.

He'll watch the horologe a double set,

If drink rock not his cradle.

122–4	*'Tis ... cradle:* he always drinks before sleeping. He'll remain awake twice around the clock ('horologe') [for twenty-four hours], if alcohol doesn't put him to sleep

MONTANO

It were well

125 The general were put in mind of it.

Perhaps he sees it not, or his good nature

Prizes the virtue that appears in Cassio

And looks not on his evils. Is not this true?

Enter RODERIGO.

	[aside to him]: Iago speaks to Roderigo, and Montano and the others on stage do not hear what he says

IAGO *[aside to him]*

How now, Roderigo!

130 I pray you, after the lieutenant. Go.

Exit RODERIGO.

MONTANO

And 'tis great pity that the noble Moor

Should hazard such a place as his own second

With one of an ingraft infirmity.

It were an honest action to say so

132–3	*hazard ... infirmity:* risk appointing a man with such a deep-rooted weakness as his deputy

135 To the Moor. ···················

IAGO

Not I, for this fair island!

I do love Cassio well and would do much

To cure him of this evil.

VOICES *[cry within]*

Help! help!

IAGO

But, hark! What noise?

Enter CASSIO, driving in RODERIGO.

CASSIO
Zounds, you rogue, you rascal!

MONTANO
What's the matter, lieutenant?

CASSIO
A knave, teach me my duty! But I'll beat the knave into   140
a wicker bottle.

RODERIGO
Beat me?

CASSIO
Dost thou prate, rogue? *[striking Roderigo]*

MONTANO
Good lieutenant, pray sir, hold your hand.

CASSIO
Let me go, sir, or I'll knock you o'er the mazzard.   145

MONTANO
Come, come, you are drunk.

CASSIO
Drunk?

They fight.

IAGO *[aside to Roderigo]*
Away I say, go out and cry a mutiny.

Exit RODERIGO.
Nay, good lieutenant. God's will, gentlemen!
Help, ho! Lieutenant! Sir! Montano! Sir!   150
Help, masters! Here's a goodly watch indeed!

A bell rings.
Who's that which rings the bell? Diablo, ho!
The town will rise. God's will, lieutenant,
You'll be ashamed forever.

Enter OTHELLO and GENTLEMEN, with weapons.

OTHELLO
What's the matter here?

MONTANO
                         Zounds, I bleed still,   155
I am hurt, to the death.

OTHELLO
                         Hold, for your lives!

140   *knave:* scoundrel, rogue
141   *wicker bottle:* wicker-covered bottle

143   *prate:* speak, answer back

145   *mazzard:* head

148   *cry a mutiny:* call out that there's a riot

149   *God's will:* let God's will be done. Iago is calling for a stop to the fighting at the same time as he is shouting in order to spread alarm and confusion

152   *Diablo:* devil
153   *rise:* grow riotous
154   *ashamed:* disgraced

156   *to the death:* fatally

156   *Hold ... lives:* stop, or you die

IAGO

Hold, hold,
Lieutenant. Sir. Montano. Gentlemen!

Have you forgot all place of sense and duty?

Hold, the general speaks to you. Hold, hold, for shame!

OTHELLO

160   Why, how now, ho! From whence arises this?

Are we turn'd Turks, and to ourselves do that

Which heaven has forbid the Ottomites?

For Christian shame, put by this barbarous brawl.

He that stirs next, to carve for his own rage,

165   Holds his soul light, he dies upon his motion.

Silence that dreadful bell, it frights the isle

From her propriety. What's the matter, masters?

Honest Iago, that looks dead with grieving,

Speak. Who began this? On thy love, I charge thee.

IAGO

170   I do not know. Friends all but now, even now,

In quarter and in terms like bride and groom,

Devesting them for bed, and then but now,

As if some planet had unwitted men,

Swords out and tilting one at other's breast

175   In opposition bloody. I cannot speak

Any beginning to this peevish odds

And would in action glorious I had lost

Those legs that brought me to a part of it!

OTHELLO

How comes it, Michael, you are thus forgot?

CASSIO

180   I pray you pardon me, I cannot speak.

OTHELLO

Worthy Montano, you were wont be civil,

The gravity and stillness of your youth

The world hath noted, and your name is great

In mouths of wisest censure. What's the matter

185   That you unlace your reputation thus,

And spend your rich opinion for the name

Of a night-brawler? Give me answer to't.

MONTANO

Worthy Othello, I am hurt to danger.

Your officer Iago can inform you —

---

160 *From whence:* from where

161–2 *Are ... Ottomites:* are we going to kill each other, and so do what heaven has prevented the Turks from doing to us (by destroying them at sea)?

164 *carve ... rage:* gratify his anger

165 *Holds ... motion:* puts very little value on his life, as he will die as soon as he moves

167 *propriety:* natural peace and quiet

171 *In quarter:* on good terms, or, more probably, on duty

172 *Devesting:* undressing

173 *As ... men:* as if they came under the evil influence of some planet and so were deprived of their wits

175–6 *speak ... odds:* say what began this silly quarrel

179 *How ... forgot:* Michael, how did you come to neglect your responsibility?

182 *stillness:* sober habits

184 *wisest censure:* most reliable judgement

185 *unlace:* undo or do damage to

186 *spend ... opinion:* throw away the good opinion people have formed of you

188 *hurt to danger:* have a serious wound

While I spare speech, which something now offends me — 190
Of all that I do know, nor know I aught
By me that's said or done amiss this night,
Unless self-charity be sometime a vice,
And to defend ourselves it be a sin
When violence assails us.

OTHELLO

            Now, by heaven, 195
My blood begins my safer guides to rule,
And passion, having my best judgement collied,
Assays to lead the way. Zounds, if I stir
Or do but lift this arm, the best of you
Shall sink in my rebuke. Give me to know 200
How this foul rout began, who set it on,
And he that is approv'd in this offence,
Though he had twinn'd with me, both at a birth,
Shall lose me. What, in a town of war,
Yet wild, the people's hearts brim-full of fear, 205
To manage private and domestic quarrels
In night, and on the court and guard of safety!
'Tis monstrous. Iago, who began't?

190 *While ... me:* I must be sparing of my speech, because, being badly wounded, speaking hurts me

193 *Unless ... vice:* unless it is sometimes wrong to act on one's own interests

195–208 Montano's evasive answer causes Othello to lose his patience and temper. Iago makes deadly use of his experience of this fact in Act 3, Scene 3

196–8 *My ... way:* emotion is beginning to overpower my reason, and passion, clouding my judgement, tries to lead me on

202 *approv'd:* proved guilty

204 *town of war:* garrison town

206 *manage:* conduct

How comes it, Michael, you are thus forgot?
OTHELLO, Act 2, Scene 3, 179

MONTANO

If partially affin'd, or leagu'd in office,

210   Thou dost deliver more or less than truth,

Thou art no soldier.

IAGO

                Touch me not so near,

I had rather ha' this tongue cut from my mouth

Than it should do offence to Michael Cassio,

Yet I persuade myself to speak the truth

215   Shall nothing wrong him. Thus it is, general:

Montano and myself being in speech,

There comes a fellow crying out for help,

And Cassio following him with determin'd sword

To execute upon him. Sir, this gentleman

220   Steps in to Cassio and entreats his pause;

Myself the crying fellow did pursue,

Lest by his clamour (as it so fell out)

The town might fall in fright. He, swift of foot,

Outran my purpose, and I return'd, the rather,

225   For that I heard the clink and fall of swords

And Cassio high in oaths, which till to-night

I ne'er might say before. When I came back —

For this was brief — I found them close together

At blow and thrust, even as again they were

230   When you yourself did part them.

More of this matter can I not report,

But men are men, the best sometimes forget.

Though Cassio did some little wrong to him,

As men in rage strike those that wish them best,

235   Yet surely Cassio, I believe, receiv'd

From him that fled some strange indignity,

Which patience could not pass.

OTHELLO

                I know, Iago,

Thy honesty and love doth mince this matter,

Making it light to Cassio. Cassio, I love thee,

240   But never more be officer of mine.

Enter DESDEMONA, with others.

Look, if my gentle love be not rais'd up!

I'll make thee an example.

Notes (left margin)

209 *If partially ... office:* if you [Iago] are favourably disposed [to Cassio] either because you are related or because you are his fellow-officer

211 *Touch ... near:* Iago is asking Montano and Othello not to press him too hard

211–37 A virtuoso display of Iago's opportunism. Granville-Barker comments that Iago 'has only – how conveniently! – to speak the truth. He gives it convincing clarity and circumstance, falsifies it ever so slightly. It is not the whole truth, that is all!' Notice also how cleverly Iago makes Cassio guilty in Othello's eyes, while at the same time pretending to look for excuses for Cassio's behaviour

214–15 *I persuade ... him:* I am convinced that if I give a truthful account I shall not wrong him

216 *in speech:* engaged in conversation

219 *this gentleman:* Montano

220 *entreats his pause:* begs him to stop

221 *the crying fellow:* Roderigo, who was shouting

224 *the rather:* more quickly

225 *For that:* because

226 *high in oaths:* swearing freely

236 *strange indignity:* insult of which I was unaware

237 *not pass:* not let pass

238 *mince:* give only a partial account of

239 *Making ... to Cassio:* toning it down in favour of Cassio. Note Othello's switch to a more formal mode of address; this shows him distancing himself from Cassio, whom he previously addressed as 'Michael' (see lines 1, 7 and 179 of this scene)

DESDEMONA
What's the matter?

OTHELLO
All's well now, sweeting, come away to bed.
Sir, for your hurts, myself will be your surgeon;   245
Lead him off.

MONTANO is led off.
Iago, look with care about the town
And silence those whom this vile brawl distracted.
Come, Desdemona, 'tis the soldiers' life,
To have their balmy slumbers wak'd with strife.   250

Exeunt all but IAGO and CASSIO.

IAGO
What, are you hurt, lieutenant?

CASSIO
Ay, past all surgery.

IAGO
Marry, heaven forbid!

CASSIO
Reputation, reputation, reputation! O, I have lost my
reputation. I have lost the immortal part of myself,   255
and what remains is bestial. My reputation, Iago, my
reputation.

IAGO
As I am an honest man, I thought you had receiv'd
some bodily wound. There is more offence in that
than in reputation: reputation is an idle and most false   260
imposition, oft got without merit and lost without
deserving. You have lost no reputation at all, unless
you repute yourself such a loser. What, man, there are
ways to recover the general again: you are but now
cast in his mood, a punishment more in policy than   265
in malice, even so as one would beat his offenceless
dog to affright an imperious lion. Sue to him again
and he's yours.

CASSIO
I will rather sue to be despis'd than to deceive so
good a commander with so light, so drunken and   270

245 *Sir:* Montano

248 *distracted:* agitated

259 *offence:* hurt, injury
260–1 *idle ... imposition:* useless and false thing imposed
on people from the outside

264 *recover the general:* get back to Othello's favour

265 *cast in his mood:* dismissed from your post because
of his angry mood
265–6 *more ... malice:* dictated more by political necessity
than by ill feeling
266 *even so:* just
267 *Sue:* petition

270 *light:* irresponsible

271 *speak parrot:* talk nonsense

272 *discourse fustian:* talk coarse rubbish

281 *nothing wherefore:* not the reason for the quarrel

282 *an enemy:* drink

283 *pleasance:* pleasure

284 *applause:* the desire to win the admiration of our fellow revellers

288 *wrath:* anger
unperfectness: imperfection, flaw

290 *moraller:* moralist or moraliser

295 *Hydra:* a mythological snake that grew two heads for each one cut off

296 *sensible:* possessing all one's faculties

298 *inordinate:* excessive
ingredience: ingredient, the main component of the mixture

indiscreet an officer. Drunk? And speak parrot? And squabble? Swagger? Swear? And discourse fustian with one's own shadow? O thou invisible spirit of wine, if thou hast no name to be known by, let us call
275 thee devil!

IAGO

What was he that you followed with your sword? What had he done to you?

CASSIO

I know not.

IAGO

Is't possible?

CASSIO

280 I remember a mass of things, but nothing distinctly; a quarrel, but nothing wherefore. O God, that men should put an enemy in their mouths to steal away their brains; that we should, with joy, pleasance, revel and applause, transform ourselves into beasts!

IAGO

285 Why, but you are now well enough: how came you thus recovered?

CASSIO

It hath pleas'd the devil drunkenness to give place to the devil wrath. One unperfectness shows me another, to make me frankly despise myself.

IAGO

290 Come, you are too severe a moraller. As the time, the place, the condition of this country stands, I could heartily wish this had not so befallen, but since it is as it is, mend it for your own good.

CASSIO

I will ask him for my place again. He shall tell me I
295 am a drunkard. Had I as many mouths as Hydra, such an answer would stop 'em all. To be now a sensible man, by and by a fool, and presently a beast! Every inordinate cup is unblessed, and the ingredience is a devil.

IAGO

Come, come, good wine is a good familiar creature if it be well us'd. Exclaim no more against it. And, good lieutenant, I think you think I love you.

CASSIO

I have well approved it, sir — I drunk!

IAGO

You, or any man living, may be drunk at some time. I'll tell you what you shall do. Our general's wife is now the general; I may say so in this respect, for that he has devoted and given up himself to the contemplation, mark and denotement of her parts and graces. Confess yourself freely to her, importune her. She'll help to put you in your place again. She is so free, so kind, so apt, so blessed a disposition that she holds it a vice in her goodness not to do more than she is requested. This brawl between you and her husband entreat her to splinter, and, my fortunes against any lay worth naming, this crack of your love shall grow stronger than 'twas before.

CASSIO

You advise me well.

IAGO

I protest in the sincerity of love and honest kindness.

CASSIO

I think it freely, and betimes in the morning will I beseech the virtuous Desdemona to undertake for me. I am desperate of my fortunes, if they check me here.

IAGO

You are in the right. Good night, lieutenant, I must to the watch.

CASSIO

Good night, honest Iago.

Exit.

300

305

310

315

320

325

300 *familiar:* friendly

303 *well approved it:* clearly proved it, given good evidence of it. This is a fine example of irony

306–8 *I may ... parts:* I base my observation on the fact that Othello has given himself over to the study of Desdemona's qualities

309 *importune her:* ask Desdemona urgently and persistently

314 *splinter:* mend (apply splints to)

315 *lay:* wager

319 *think it freely:* readily believe it
betimes: early

320 *undertake:* plead my case

321 *check:* rebuke, repulse

IAGO

And what's he then that says I play the villain,

When this advice is free I give, and honest,

Probal to thinking, and indeed the course

To win the Moor again? For 'tis most easy

330   The inclining Desdemona to subdue

In any honest suit; she's fram'd as fruitful

As the free elements; and then for her

To win the Moor, were't to renounce his baptism,

All seals and symbols of redeemed sin;

335   His soul is so infetter'd to her love

That she may make, unmake, do what she list,

Even as her appetite shall play the god

With his weak function. How am I then a villain,

To counsel Cassio to this parallel course

340   Directly to his good? Divinity of hell!

When devils will their blackest sins put on,

They do suggest at first with heavenly shows,

As I do now. For whiles this honest fool

Plies Desdemona to repair his fortunes,

345   And she for him pleads strongly to the Moor,

I'll pour this pestilence into his ear:

That she repeals him for her body's lust,

And by how much she strives to do him good,

She shall undo her credit with the Moor;

350   So will I turn her virtue into pitch,

And out of her own goodness make the net

That shall enmesh 'em all.

Enter RODERIGO.

How now, Roderigo?

RODERIGO

I do follow here in the chase, not like a hound that

hunts, but one that fills up the cry. My money is

355   almost spent; I ha' been to-night exceedingly well

cudgel'd; and I think the issue will be I shall have so

much experience for my pains, as that comes to, and

no money at all, and with that wit return to Venice.

Iago's Fourth Soliloquy

327   *free:* frank, generous

328   *Probal to:* proved or confirmed by

330   *inclining:* inclined to be helpful

331–2   *she's fram'd ... elements:* nature has made her as generous as itself

332–8   *and then ... function:* she could persuade Othello to anything, even if it meant betraying his religion; he is so much the prisoner of his love that she can order as she likes and do what she likes, just as his desire for her dominates his vulnerable nature

334   *seals ... sin:* the marks of Othello's Christianity

338   *his weak function:* Othello's ability to resist Desdemona is weak

339–40   *parallel ... good:* course of action coinciding with his wish or purpose

340   *Divinity of hell:* Iago's god is the devil; the 'divinity' in question is the teaching offered by the devil, which Iago takes to heart

341–2   *When ... shows:* when evil men want to advance their evil purposes, they first take on a heavenly appearance (to tempt the unwary)

344   *Plies:* urges, petitions, begs

347   *repeals:* asks for him to be called back into favour

350   *pitch:* suggests blackness and filth

354   *fills up the cry:* fills up the pack (hunting metaphor). Roderigo is saying that he does not have a very significant part to play

356   *cudgel'd:* beaten

358   *wit:* sense

IAGO

How poor are they that have not patience!

What wound did ever heal but by degrees? 360

Thou knowest we work by wit, and not by witchcraft,

And wit depends on dilatory time.

Does't not go well? Cassio hath beaten thee,

And thou, by that small hurt, hast cashier'd Cassio.

Though other things grow fair against the sun, 365

But fruits that blossom first, will first be ripe.

Content thyself awhile. By the mass, 'tis morning;

Pleasure and action make the hours seem short.

Retire thee, go where thou art billeted.

Away I say. Thou shalt know more hereafter. 370

Nay, get thee gone.

Exit RODERIGO.

　　　　　　Two things are to be done.

My wife must move for Cassio to her mistress;

I'll set her on.

Myself awhile to draw the Moor apart,

And bring him jump when he may Cassio find 375

Soliciting his wife. Ay, that's the way,

Dull not device by coldness and delay.

Exit.

359 Iago is quoting a common proverb: 'He that has no patience has nothing'

361 *wit:* quickness of understanding

362 *dilatory:* protracted, extended, slow

364 *cashier'd:* dismissed from his position of command

365–6 *Though ... ripe:* the first line seems to mean that some things (i.e. plots) thrive in spite of the conditions. The second line tells us that the fruits (i.e. plots) that ripen first are those that blossom first. The exact relevance of this to the context is not clear, which can also be said of some of Iago's other proverbs

367 *'tis morning:* as the scene opens at ten o'clock in the evening, Shakespeare has made the twenty minutes of stage time it takes to play this scene do duty for perhaps nine hours of represented time

372 *move:* petition

374 *awhile:* at the same time

375 *jump:* at the exact time and place

377 *device:* plot

Key points

Othello trusts Cassio to keep the celebrations under control. Cassio notes that Iago has taken care of matters and Othello, in one of the recurring ironies of the play, pays tribute to Iago's honesty.

- Iago's and Cassio's discussion of Desdemona underlines an essential contrast between these two men: Iago's coarseness is set against Cassio's delicacy.

- This brawl scene is a miniature play within the main play. Iago is the scriptwriter and producer as well as the main actor. He creates and manages the situation with skill and cunning.

- One of Iago's most remarkable talents is his ability to adapt to changing circumstances. He begins as a companion to Cassio, full of good cheer. Having succeeded in getting Cassio drunk, he takes on a more sinister role and lies effectively to Montano about Cassio's 'infirmity' (addiction to alcohol; line 120). He makes this supposed revelation all the more convincing by also paying tribute to Cassio's abilities as a soldier. It is as if he is saying to Montano: Cassio is an outstanding soldier, but it is a great pity that he gets drunk so often.

- Iago changes from hypocrite to outright villain when he puts Roderigo to work making further mischief ('go out and cry a mutiny'; line 148).

- Next Iago takes on the role of upholder of law and order, asking all present to show due respect for Othello.

- As Othello investigates the brawl, Iago plays the part that suits him best: he becomes honest Iago, straining to give an impartial account of what has happened. He impresses Othello with his pained reaction to Cassio's lapse. His talent for hypocrisy is again to the fore as he tells his story against Cassio with a fine show of reluctance and misgiving.

- Having performed to his own advantage what everyone else admires as a public duty, Iago switches to the role of faithful counsellor and consoler of Cassio. He is able to convince Cassio that he can regain Othello's favour by employing Desdemona to plead with her husband to reinstate him.

- The real Iago fully emerges in his great soliloquy (lines 326–52). Here he is the self-confessed evildoer whose god is the devil, and whose method is to conceal his 'blackest sins' under 'heavenly shows'.

- Iago uses his powers of reasoning to ease Roderigo's troubled mind. He points out that, for the price of a minor injury, Roderigo has secured the dismissal of Cassio (his apparent rival for Desdemona's affections).

- The scene also throws important light on Othello's character, and on the reasons for Iago's success in destroying Othello's faith in Desdemona.

- Othello has placed his trust in Cassio. Now that Cassio has disappointed him, he finds his faith in his own judgement weakened, and he will be all the more easily tempted to question Desdemona's fidelity to him when Iago comes to cast doubt on that.

- Meanwhile, Othello's belief in Iago's honesty, goodness and wisdom is further strengthened. He is convinced that Iago has done his best to shield Cassio from the consequences of his drunkenness, without betraying the interests of Venice. He sees Iago as both a loyal friend and a patriot.

- Having thus gained Othello's total trust, Iago will later be able to arouse his suspicions of Desdemona and Cassio without being suspected of having evil motives.

- The relationship shown here between Iago (beloved, trusted servant and friend) and Othello (trusting, grateful master and friend) will also be evident in the temptation scene (Act 3, Scene 3), when Othello will again praise Iago for his love and honesty.

- The brawl scene reveals a dangerous side of Othello's character: his nature inclines him to take action without making a full and painstaking examination of the evidence. He cannot tolerate uncertainty; he must know quickly who is responsible for the brawl. When he finds out, he acts immediately and decisively.

- We also see that Othello likes to regard himself as a just man, even as an instrument of justice, and is ready to perform harsh acts of punishment without taking time to reflect. For example, he is quick to dismiss Cassio, his trusted lieutenant and friend. This determination to act justly, whatever the implications, will be fatally evident in his dealings with Desdemona.

- Iago will exploit these aspects of Othello's personality. Knowing Othello as he does, all Iago has to do is arouse suspicion and call it proof; he can then leave it to his victim to take swift and unconsidered action against Desdemona.

Useful quotes

I fear the trust Othello puts him in,
On some odd time of his infirmity,
Will shake this island.

(Iago, lines 119–21)

I know, Iago,
Thy honesty and love doth mince this matter,
Making it light to Cassio. Cassio, I love thee,
But never more be officer of mine.

(Othello, lines 237–40)

And 'tis great pity that the noble Moor
Should hazard such a place as his own second
With one of an ingraft infirmity.
It were an honest action to say so
To the Moor.

(Montano, lines 131–5)

And by how much she strives to do him good,
She shall undo her credit with the Moor;
So will I turn her virtue into pitch,
And out of her own goodness make the net
That shall enmesh 'em all.

(Iago, lines 348–52)

My blood begins my safer guides to rule,
And passion, having my best judgement collied,
Assays to lead the way. Zounds, if I stir
Or do but lift this arm, the best of you
Shall sink in my rebuke.

(Othello, lines 196–200)

Questions ?

1 Othello's form of address to Cassio at the beginning of the scene is significant. What attitude does it suggest? How does his tone towards Cassio change later in the scene?

2 What does the Cassio–Iago dialogue on the subject of Desdemona (lines 13–26) tell you about each of these characters?

3 How does Iago manage to get Cassio drunk?

4 What opinion do you form of Cassio on the evidence of his behaviour during the drinking episode (lines 60–112)?

5 How does Iago display his cunning in dealing with Othello and Montano?

6 What aspects of Othello's character are displayed in this scene?

7 Describe the Othello–Iago relationship in this scene.

8 Explain the success of Iago's schemes in this scene.

9 What does Iago reveal in his soliloquy (lines 326–52) about his own nature and purposes?

10 What evidence is there that Iago has been enjoying his deadly activities?

ACT 2 ⚟ Key moments

Scene 1

- A storm has destroyed the Turkish fleet. Othello is therefore free to come ashore in Cyprus and be reunited with Desdemona, and Iago can concentrate on his plans to undermine Othello's marriage and discredit Cassio.
- Cassio's absolute loyalty to Othello and devotion to Desdemona are established.
- Iago convinces Roderigo that Desdemona is in love with Cassio. Iago will use Roderigo's anger to further his own plans.
- In a soliloquy, Iago shares his hatred for Othello with the audience, but also acknowledges Othello's good qualities. He claims that Othello and Cassio have betrayed him and he intends to get even with both men.

Scene 2

- A herald proclaims that Othello has declared an evening of festivities to celebrate both the destruction of the Turkish fleet and his recent marriage to Desdemona.

Scene 3

- Iago succeeds in making Cassio drunk while on duty. He convinces Montano that Cassio is often drunk.
- Roderigo, incited by Iago, provokes Cassio to a fight. A riot erupts.
- Othello intervenes and Iago manipulates the situation to make sure that Othello blames Cassio and dismisses him as his lieutenant.
- Pretending to console Cassio, Iago persuades him to ask Desdemona to intervene with Othello on his behalf.
- Iago decides that he will also get Emilia to plead Cassio's case with Desdemona. This will influence Desdemona to take Cassio's request seriously when he asks for her help.
- Iago plans to bring Othello to where he will find Cassio and Desdemona together, hoping that this will arouse Othello's suspicions.

ACT 2 ⚟ Speaking and listening

1 In small groups, choose one member to play the role of Iago. Take turns to question Iago on his opinion of the other characters, his attitudes on, for example, women, love and friendship, and the motives for his behaviour. As a group, seek to establish Iago's reasons for wanting revenge on Othello and Cassio and decide whether they are justified. Report your conclusions back to the class.

2 In groups of four, assign the roles of Iago, Desdemona, Cassio and Othello. Each person should choose and recite a short speech (from either of the first two Acts) that indicates their character's true nature. As a group, identify and discuss the characteristics revealed.

Plot summary

I T IS MORNING AND Cassio has hired musicians to entertain Othello and Desdemona. Othello does not care much for the music, and sends a clown, or professional jester, to banish the musicians. He does this in an amusing way, providing the only humorous episode in a grim play (if we exclude Cassio's drunken comments). Iago sends Emilia to Cassio, promising to get Othello out of the way so that they may speak freely. Emilia brings good news: Othello will restore Cassio to his previous position at the earliest opportunity. Cassio should be satisfied with this promise, but instead thinks he will have a better chance if he speaks to Desdemona. He persuades Emilia to arrange a private meeting between Desdemona and himself.

There's a poor piece of gold for thee: if the gentlewoman that attends the general's wife be stirring, tell her there's one Cassio entreats her a little favour of speech.

CASSIO, Act 3, Scene 1, 23–6

1 *content your pains:* reward you for your trouble

2 Cassio, anxious to recover Othello's favour, is asking the musicians to play a morning serenade in his honour, intended to put Othello in good humour

4 *i' the nose:* the clown (a jester or fool) may be referring to the nasal tone associated with Naples

7 *marry are they:* by the Virgin Mary, they are

8 *thereby ... tail:* there's a story attached to that; also a pun concerning flatulence. A pun is a joke based on a word having two distinct meanings or associations. Puns are a common feature of Shakespeare's plays

15 *to't:* play it

18 *ha' none such:* have no such music (i.e. no music that cannot be heard)

Cyprus. Before the citadel.

Enter CASSIO and MUSICIANS.

CASSIO
Masters, play here. I will content your pains.
Something that's brief, and bid 'Good morrow, general.'

They play. Enter CLOWN.

CLOWN
Why, masters, ha' your instruments been at Naples
That they speak i' the nose thus?

FIRST MUSICIAN
5   How, sir, how?

CLOWN
Are these, I pray, call'd wind-instruments?

FIRST MUSICIAN
Ay, marry are they, sir.

CLOWN
O, thereby hangs a tail.

FIRST MUSICIAN
Whereby hangs a tale, sir?

CLOWN
10   Marry, sir, by many a wind-instrument that I know.
But, masters, here's money for you, and the general
so likes your music that he desires you, for love's sake,
to make no more noise with it.

FIRST MUSICIAN
Well, sir, we will not.

CLOWN
15   If you have any music that may not be heard, to't
again. But, as they say, to hear music the general does
not greatly care.

FIRST MUSICIAN
We ha' none such, sir.

CLOWN
Then put up your pipes in your bag, for I'll away. Go,
20   vanish away!

Exeunt MUSICIANS.

CASSIO

Dost thou hear, my honest friend?

CLOWN

No, I hear not your honest friend. I hear you.

CASSIO

Prithee, keep up thy quillets. There's a poor piece of gold for thee: if the gentlewoman that attends the general's wife be stirring, tell her there's one Cassio entreats her a little favour of speech. Wilt thou do this?

25

23 *Prithee ... quillets:* please give up your puns

CLOWN

She is stirring, sir, if she will stir hither, I shall seem to notify unto her.

Enter IAGO.

28–9 The clown appears to be mocking Cassio's polite, formal speech
seem: arrange, go about the business of

CASSIO

Do, good my friend.

Exit CLOWN.

         In happy time, Iago.

30

30 *In happy time:* I am glad to see you

IAGO

You have not been a-bed, then?

31 *a-bed:* to bed

CASSIO

Why no, the day had broke before we parted.
I ha' made bold, Iago,
To send in to your wife. My suit to her
Is that she will to virtuous Desdemona
Procure me some access.

35

34 *suit:* petition

IAGO

         I'll send her to you presently,
And I'll devise a mean to draw the Moor
Out of the way, that your converse and business
May be more free.

36 *presently:* at once
37 *mean:* means

39 *more free:* less inhibited, less restricted

CASSIO

I humbly thank you for it.

Exit IAGO.

         I never knew
A Florentine more kind and honest.

Enter EMILIA.

40

40–1 *I never ... honest:* Cassio, in his simplicity of heart, is saying that he has never met the kindness and honesty of Iago (a Venetian) among his own Florentine countrymen

43 *displeasure:* being out of favour

47 *great affinity:* has relatives of high rank

47–8 *in wholesome ... refuse you:* if he were to take common sense and prudence into account, he would have to turn down your request

49–51 *his likings ... again:* his love for you is such that he will avail of the earliest appropriate and safe opportunity to restore you to your former position

55 *bestow:* place

56 *bosom:* innermost thoughts

EMILIA

Good morrow, good lieutenant. I am sorry

For your displeasure, but all will sure be well.

The general and his wife are talking of it,

45 And she speaks for you stoutly. The Moor replies

That he you hurt is of great fame in Cyprus,

And great affinity, and that in wholesome wisdom

He might not but refuse you, but he protests he loves you,

And needs no other suitor but his likings

50 To take the safest occasion by the front

To bring you in again.

CASSIO

                    Yet, I beseech you,

If you think fit, or that it may be done,

Give me advantage of some brief discourse

With Desdemona alone.

EMILIA

                    Pray you, come in,

55 I will bestow you where you shall have time

To speak your bosom freely.

CASSIO

                    I am much bound to you.

Exeunt.

Key points

Iago's plans are aided by good luck. Cassio, tormented by his fall from grace, cannot wait patiently for Othello's pardon to take effect. Instead, he insists on taking action on the morning after the brawl.

- Othello's abrupt rejection of the music may be due to his knowledge that its source is Cassio. If this is the case, Cassio is remiss in not being able to read the meaning of Othello's gesture, and act accordingly.

- Without knowing it, Cassio is playing into Iago's hands. Iago will use the meeting between Cassio and Desdemona to raise doubts in Othello's mind about his wife's relationship with Cassio.

- In forcing an immediate interview with Desdemona, Cassio unwittingly assists in her undoing. In the temptation scene (Act 3, Scene 3), Desdemona's childlike persistence in trying to have Cassio reinstated irritates Othello beyond patience.

- Iago, as always, turns up at the moment when he can most effectively advance his own designs.

- He is greeted by Cassio's 'In happy time, Iago' (line 30), one of the numerous instances in the play when the speaker is totally blind to the implications of what he is saying.

- Cassio, a native of Florence, pays one of many ironic tributes to Iago: 'I never knew a Florentine more kind and honest' (lines 40–1). The point here is that Cassio is so impressed by Iago's apparent sincerity that he considers the character and behaviour of the Venetian Iago worthy of his Florentine countrymen. Such behaviour as Iago's in a Venetian was bound to seem surprising to Cassio, since Venetians had a reputation for cunning and self-interest.

- It should be noted that Cassio is bound to be favourably impressed, indeed deeply touched, by Iago's apparent concern and activity on his behalf. After all, if Desdemona's appeal (engineered by Iago) is successful, then Iago's chance of replacing him as Othello's lieutenant will be lost.

Useful quotes

> I ha' made bold, Iago,
> To send in to your wife. My suit to her
> Is that she will to virtuous Desdemona
> Procure me some access.
>
> (Cassio, lines 33–6)

> And I'll devise a mean to draw the Moor
> Out of the way, that your converse and business
> May be more free.
>
> (Iago, lines 37–9)

Questions ?

1 What is the purpose of this brief scene?

2 What type of music would you expect the musicians to play? Give reasons for your answer.

3 What significance is there in Othello's message to the effect that he does not like the music arranged for him by Cassio?

4 If you were staging a performance of *Othello,* how would you portray the Clown? Consider issues such as costume, make-up, props, choice of actor, voice and movement in your answer.

5 Comment on the timing of Iago's arrival on the scene.

6 What sense do you get of the relationship between Emilia and Desdemona in this scene?

7 Describe Cassio's behaviour in this scene.

8 How does Cassio create new problems for Desdemona?

9 It has been said of this scene that none of the characters in it, apart from Iago, can possibly understand what is really happening to them. Can you find evidence for this point of view?

10 There are various ironies in this scene. Comment on these. (See also Themes: Tragic irony, p. 211.)

ACT 3 ✝ Scene 2

Plot summary

THIS, THE SHORTEST SCENE in the play, features a further irony. Othello is inspecting the Venetian defences against the enemy, little thinking that his personal defences are soon to be undermined by an enemy within: Iago. The fact that he is inspecting the defences may be a further indication of Iago's ingenuity, since this may be the means he uses to 'draw the Moor out of the way' (Act 3, Scene 1, lines 37–8), thus fulfilling the promise he made to Cassio.

Cyprus. The citadel.

Enter OTHELLO, IAGO, and GENTLEMEN.

OTHELLO
These letters give, Iago, to the pilot,
And by him do my duties to the senate.
That done, I will be walking on the works,
Repair there to me.

IAGO
                     Well, my good lord, I'll do't.

OTHELLO
This fortification, gentlemen, shall we see't?

GENTLEMEN
We wait upon your lordship.

Exeunt.

2 *by him ... senate:* the pilot will convey Othello's respects and see to it that his dispatches reach the Venetian authorities

3 *works:* fortifications

4 *Repair:* go

5 Iago may have suggested this inspection to Othello in order to enable Cassio to see Desdemona alone

5

ACT 3 ✟ Scene 3

Plot summary

THIS IS THE 'TEMPTATION scene', the longest and most important in the play. Iago's plot comes to a head in this pivotal scene, which falls naturally into five parts.

1 CASSIO'S SUIT (LINES 1–41): Desdemona assures Cassio that she will plead energetically with Othello on his behalf. Her promise is made with frank, almost childlike, enthusiasm. Emilia is not aware of Iago's true intentions: when she tells Cassio that his predicament grieves Iago, she is speaking the truth as she sees it. Cassio's sudden anxiety to leave Desdemona as Othello approaches is, presumably, because he is ashamed of his recent behaviour. However, it gives Iago the opportunity to suggest a more sinister interpretation.

2 DESDEMONA'S PLEA (LINES 42–93): Othello's mind is troubled by Iago's comments and the furtive manner of Cassio's departure. Matters are not improved by Desdemona's insistent, irritating and repetitious pleas on Cassio's behalf. Othello dismisses her with barely concealed impatience. The conversation marks a distinct deterioration in their relationship.

3 IAGO'S FIRST TEMPTATION OF OTHELLO (LINES 94–283): Iago sets to work, concentrating first on Cassio's role as a go-between in Othello's wooing of Desdemona, and allows Othello to recall the nature of Cassio's recent departure and his reservations about it. Iago's strategy is to throw out mysterious hints of something unpleasant that he does not wish to bother Othello with, certain at the same time that his victim will want to hear more. Othello is hooked. He cannot let the matter drop and his suspicions grow. Iago warns him of the dangers of jealousy, and subtly mentions the unhappy lot of the deceived husband. He then proceeds to make Othello even more jealous. Iago (the Venetian insider) tells Othello (the Moorish outsider) that Venetian women (Desdemona being one of them) are notorious for their infidelity to their husbands. He reminds Othello of Desdemona's deception of her father in marrying him (the suggestion being that if she can deceive her father, she is quite capable of deceiving her husband). Then he remarks how unnatural it was for her to prefer Othello to a man of her own race (implying that she will inevitably regret her marriage and look elsewhere).

Othello's first soliloquy in the play (lines 262–81) reveals the moral and psychological damage Iago has been able to inflict on him. Othello is so convinced of Iago's honesty and knowledge of human nature that he searches for reasons for Desdemona's 'infidelity' as though it is an established fact.

4 LOSS OF THE HANDKERCHIEF (LINES 283–334): The sight of Desdemona causes confusion in Othello's mind. Desdemona notices a distressing change in his attitude and behaviour. In trying to help, she drops her handkerchief (a gift to her from Othello, and a token to which he attaches enormous significance). Emilia picks up the handkerchief and gives it to Iago, who has often asked her to steal it. Iago decides to plant the handkerchief at Cassio's lodgings.

5 IAGO'S SECOND TEMPTATION OF OTHELLO (LINES 335–486): Othello has lost his sense of proportion. His speech becomes disordered and he grasps vainly at contradictory ways of relieving his mind, first abusing Iago for having opened his eyes to Desdemona's 'infidelity', and then demanding proof of her guilt. Iago, of course, has no proof to offer, but argues that strong circumstantial evidence ought to be enough to satisfy Othello. He cleverly mentions two pieces of manufactured evidence: Cassio's dream, the falsehood of which cannot be detected, and Cassio's possession of Desdemona's handkerchief. Othello orders Iago to see to Cassio's death, decides to kill Desdemona, and makes Iago his lieutenant in place of Cassio.

For thy solicitor shall rather die
Than give thy cause away.
DESDEMONA, Act 3, Scene 3, 27–8

Cyprus. The garden of the citadel.

Enter DESDEMONA, EMILIA, and CASSIO.

DESDEMONA

Be thou assur'd, good Cassio, I will do

All my abilities in thy behalf.

EMILIA

Good madam, do. I know it grieves my husband,

As if the case were his.

DESDEMONA

O, that's an honest fellow — do not doubt, Cassio,   5

But I will have my lord and you again

As friendly as you were.

CASSIO

                    Bounteous madam,

Whatever shall become of Michael Cassio,

He's never anything but your true servant.

DESDEMONA

O sir, I thank you; you do love my lord,   10

You have known him long, and be you well assur'd

He shall in strangeness stand no farther off

Than in a politic distance.

CASSIO

                    Ay, but, lady,

The policy may either last so long,

Or feed upon such nice and wat'rish diet,   15

Or breed itself so out of circumstance,

That I being absent and my place supplied,

My general will forget my love and service.

DESDEMONA

Do not doubt that. Before Emilia here

I give thee warrant of thy place; assure thee,   20

If I do vow a friendship, I'll perform it

To the last article; my lord shall never rest,

I'll watch him tame, and talk him out of patience;

His bed shall seem a school, his board a shrift,

I'll intermingle everything he does   25

With Cassio's suit. Therefore be merry, Cassio,

---

2   *All my abilities:* the best I can

5   *O ... fellow:* Iago's victims – Othello, Cassio, Desdemona – all pay heartfelt tribute to their tormentor's honesty

12–13   *He ... distance:* for reasons of policy he will be obliged to distance himself from you somewhat, but he will not do this more than is necessary

14–16   *The ... circumstance:* he may decide that it is appropriate to keep me out of employment so long, or he may keep me out for trivial and weak reasons, or else circumstances may arise to make him think that it is no longer proper for him to re-employ me

17   *supplied:* filled

19   *doubt:* fear

20   *give thee warrant:* guarantee you

23   *watch him tame:* keep him awake and so wear down his resistance to my plan

24   *his ... shrift:* his dining-table will be like a confessional. She will presumably, in the guise of Othello's confessor, impose Cassio's re-employment on Othello by way of penance

27–8 *thy solicitor ... away:* the person [Desdemona] who pleads for you [Cassio] would die rather than abandon your cause. This is one of the most poignant ironies in the play

33 *Unfit ... purposes:* I'm not fit to plead my case

34 *do your discretion:* act as you think fit. This particular 'discretion' will help to unmake Cassio

35 Iago begins his temptation of Othello

43 *suitor:* petitioner

For thy solicitor shall rather die

Than give thy cause away.

Enter OTHELLO and IAGO.

EMILIA
Madam, here comes my lord.

CASSIO
30 Madam, I'll take my leave.

DESDEMONA
Why, stay and hear me speak.

CASSIO
Madam, not now, I am very ill at ease,

Unfit for mine own purposes.

DESDEMONA
Well, do your discretion.

Exit CASSIO.

IAGO
35 Ha! I like not that.

OTHELLO
What dost thou say?

IAGO
Nothing, my lord, or if … I know not what.

OTHELLO
Was not that Cassio parted from my wife?

IAGO
Cassio, my lord? No, sure, I cannot think it,

40 That he would sneak away so guilty-like,

Seeing you coming.

OTHELLO
                              I do believe 'twas he.

DESDEMONA
How now, my lord?

I have been talking with a suitor here,

A man that languishes in your displeasure.

OTHELLO
45 Who is't you mean?

DESDEMONA

Why, your lieutenant, Cassio, good my lord.

If I have any grace or power to move you,

His present reconciliation take;

For if he be not one that truly loves you,

That errs in ignorance, and not in cunning,   50

I have no judgement in an honest face.

I prithee call him back.

OTHELLO

              Went he hence now?

DESDEMONA

Yes, faith, so humbled

That he has left part of his grief with me,

To suffer with him. Good love, call him back.   55

OTHELLO

Not now, sweet Desdemona, some other time.

DESDEMONA

But shall't be shortly?

OTHELLO

             The sooner, sweet, for you.

DESDEMONA

Shall't be to-night at supper?

OTHELLO

               No, not to-night.

DESDEMONA

To-morrow dinner then?

OTHELLO

              I shall not dine at home,

I meet the captains at the citadel.   60

DESDEMONA

Why then to-morrow night, or Tuesday morn,

On Tuesday noon, or night, or Wednesday morn.

I prithee name the time, but let it not

Exceed three days. In faith, he's penitent,

And yet his trespass, in our common reason   65

(Save that they say the wars must make examples

Out of their best), is not almost a fault

---

48 *His ... take:* accept his apology for what he has done and be reconciled to him immediately

50 *That ... cunning:* his fault was not due to malice, but to ignorance of what he was doing

59 *To-morrow dinner:* at midday tomorrow

61–2 This presentation of the matter can only irritate Othello

64 *penitent:* sorry for what he did

65–8 *his trespass ... check:* it should be obvious to common sense that Cassio's offence is hardly serious enough to warrant a private rebuke (although the fact that it was committed during wartime makes it more grave as examples must be made to maintain discipline)

To incur a private check. When shall he come?

Tell me, Othello. I wonder in my soul

70   What you would ask me that I should deny?

Or stand so mammering on? What? Michael Cassio,

That came a-wooing with you, and so many a time

When I have spoke of you dispraisingly

Hath ta'en your part, to have so much to-do

75   To bring him in? By'r lady, I could do much …

OTHELLO

Prithee, no more. Let him come when he will,

I will deny thee nothing.

DESDEMONA

                 Why, this is not a boon.

'Tis as I should entreat you wear your gloves,

Or feed on nourishing dishes, or keep you warm,

80   Or sue to you to do a peculiar profit

To your own person. Nay, when I have a suit

Wherein I mean to touch your love indeed

It shall be full of poise and difficulty,

And fearful to be granted.

OTHELLO

                 I will deny thee nothing,

85   Whereon I do beseech thee grant me this:

To leave me but a little to myself.

DESDEMONA

Shall I deny you? No. Farewell, my lord.

OTHELLO

Farewell, my Desdemona, I'll come to thee straight.

DESDEMONA

Emilia, come. *[to Othello]* Be it as your fancies teach you,

90   Whate'er you be, I am obedient.

Exeunt DESDEMONA and EMILIA.

OTHELLO

Excellent wretch, perdition catch my soul

But I do love thee, and when I love thee not,

Chaos is come again.

IAGO

My noble lord …

---

71 *mammering:* hesitating

73 *dispraisingly:* disparagingly, critically

74–5 *to-do … him in:* difficulty to have him restored to his position

75 *By'r lady:* by Our Lady (an oath)

77 *boon:* favour. Desdemona is taking up his 'I will deny you nothing', and telling him that by reinstating Cassio he is not doing her a favour; she goes on to tell him that he will be doing himself a favour

80–1 *to do … person:* to confer an exclusively personal benefit on yourself

81–4 *when I … granted:* when I have some real favour to beg of you that will really test ('touch') your love for me, it will be a weighty one, difficult for you to grant, and one about which I shall be rightly apprehensive (unlike this one). Her point throughout is that Cassio's request should be granted without fuss or delay

88 *straight:* at once

89 *Be … teach you:* act according to your inclinations. The irony here is that Othello does just this, with fatal consequences for both of them

91 *wretch:* used here as a term of endearment, not of contempt

91–3 *perdition … again:* may my soul be damned if I do not love you, and if the time comes when I cease to love you, I will be overwhelmed by the kind of darkness and confusion that engulfed the primitive world

OTHELLO
What dost thou say, Iago?

IAGO
Did Michael Cassio, when you woo'd my lady,   95
Know of your love?

OTHELLO
He did from first to last. Why dost thou ask?

IAGO
But for a satisfaction of my thought,
No further harm.

OTHELLO
Why of thy thought, Iago?

IAGO
I did not think he had been acquainted with her.   100

OTHELLO
O yes, and went between us very oft.

IAGO
Indeed?

OTHELLO
Indeed? Ay, indeed. Discern'st thou aught in that?
Is he not honest?

IAGO
Honest, my lord?   105

OTHELLO
Honest? Ay, honest.

IAGO
My lord, for aught I know.

OTHELLO
What dost thou think?

IAGO
Think, my lord?

OTHELLO
Think, my lord? By heaven, he echoes me   110
As if there were some monster in his thought
Too hideous to be shown! Thou didst mean something;
I heard thee say, but now, thou lik'dst not that,
When Cassio left my wife. What didst not like?

95–6 The real menace of such a question is that Iago pretends not to want to pursue its imaginary implications, thereby making Othello think that it points to some significant fact

99 *No further harm:* Iago is implying the opposite

101 *went ... oft:* often acted as our messenger

103 *Discern'st thou aught:* do you see any significance

104–6 *honest:* the word is used ambiguously in this exchange as it can mean either honourable or sexually moral. A word is ambiguous when it has more than one possible meaning or interpretation

113 *but:* just

115	*of my counsel:* in my confidence
119	*conceit:* idea, or its image
122–4	There is irony in everything Othello says here
124	*stops:* pauses, hesitations
126	*tricks of custom:* customary tricks
127	*close denotements:* hints denoting or indicating something hidden
130–1	Another of Iago's many brazen ironies
131	*none:* not men at all
132	*Certain:* for sure, without doubt
133	*Why ... man:* Iago is saying that Cassio must be honest because he seems honest, on the premise that men should be what they seem. He misuses logic for his own purposes, i.e. to raise fresh doubts in Othello's mind
136	*ruminate:* turn over in the mind
136–7	*give ... word:* if you are thinking ill of him [Cassio], speak ill of him. Othello is now inviting Iago to incriminate Cassio

115 And when I told thee he was of my counsel
In my whole course of wooing, thou criedst 'Indeed?'
And didst contract and purse thy brow together
As if thou then hadst shut up in thy brain
Some horrible conceit. If thou dost love me,
120 Show me thy thought.

IAGO
My lord, you know I love you.

OTHELLO
                I think thou dost.
And for I know thou art full of love and honesty
And weighest thy words before thou give 'em breath,
Therefore these stops of thine fright me the more;
125 For such things in a false disloyal knave
Are tricks of custom, but in a man that's just,
They are close denotements, working from the heart
That passion cannot rule.

IAGO
             For Michael Cassio,
I dare be sworn, I think that he is honest.

OTHELLO
130 I think so too.

IAGO
            Men should be what they seem,
Or those that be not, would they might seem none!

OTHELLO
Certain, men should be what they seem.

IAGO
Why then I think Cassio's an honest man.

OTHELLO
Nay, yet there's more in this.
135 I prithee, speak to me as to thy thinkings,
As thou dost ruminate, and give the worst of thought
The worst of word.

IAGO
          Good my lord, pardon me.
Though I am bound to every act of duty,

I am not bound to that all slaves are free to.

Utter my thoughts? Why, say they are vile and false: 140

As where's that palace whereinto foul things

Sometimes intrude not? Who has a breast so pure,

But some uncleanly apprehensions

Keep leets and law-days, and in session sit

With meditations lawful?   145

OTHELLO

Thou dost conspire against thy friend, Iago,

If thou but thinkest him wrong'd and makest his ear

A stranger to thy thoughts.

IAGO

              I do beseech you,

Though I perchance am vicious in my guess

(As I confess it is my nature's plague   150

To spy into abuses, and oft my jealousy

Shapes faults that are not), I entreat you then,

From one that so imperfectly conjects,

You'd take no notice nor build yourself a trouble

Out of my scattering and unsure observance.   155

It were not for your quiet nor your good,

Nor for my manhood, honesty or wisdom,

To let you know my thoughts.

OTHELLO

              Zounds!

IAGO

Good name in man and woman, dear my lord,

Is the immediate jewel of their souls.   160

Who steals my purse, steals trash; 'tis something, nothing;

'Twas mine, 'tis his, and has been slave to thousands.

But he that filches from me my good name,

Robs me of that which not enriches him,

And makes me poor indeed.   165

OTHELLO

By heaven, I'll know thy thoughts!

IAGO

You cannot, if my heart were in your hand,

Nor shall not, whilst 'tis in my custody.

O beware, my lord, of jealousy!

[Handwritten margin note: Iago talking about a good name]

142–5 *Who … lawful:* whose mind is so pure that from time to time foul ideas ('uncleanly apprehensions') do not share a place in it with decent ones

144–5 *keep leets … lawful:* this is a legal metaphor: 'leets and law-days' are days on which local courts sit; at such 'sessions' (another legal term) good and evil thoughts are imagined by Iago as sitting side by side, the courthouse being the human mind

146 *thy friend:* me [Othello]

149 *perchance:* perhaps
vicious: incorrect

150 *plague:* curse, weakness

151–2 *oft … are not:* by admitting that his suspicions are often unjustified, Iago adds credibility to his suggestions

153 *conjects:* conjectures, guesses

155 *scattering:* random, haphazard
observance: observations

156–8 *It were … thoughts:* it would disturb you severely if you knew my thoughts. Iago is making sure that Othello wants to know those thoughts

158 *Zounds:* by God's wounds (an oath). This exclamation conveys Othello's loss of self-control

159–65 *Good … indeed:* notice the contrast between the high value Iago places on one's reputation here, and his completely opposite view, expressed to Cassio in Act 2, Scene 3, lines 259–63, where he dismisses reputation as a useless and false thing

160 *immediate:* closest, dearest

163 *filches:* steals

170–1 *green-ey'd ... on:* Iago is depicting jealousy as the beast mocking its victim while it devours his heart

171 *cuckold:* husband of an unfaithful wife

172 *wronger:* here it means his wife

173–4 A cruel, and deadly accurate, anticipation of Othello's fate

173 *tells:* counts

174 *fondly:* foolishly

177 *fineless:* endless

181 *I'ld:* I would

182–3 *To follow ... suspicions:* to have new suspicions with every phase of the moon

183–4 *to be once ... resolv'd:* I cannot bear to be in doubt; if I am, I have to rid myself of my doubt immediately, one way or another

184–7 *Exchange ... inference:* I would rather be a goat than take seriously such exaggerated and inflated speculations as you imply

191–2 *Nor ... revolt:* the fact that my merits may be slight will not lead me to suspect that Desdemona may waver in her allegiance to me

194–6 *I'll ... jealousy:* before I suspect, I shall need the evidence of my eyes, and if I then suspect, I will require proof, one way or another; when I get this, I will cast aside either my love or my jealousy

199 *franker:* more open, candid

202 *not jealous, nor secure:* neither jealous nor free from suspicion

---

170 It is the green-ey'd monster which doth mock

The meat it feeds on. That cuckold lives in bliss,

Who, certain of his fate, loves not his wronger;

But O, what damned minutes tells he o'er

Who dotes yet doubts, suspects yet fondly loves!

OTHELLO

175 O misery!

IAGO

Poor and content is rich, and rich enough;

But riches, fineless, is as poor as winter

To him that ever fears he shall be poor.

Good God, the souls of all my tribe defend

180 From jealousy!

OTHELLO

               Why, why is this?

Think'st thou I'ld make a life of jealousy?

To follow still the changes of the moon

With fresh suspicions? No, to be once in doubt,

Is once to be resolv'd. Exchange me for a goat

185 When I shall turn the business of my soul

To such exsufflicate and blown surmises,

Matching thy inference. 'Tis not to make me jealous

To say my wife is fair, feeds well, loves company,

Is free of speech, sings, plays and dances well;

190 Where virtue is, these are more virtuous.

Nor from mine own weak merits will I draw

The smallest fear or doubt of her revolt,

For she had eyes and chose me. No, Iago,

I'll see before I doubt, when I doubt, prove,

195 And on the proof, there is no more but this:

Away at once with love or jealousy!

IAGO

I am glad of it, for now I shall have reason

To show the love and duty that I bear you

With franker spirit. Therefore, as I am bound,

200 Receive it from me. I speak not yet of proof.

Look to your wife, observe her well with Cassio.

Wear your eye thus: not jealous, nor secure.

I would not have your free and noble nature

Out of self-bounty be abused. Look to't.

I know our country disposition well: 205

In Venice they do let God see the pranks

They dare not show their husbands: their best conscience

Is not to leave undone, but keep unknown.

OTHELLO

Dost thou say so?

IAGO

She did deceive her father, marrying you.   210

And when she seem'd to shake and fear your looks,

She lov'd them most.

OTHELLO

                    And so she did.

IAGO

                           Why, go to then.

She that so young could give out such a seeming

To seal her father's eyes up, close as oak,

He thought 'twas witchcraft. But I am much to blame,   215

I humbly do beseech you of your pardon,

For too much loving you.

OTHELLO

                       I am bound to thee for ever.

IAGO

I see this hath a little dash'd your spirits.

OTHELLO

Not a jot, not a jot.

IAGO

                 I' faith I fear it has.

I hope you will consider what is spoke   220

Comes from my love. But I do see you're mov'd.

I am to pray you not to strain my speech

To grosser issues, nor to larger reach

Than to suspicion.

OTHELLO

I will not.   225

---

203 *free:* generous

204 *self-bounty:* innate kindness or generosity

205 *disposition:* temperament, natural inclination

206 *pranks:* infidelities

207–8 *their best ... unknown:* their moral code permits adultery, but prevents it from being found out. This disturbing version of Venetian morality is bound to unsettle the comparative outsider, Othello; harping on the latter's social inexperience is Iago's most effective stratagem. Othello's inexperience leaves him vulnerable to these suggestions and his tragic error may be seen to arise from his failure to recognise that Desdemona is exceptional among Venetians

212 *go to then:* well, then, what more do you want me to say

213 *seeming:* false appearance

214–15 *To seal ... witchcraft:* to blind her father to her real purposes so that he thought she must have been bewitched
close as oak: tightly

222–3 *strain ... issues:* read more into my words than is intended by them (by exaggerating them to draw large conclusions). This is a splendid irony

223–4 *larger ... suspicion:* Iago is telling Othello that his words do not warrant anything greater than suspicion

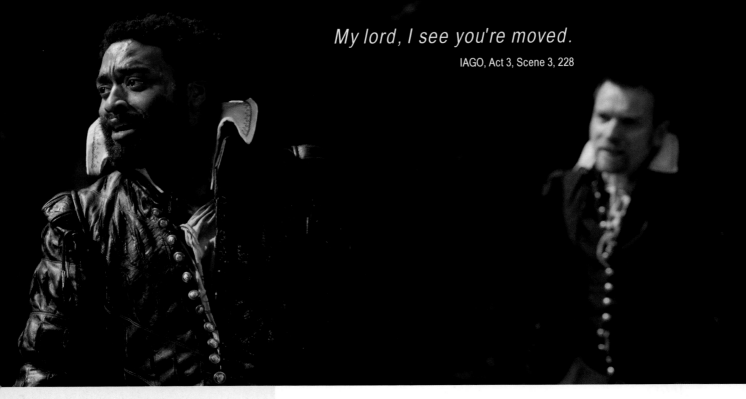

My lord, I see you're moved.

IAGO, Act 3, Scene 3, 228

IAGO

Should you do so, my lord,

My speech should fall into such vile success

As my thoughts aim not at. Cassio's my worthy friend.

My lord, I see you're mov'd.

OTHELLO

No, not much mov'd.

I do not think but Desdemona's honest.

IAGO

230 Long live she so, and long live you to think so!

OTHELLO

And yet, how nature erring from itself …

IAGO

Ay, there's the point. As, to be bold with you,

Not to affect many proposed matches

Of her own clime, complexion and degree,

235 Whereto we see in all things nature tends;

Fie, we may smell in such a will most rank,

Foul disproportion; thoughts unnatural.

But pardon me, I do not in position

Distinctly speak of her; though I may fear

240 Her will, recoiling to her better judgement,

May fall to match you with her country forms,

And happily repent.

226 *My ... success:* my words would have horrible consequences

229 *but:* otherwise than that

230 Iago's implication here is that Othello would thus be living in a fool's paradise

232–7 *Ay ... unnatural:* Iago picks up Othello's hint that Desdemona's marriage to him may be an example of an unnatural choice on her part. To be honest with you, Iago tells him, one may detect signs of a corrupted will and an unnatural lack of discretion in a woman who did not favour ('affect') a marriage with one of the many suitors of her own country, colour and rank (but chose a Moor instead)

234 *clime ... degree:* land, colour and social rank

235 *Whereto ... tends:* all things in nature seek out their own kind

236 *rank:* wanton

238–42 *I do ... repent:* I am not, by way of argument, speaking specifically of Desdemona; although I must say that I fear she may, through lapse of judgement, happen to compare your appearance with the appearance of her compatriots, and perhaps ('happily') regret her original choice

OTHELLO

Farewell, if more

Thou dost perceive, let me know more. Set on

Thy wife to observe. Leave me, Iago.

IAGO

[going] My lord, I take my leave.   245

OTHELLO

Why did I marry? This honest creature doubtless

Sees and knows more, much more, than he unfolds.

IAGO

[returning] My lord, I would I might entreat your honour

To scan this thing no further. Leave it to time.

Though it be fit that Cassio have his place,   250

For sure he fills it up with great ability,

Yet if you please to hold him off awhile,

You shall by that perceive him and his means.

Note if your lady strain his entertainment

With any strong or vehement importunity,   255

Much will be seen in that. In the mean time,

Let me be thought too busy in my fears

(As worthy cause I have to fear I am)

And hold her free, I do beseech your honour.

OTHELLO

Fear not my government.   260

IAGO

I once more take my leave.

Exit.

OTHELLO

This fellow's of exceeding honesty,

And knows all qualities, with a learned spirit,

Of human dealings. If I do prove her haggard,

Though that her jesses were my dear heart-strings,   265

I'ld whistle her off and let her down the wind

To prey at fortune. Haply, for I am black

And have not those soft parts of conversation

That chamberers have, or for I am declin'd

Into the vale of years — yet that's not much —   270

She's gone. I am abus'd and my relief

[handwritten note: Othello doubting his relationship with Desdemona]

249 *scan:* examine, consider
Leave it to time: Iago does not really want Othello to do this, and knows he will not

253 *his means:* the methods he uses to get his job back

254–5 *strain ... importunity:* press strongly for his reinstatement with particularly vehement pleading (Iago knows she will do this)

257 *busy:* prying, interfering

259 *free:* innocent

260 *government:* conduct, discretion, self-control

263–4 *And ... dealings:* Iago is well schooled in all the features of human conduct

264 *haggard:* a wild female hawk caught when in her adult plumage; here it is applied figuratively to a wild female person

265–7 *Though ... fortune:* Othello is imagining Desdemona as a poorly tamed hawk that has gone wild again; if he should prove she has, he would give her the freedom to try her fortune (fend for herself) elsewhere, however dear she is to him

265 *jesses:* straps binding the hawk's legs to the trainer's wrist

267–9 *Haply ... chamberers have:* it may be because I am black, and do not possess the refinement and social graces of men of fashion

271 *abus'd:* deceived

273 *delicate:* exquisite

274 *appetites:* desires

277–8 *'tis ... base:* men of high degree are more vulnerable to this curse than their inferiors

278 *Prerogatv'd:* privileged

279–81 *'Tis ... quicken:* betrayal by unfaithful wives is the destiny of men; it is as inevitable as death, fated upon us in the womb

282 *If ... itself:* the sight of Desdemona momentarily dispels Othello's suspicions: if she is unfaithful, he says, heaven's own truth is false

284 *generous:* well-bred, noble-minded

289 *watching:* staying awake

291 *napkin:* handkerchief (that she was going to bind his head with). Desdemona's concern for Othello causes her to neglect the precious handkerchief; its loss will prove momentous

Must be to loathe her. O curse of marriage
That we can call these delicate creatures ours
And not their appetites! I had rather be a toad,
275 And live upon the vapour of a dungeon,
Than keep a corner in the thing I love
For others' uses. Yet 'tis the plague of great ones,
Prerogativ'd are they less than the base.
'Tis destiny, unshunnable, like death.
280 Even then this forked plague is fated to us
When we do quicken.

Enter DESDEMONA and EMILIA.

                  Desdemona comes.
If she be false, O, then heaven mocks itself.
I'll not believe it.

DESDEMONA
            How now, my dear Othello?
Your dinner, and the generous islanders
285 By you invited, do attend your presence.

OTHELLO
I am to blame.

DESDEMONA
Why is your speech so faint? Are you not well?

OTHELLO
I have a pain upon my forehead, here.

DESDEMONA
Faith, that's with watching; 'twill away again;
290 Let me but bind your head, within this hour
It will be well again.

OTHELLO
                Your napkin is too little.

She drops her handkerchief.
Let it alone, come, I'll go in with you.

DESDEMONA
I am very sorry that you are not well.

Exeunt OTHELLO and DESDEMONA.

Let me but bind your head, within this hour
It will be well again.

DESDEMONA, Act 3, Scene 3, 290–1

295 **remembrance:** keepsake

296 **wayward:** unpredictable

298 **he conjur'd:** Othello solemnly urged

300 **work ta'en out:** embroidery copied

303 **fantasy:** whim

305 **chide:** scold, rebuke

306 **common thing:** sexual innuendo, with 'common' meaning (a) ordinary and (b) used by everybody. A sexual innuendo involves a word or phrase with more than one meaning, one of which is risqué or immodest

316 **to the advantage:** as luck would have it

EMILIA

I am glad I have found this napkin;

295 This was her first remembrance from the Moor.

My wayward husband hath a hundred times

Woo'd me to steal it; but she so loves the token,

For he conjur'd her she should ever keep it,

That she reserves it evermore about her,

300 To kiss and talk to. I'll ha' the work ta'en out,

And give't Iago. What he will do with it

Heaven knows, not I.

I nothing but to please his fantasy.

Enter IAGO.

IAGO

How now, what do you here alone?

EMILIA

305 Do not you chide, I have a thing for you.

IAGO

A thing for me? It is a common thing …

EMILIA

Ha?

IAGO

To have a foolish wife.

EMILIA

O, is that all? What will you give me now

310 For that same handkerchief?

IAGO

What handkerchief?

EMILIA

What handkerchief?

Why, that the Moor first gave to Desdemona,

That which so often you did bid me steal.

IAGO

Hast stole it from her?

EMILIA

315 No, faith, she let it drop by negligence,

And, to the advantage, I being here took't up.

Look, here it is.

IAGO

A good wench, give it me.

EMILIA

What will you do with it, that you have been

So earnest to have me filch it?

IAGO

[taking it] Why, what's that to you?   320

EMILIA

If it be not for some purpose of import,

Give me't again. Poor lady, she'll run mad

When she shall lack it.

IAGO

Be not acknown on't. I have use for it —

Go, leave me.   325

Exit EMILIA.

I will in Cassio's lodging lose this napkin,

And let him find it. Trifles light as air

Are, to the jealous, confirmations strong

As proofs of Holy Writ. This may do something.

The Moor already changes with my poison.   330

Dangerous conceits are in their natures poisons,

Which at the first are scarce found to distaste,

But with a little act upon the blood

Burn like the mines of sulphur. I did say so.

Enter OTHELLO.

Look where he comes. Not poppy, nor mandragora,   335

Nor all the drowsy syrups of the world,

Shall ever medicine thee to that sweet sleep

Which thou owed'st yesterday.

OTHELLO

Ha, ha, false to me, to me?

IAGO

Why, how now, general? No more of that.   340

OTHELLO

Avaunt, be gone. Thou hast set me on the rack.

I swear 'tis better to be much abus'd

Than but to know't a little.

319	*filch:* steal
321	*purpose of import:* some important use
323	*lack:* miss
324	*Be ... on't:* don't admit you know anything about it
326	*lose:* drop
327–9	*Trifles ... Writ:* jealous people put as much faith in trivial details as they do in the Bible itself
331	*conceits:* imaginings
332	*scarce ... distaste:* hardly found to be distasteful
333	*act:* action *blood:* emotions, passions
335–8	*Not poppy ... yesterday:* no opium, no narcotic, no sleep-giving syrup, will restore to you the sweet sleep that you enjoyed yesterday
341	*Avaunt:* away with you *rack:* an instrument of torture, used in Shakespeare's day to twist and stretch the limbs of victims; here it is a metaphor for Othello's tortured state of mind
342	*abus'd:* wronged

IAGO

                              How now, my lord?

OTHELLO

What sense had I of her stol'n hours of lust?

345   I saw't not, thought it not, it harm'd not me,

I slept the next night well, was free and merry,

I found not Cassio's kisses on her lips.

He that is robb'd, not wanting what is stol'n,

Let him not know't and he's not robb'd at all.

IAGO

350   I am sorry to hear this.

OTHELLO

I had been happy if the general camp,

Pioners and all, had tasted her sweet body,

So I had nothing known. O, now for ever

Farewell the tranquil mind! Farewell content!

355   Farewell the plumed troops and the big wars

That make ambition virtue! O, farewell!

Farewell the neighing steed and the shrill trump,

The spirit-stirring drum, th'ear-piercing fife,

The royal banner, and all quality,

360   Pride, pomp and circumstance of glorious war!

And O, you mortal engines, whose wide throats

The immortal Jove's great clamour counterfeit,

Farewell! Othello's occupation's gone!

IAGO

Is't possible, my lord?

OTHELLO

365   Villain, be sure thou prove my love a whore,

Be sure of it. Give me the ocular proof

Or, by the worth of man's eternal soul,

Thou hadst been better have been born a dog

Than answer my wak'd wrath.

IAGO

                              Is't come to this?

OTHELLO

370   Make me to see't, or at the least so prove it

That the probation bear no hinge nor loop

To hang a doubt on, or woe upon thy life!

344–9 Othello is now convinced that Desdemona is unfaithful to him

344 *sense:* awareness, consciousness

348–9 *He ... all:* if a man does not need what a thief has stolen, and doesn't know it has been stolen, it is the same as if nothing has been stolen at all

351 *general camp:* entire army

352 *Pioners:* sappers, the lowest military rank

353 *So:* if, provided that

356 *That ... virtue:* that turn ambition into a virtue

357 *trump:* trumpet

360 *circumstance:* pageantry, ceremony

361 *mortal engines:* deadly weapons (cannons, etc.)

362 *The ... counterfeit:* imitate thunder

363 *occupation:* career as a soldier

366 *ocular:* visible

369 *Than ... wrath:* than suffer the consequences of my roused anger

370–2 *Make ... doubt on:* you must give me either visible evidence or absolute proof

371 *probation:* proof

IAGO

My noble lord …

OTHELLO

If thou dost slander her and torture me,

Never pray more, abandon all remorse,   375

On horror's head horrors accumulate,

Do deeds to make heaven weep, all earth amaz'd,

For nothing canst thou to damnation add

Greater than that.

IAGO

               O grace, O heaven forgive me!

Are you a man? Have you a soul or sense?   380

God buy you, take mine office — O wretched fool,

That livest to make thine honesty a vice!

O monstrous world, take note. Take note, O world,

To be direct and honest is not safe.

I thank you for this profit, and from hence   385

I'll love no friend, since love breeds such offence.

OTHELLO

Nay, stay, thou shouldst be honest.

IAGO

I should be wise, for honesty's a fool

And loses that it works for.

OTHELLO

               By the world,

I think my wife be honest, and think she is not.   390

I think that thou art just, and think thou art not.

I'll have some proof. My name, that was as fresh

As Dian's visage, is now begrim'd and black

As mine own face. If there be cords or knives,

Poison or fire, or suffocating streams,   395

I'll not endure it. Would I were satisfied!

IAGO

I see, sir, you are eaten up with passion.

I do repent me that I put it to you.

You would be satisfied?

OTHELLO

               Would? Nay, I will.

374–9   Othello has his hands on Iago's throat

375   *abandon all remorse:* give up all hope of repentance, therefore of salvation

381   *God …office:* goodbye, take away my position

381–2   *wretched … vice:* Iago is describing himself as a fool, so excessively honest that his honesty has become a danger to himself (by incurring Othello's wrath)

385   *profit:* profitable lesson

386   *offence:* danger. Iago makes as if to leave at this point

387   *thou … honest:* it cannot be but that you are honest

388–9   *I … works for:* wisdom is better than honesty; I have learned from you that an honest man is a fool, since he loses the friendship of those he is giving honest advice to

390   *honest:* chaste, faithful

391   *just:* truthful, honest

392   *name:* reputation, honour

393   *Dian's visage:* face of Diana (the Roman goddess of chastity and of the moon)

394–6   *If … endure it:* Othello is considering suicide

396   *satisfied:* in possession of the truth

401–2 *Would ... topp'd:* would you, as an onlooker, like to see her engaged in sexual congress

403 *tedious difficulty:* difficult thing to arrange

404 *prospect:* situation

405–6 Iago is pretending that the real 'difficulty' in finding ocular proof is that Cassio and Desdemona will ensure that they will 'bolster' (i.e. share the same pillow) in private

409–11 These are images of lust

412–14 *If ... ha't:* if you want the kind of circumstantial evidence that will make it possible for you to arrive directly at the truth, you may have it

415 *living:* good, real

416 *office:* task

417 *sith:* since

418 *Prick'd:* spurred on

419 *lay:* shared a bed; beds were expensive items and were therefore commonly shared

422 *loose of soul:* careless with secrets

427 *gripe:* grip hard, squeeze

IAGO

400 And may. But how, how satisfied, my lord?

Would you, the supervisor, grossly gape on,

Behold her topp'd?

OTHELLO

Death and damnation! O!

IAGO

It were a tedious difficulty, I think,

To bring 'em to that prospect. Damn 'em then,

405 If ever mortal eyes do see them bolster

More than their own! What then? How then?

What shall I say? Where's satisfaction?

It is impossible you should see this,

Were they as prime as goats, as hot as monkeys,

410 As salt as wolves in pride, and fools as gross

As ignorance made drunk. But yet I say,

If imputation and strong circumstances,

Which lead directly to the door of truth,

Will give you satisfaction, you may ha't.

OTHELLO

415 Give me a living reason she's disloyal.

IAGO

I do not like the office,

But sith I am enter'd in this cause so far,

Prick'd to't by foolish honesty and love,

I will go on. I lay with Cassio lately,

420 And being troubled with a raging tooth,

I could not sleep.

There are a kind of men so loose of soul

That in their sleeps will mutter their affairs.

One of this kind is Cassio.

425 In sleep I heard him say, 'Sweet Desdemona,

Let us be wary, let us hide our loves.'

And then, sir, would he gripe and wring my hand,

Cry out 'Sweet creature!' and then kiss me hard

As if he pluck'd up kisses by the roots

430 That grew upon my lips, then laid his leg

Over my thigh, and sigh'd, and kiss'd, and then

Cried, 'Cursed fate, that gave thee to the Moor!'

OTHELLO

O monstrous, monstrous!

IAGO

Nay, this was but his dream.

OTHELLO

But this denoted a foregone conclusion.

> 434 *denoted ... conclusion:* indicated something that had previously taken place

IAGO

'Tis a shrewd doubt, though it be but a dream,   435

And this may help to thicken other proofs

That do demonstrate thinly.

> 435 *shrewd doubt:* penetrating guess

> 436–7 *this may ... thinly:* it may help to reinforce other evidence that may not be so convincing on its own

OTHELLO

I'll tear her all to pieces.

IAGO

Nay, but be wise, yet we see nothing done.

She may be honest yet. Tell me but this: 440

Have you not sometimes seen a handkerchief,

Spotted with strawberries, in your wife's hand?

> 442 *Spotted:* patterned, embroidered

I'll tear her all to pieces.

OTHELLO, Act 3, Scene 3, 438

443 The handkerchief is an important symbol in the play. It represents different things for different characters

448 *other proofs:* there are, of course, no proofs of any kind, but Iago knows that Othello's emotional balance is so disturbed that he cannot see or think clearly. Indeed, Othello readily accepts that there is proof

449 *slave:* Desdemona or, more probably, Cassio

454 *cell:* lair; vengeance is seen as a dark monster emerging from its hellish lair

455–6 *Yield ... hate:* let love surrender its power, and its seat in the heart, to the tyranny of hatred

456 *fraught:* freight, burden (i.e. the weight of sorrow)

457 *aspics' tongues:* the tongues of asps (venomous serpents)

460–7 Othello is now determined to find relief from the torment of his murderous thoughts in an appropriate form of revenge

460 *Pontic sea:* Black Sea, which flows strongly through the Bosphorous and the Dardanelles into the Mediterranean Sea

461 *compulsive:* driving or forcing onward

463 *Propontic:* Sea of Marmara
Hellespont: Dardanelles

466 *capable and wide:* adequate and far-reaching

OTHELLO

I gave her such a one; 'twas my first gift.

IAGO

I know not that; but such a handkerchief —
445 I am sure it was your wife's — did I to-day
See Cassio wipe his beard with.

OTHELLO

                                    If't be that …

IAGO

If it be that, or any that was hers,
It speaks against her, with the other proofs.

OTHELLO

O, that the slave had forty thousand lives!
450 One is too poor, too weak for my revenge.
Now do I see 'tis true. Look here, Iago,
All my fond love thus do I blow to heaven.
'Tis gone.
Arise, black vengeance, from thy hollow cell;
455 Yield up, O love, thy crown and hearted throne
To tyrannous hate; swell, bosom, with thy fraught,
For 'tis of aspics' tongues!

He kneels.

IAGO

Pray be content.

OTHELLO

                    O blood, blood, blood!

IAGO

Patience, I say. Your mind perhaps may change.

OTHELLO

460 Never, Iago. Like to the Pontic sea,
Whose icy current and compulsive course
Ne'er feels retiring ebb, but keeps due on
To the Propontic and the Hellespont,
Even so my bloody thoughts with violent pace
465 Shall ne'er look back, ne'er ebb to humble love,
Till a capable and wide revenge

Swallow them up. Now by yond marble heaven,

In the due reverence of a sacred vow,

I here engage my words.

IAGO
                              Do not rise yet.

IAGO kneels.

Witness you ever-burning lights above,   470

You elements that clip us round about,

Witness that here Iago doth give up

The execution of his wit, hands, heart

To wrong'd Othello's service: let him command,

And to obey shall be in me remorse,   475

What bloody business ever.

They rise.

OTHELLO
                              I greet thy love,

Not with vain thanks but with acceptance bounteous,

And will upon the instant put thee to't:

Within these three days, let me hear thee say

That Cassio's not alive.

IAGO
                              My friend is dead: 480

'Tis done as you request; but let her live.

OTHELLO

Damn her, lewd minx! O, damn her!

Come, go with me apart. I will withdraw

To furnish me with some swift means of death

For the fair devil. Now art thou my lieutenant.   485

IAGO

I am your own for ever.

Exeunt.

467 *yond marble heaven:* the shining heaven up there. Othello is still kneeling, which gives additional force to his oath

469 *engage my words:* pledge my word of honour

470 *lights:* stars

471 *clip:* enclose, surround, embrace

472 *give up:* dedicate

473 *execution:* workings, exercise

475–6 *And ... ever:* Iago will perform any bloody deed that Othello commands him to, and consider it an act of pity ('remorse') since he will be doing it for the poor victim [Othello]

477 *vain:* empty
     bounteous: full-hearted

478 *upon ... to't:* at once set you to do the kind of work you are willing to do

481 *her:* Desdemona

483 *apart:* away from here

485 *lieutenant:* Iago has reached the summit of his ambitions: he has destroyed Othello's peace of mind and Cassio's career, and secured his own much-desired promotion

Key points

Iago has the dominant role in this scene. His ingenuity, inventiveness, cunning and hypocrisy – all aided by sheer good luck – are evident throughout. An analysis of the various critical stages in Iago's assault on Othello's peace of mind, and on the reputations of Cassio and Desdemona, reveals the depth of Iago's genius for evildoing.

- At the beginning of the scene, Othello is a happily married man. By the end, he has decided to murder his wife and to have Cassio murdered. Iago alone contrives this extraordinary transformation in Othello's mind and heart.

- Iago's first tentative move proves abortive. He tries to make Othello see a sinister meaning in Cassio's 'guilty-like' (line 40) departure. This does not appear to have a major effect on Othello, so Iago is obliged to begin again.

- He succeeds in troubling Othello's mind with his reference to Cassio's part in the wooing of Desdemona, and his provocative, nagging repetition of Othello's words. Othello is convinced that Iago is concealing some damaging information about Cassio.

- Further suggestive hints from Iago culminate in Othello's demand, 'By heaven, I'll know thy thoughts!' (line 166). Iago's refusal only adds to Othello's anxiety.

- Then comes Iago's solemn warning against the very jealousy he is trying to inflame: 'O beware, my lord, of jealousy!' (line 169). Iago's reference in the same speech to the unfortunate husband 'who dotes yet doubts, suspects yet fondly loves' (line 174) inevitably causes Othello to associate Desdemona with the warning against jealousy. It is easy to imagine Iago gloating inwardly over his cleverness in converting Othello into the unfortunate husband he is describing.

- Othello, now thoroughly jealous, tells Iago that he cannot go on living in doubt, suspicion and jealousy. Hearing this, Iago proceeds to multiply Othello's doubts, suspicions and jealousies by reflecting on the infidelity of Venetian women, and the general tolerance shown to such behaviour in Venice (lines 206–8).

- Iago now moves on from mere speculation to introduce some facts about Desdemona. She did deceive her father in marrying Othello, and before that she sought to deceive Othello himself: 'when she seem'd to shake and fear your looks, she lov'd them most' (lines 211–12). Iago wants Othello to think that Desdemona's chief talent is her ability to put on a false appearance.

- Despite this, Othello does not want to face the possibility of Desdemona's 'infidelity': 'I do not think but Desdemona's honest' (line 229). Iago's reply is a clever, destructive insinuation: 'long live you to think so' (line 230), by which he means: may you long enjoy the delusion that Desdemona is faithful to you.

- Othello's change from trusting his wife to accepting Iago's slanders as true, or likely to be true, is clearly marked. He tells the departing Iago to report to him if he finds evidence against Desdemona, and to employ Emilia to watch her (lines 242–4).

- Iago's immediate return has a strategic purpose. He urges Othello to stop wondering about Desdemona but to 'leave it to time' (line 249) to settle the matter. Iago knows that this is the one thing Othello will not do, since he wants his doubts to be dispelled without delay.

- Iago's poison has worked and Othello's torment becomes more intense. He mourns the loss of his 'tranquil mind' (line 354).

- The thought of Desdemona's 'infidelity' is now so unbearable that Othello turns on Iago for not leaving him in blissful ignorance. Then, paradoxically, he looks for further evidence of her guilt. His hands are on Iago's throat as he pronounces his deadly threat. If Iago cannot prove that Desdemona has betrayed him, he will face dire consequences: 'thou hadst been better have been born a dog' (line 368).

- Iago is able to divert Othello's anger by taking on the role of the honest friend whose advice has been rebuffed: 'To be direct and honest is not safe' (line 384).

- Othello's mind is intolerably confused and his only hope of remaining sane is expressed in his despairing cry: 'Would I were satisfied!' (line 396). Iago is prepared for this. He provides Othello with a grotesque description of imagined lustful activity involving Desdemona and Cassio, and wonders if Othello would care to witness such a scene. Then he produces another vivid image of infidelity: Cassio's imaginary dream. The graphic detail supplied by Iago affects Othello so deeply that he is ready to believe without question that such a 'dream' must reflect reality.

- Then comes Iago's second master-stroke. He mentions the handkerchief mislaid by Desdemona, another piece of circumstantial evidence. He adds the plausible lie that he has seen Cassio use it to 'wipe his beard' (line 446). By this time, Iago has so captivated Othello's intellect and judgement that he can tell him without being challenged that Cassio's possession of the handkerchief 'speaks against' Desdemona 'with the other proofs' (line 448). These 'proofs', of course, are figments of Iago's imagination.

- Othello is now convinced. He decides that Cassio and Desdemona are to die.

- The accidental loss of the handkerchief is a further example of Iago's incredible good luck as it provides him with his most potent weapon against Desdemona and Cassio.

- How you interpret Othello's character will depend very much on how you view this scene. If you see it as an exhibition of Iago's superhuman cunning, then you should see Othello as a pathetic victim, powerless to resist the devilish onslaught. If, on the other hand, you see Othello as the victim of his own jealous disposition and so playing into the hands of Iago, the scene becomes a matter of Othello's character in action, an exposure of his fatal flaw.

Useful quotes

> be merry, Cassio,
> For thy solicitor shall rather die
> Than give thy cause away.
>
> (Desdemona, lines 26–8)

> By heaven, he echoes me
> As if there were some monster in his thought
> Too hideous to be shown!
>
> (Othello, lines 110–12)

> Cassio, my lord? No, sure, I cannot think it,
> That he would sneak away so guilty-like,
> Seeing you coming.
>
> (Iago, lines 39–41)

> I'll see before I doubt, when I doubt, prove,
> And on the proof, there is no more but this:
> Away at once with love or jealousy!
>
> (Othello, lines 194–6)

> Excellent wretch, perdition catch my soul
> But I do love thee, and when I love thee not,
> Chaos is come again.
>
> (Othello, lines 91–3)

> Look to your wife, observe her well with Cassio.
> Wear your eye thus: not jealous, nor secure.
> I would not have your free and noble nature
> Out of self-bounty be abused.
>
> (Iago, lines 201–4)

? Questions

1 The first seven lines of the scene provide a good example of Shakespeare's use of irony in relation to Iago and his victims. Comment on this idea.

2 Desdemona tells Cassio: 'For thy solicitor shall rather die than give thy cause away' (lines 27–8). This is another irony of the kind that occurs throughout the play. Why is this example so particularly moving?

3 Why, do you think, does Iago's first attempt to make Othello suspicious of Desdemona – 'Ha! I like not that' (line 35) – fail?

4 Desdemona's pleadings on Cassio's behalf (lines 42–84) are not very successful. What reasons can you give for this?

5 How does Iago succeed so well in upsetting Othello's mind about Cassio's honesty in lines 95–165?

6 Othello's speech on jealousy (lines 180–96) reveals some important things about him. What are these things? How does Iago make use of them for his own purposes?

7 What doubts about Desdemona does Iago create in Othello's mind in lines 200–42?

> *Trifles light as air*
> *Are, to the jealous, confirmations strong*
> *As proofs of Holy Writ.*
>
> (Iago, lines 327–9)

> *I think my wife be honest, and think she is not.*
> *I think that thou art just, and think thou art not.*
> *I'll have some proof.*
>
> (Othello, lines 390–2)

> *Thou hast set me on the rack.*
> *I swear 'tis better to be much abus'd*
> *Than but to know't a little.*
>
> (Othello, lines 341–3)

> *my bloody thoughts with violent pace*
> *Shall ne'er look back, ne'er ebb to humble love,*
> *Till a capable and wide revenge*
> *Swallow them up.*
>
> (Othello, lines 464–7)

> *O, now for ever*
> *Farewell the tranquil mind! Farewell content!*
>
> (Othello, lines 353–4)

> *Come, go with me apart. I will withdraw*
> *To furnish me with some swift means of death*
> *For the fair devil. Now art thou my lieutenant.*
>
> (Othello, lines 483–5)

8 What is the significance of Othello's comment: 'Farewell, if more thou dost perceive, let me know more. Set on thy wife to observe' (lines 242–4)? Why do these lines mark an important stage in Othello's fall?

9 Iago advises Othello to leave the matters he has raised 'to time' (line 249). What is he hoping for here?

10 Describe Othello's state of mind in the speech beginning 'This fellow's of exceeding honesty' (line 262). How does it differ from what has gone before?

11 Desdemona's loss of the handkerchief is a vitally important incident. Consider its implications for: (a) Desdemona, (b) Cassio, (c) Othello, (d) Emilia.

12 Othello's attitude from line 365 to line 396 poses a threat to Iago. What is the nature of this threat? How does Iago deal with it?

13 During this scene Othello undergoes a remarkable change. Describe this briefly. How can it be accounted for?

14 Describe any features of Othello's character that contribute to the success of Iago's schemes.

15 Part of Iago's success in this scene depends on his good luck. Give examples of this.

ACT 3 † Scene 4

Plot summary

DESDEMONA ASKS THE clown to bring Cassio to her. She anxiously enquires of Emilia about the handkerchief. Emilia's lying reply helps to seal Desdemona's fate. Othello struggles to be civil to Desdemona. He demands the handkerchief, giving an exotic account of its origins. Desdemona lies, claiming that it is not lost, which only increases Othello's suspicions. Then she insists on pressing Cassio's case for reinstatement. Othello's fury mounts, and he leaves in a jealous rage. Emilia, despite seeing this, still fails to reveal the truth about the handkerchief and contents herself with a cynical comment on husbands. Iago urges Cassio to continue to press Desdemona to act as his advocate with Othello. Bianca's arrival heralds a further deterioration in Desdemona's chances of survival and another piece of good luck for Iago when Cassio gives Bianca the handkerchief, and asks her to copy it.

Hot, hot and moist, this hand of yours requires
A sequester from liberty
OTHELLO, Act 3, Scene 4, 35–6

Cyprus. Before the citadel.

Enter DESDEMONA, EMILIA, and CLOWN.

DESDEMONA

Do you know, sirrah, where the Lieutenant Cassio lies?

CLOWN

I dare not say he lies anywhere.

DESDEMONA

Why, man?

CLOWN

He is a soldier, and for one to say a soldier lies, is stabbing.

DESDEMONA

Go to. Where lodges he?

CLOWN

To tell you where he lodges is to tell you where I lie.

DESDEMONA

Can anything be made of this?

CLOWN

I know not where he lodges, and for me to devise a lodging, and say he lies here, or he lies there, were to lie in mine own throat.

DESDEMONA

Can you inquire him out, and be edified by report?

CLOWN

I will catechize the world for him, that is, make questions and by them answer.

DESDEMONA

Seek him, bid him come hither, tell him I have moved my lord on his behalf and hope all will be well.

CLOWN

To do this is within the compass of man and therefore I'll attempt the doing it.

Exit.

DESDEMONA

Where should I lose that handkerchief, Emilia?

5

10

15

1–18 These lines are remarkable for some particularly weak puns

1 *sirrah:* sir (usually addressed to a person of lower rank)
lies: lodges; with a pun on 'tells lies'

5 *stabbing:* running the risk of being stabbed by the offending soldier

6 *Go to:* come, come

7 *To … lie:* if I were to name a place where Cassio lodges, I would be telling a lie, because I don't know where he lodges

11 *lie … throat:* lie in the most absolute way

12 *inquire … report:* find out where he is, and be informed by what you learn. Desdemona is parodying the clown's ornate style

13 *catechize the world:* ask everywhere

13–14 *make questions … answer:* ask questions and get appropriate answers

15–16 *I have … behalf:* these eight words encompass a terrible ambiguity (Othello is 'moved', but not in the way Desdemona thinks he is), a grim irony, and a striking example of Desdemona's innocence

17 *compass:* capacity

19 *should:* did

EMILIA

20 I know not, madam.

DESDEMONA

Believe me, I had rather have lost my purse

Full of crusadoes, and but my noble Moor

Is true of mind, and made of no such baseness

As jealous creatures are, it were enough

25 To put him to ill thinking.

EMILIA

                                Is he not jealous?

DESDEMONA

Who, he? I think the sun where he was born

Drew all such humours from him.

Enter OTHELLO.

EMILIA

                                Look where he comes.

DESDEMONA

I will not leave him now till Cassio

Be called to him. How is't with you, my lord?

OTHELLO

30 Well, my good lady. *[aside]* O, hardness to dissemble!

How do you, Desdemona?

DESDEMONA

                                Well, my good lord.

OTHELLO

Give me your hand. This hand is moist, my lady.

DESDEMONA

It yet hath felt no age, nor known no sorrow.

OTHELLO

This argues fruitfulness and liberal heart.

35 Hot, hot and moist, this hand of yours requires

A sequester from liberty; fasting and prayer,

Much castigation, exercise devout;

For here's a young and sweating devil here

That commonly rebels. 'Tis a good hand,

40 A frank one.

DESDEMONA

                        You may indeed say so,

For 'twas that hand that gave away my heart.

---

22 *crusadoes:* Portuguese gold coins
but: but for the fact that

22–5 *and but … thinking:* the irony here lies in Desdemona's unwittingly accurate description of Othello's state of mind, even while she is denying its possibility

27 *humours:* characteristics. In Shakespeare's day some people still believed that the body comprised four fluids (or humours), the balance of which determined the temper of the person

30 *my good lady:* note Othello's new, more distant, mode of addressing Desdemona
hardness to dissemble: an ambiguous phrase that may refer to the difficulty Othello has in concealing his disturbed state of mind, or to his feeling that Desdemona is a consummate hypocrite

32 *moist:* a moist hand supposedly indicates a lustful nature

34 *argues:* suggests
liberal: free; with damaging overtones implying that Desdemona is unduly free with her favours

36 *sequester from liberty:* removal of freedom

37 *castigation:* chastening, penitential exercises
exercise devout: acts of religious devotion

38–9 *For … rebels:* the rebellious 'devil' is lustful desire. Othello has suggested that the cure for this involves prayer and penance

40 *A frank one:* the hand conveys an honest impression of her character and nature

OTHELLO

A liberal hand; the hearts of old gave hands,

But our new heraldry is hands, not hearts.

DESDEMONA

I cannot speak of this. Come, come, your promise.

OTHELLO

What promise, chuck?   45

DESDEMONA

I have sent to bid Cassio come speak with you.

OTHELLO

I have a salt and sullen rheum offends me,

Lend me thy handkerchief.

DESDEMONA

[offering a handkerchief to him] Here, my lord.

OTHELLO

That which I gave you.   50

DESDEMONA

I have it not about me.

OTHELLO

Not?

DESDEMONA

No, faith, my lord.

OTHELLO

                    That's a fault. That handkerchief

Did an Egyptian to my mother give.

She was a charmer, and could almost read   55

The thoughts of people. She told her, while she kept it

'Twould make her amiable, and subdue my father

Entirely to her love, but if she lost it,

Or made a gift of it, my father's eye

Should hold her loathly, and his spirits should hunt   60

After new fancies. She, dying, gave it me,

And bid me, when my fate would have me wived,

To give it her. I did so, and take heed on't,

Make it a darling, like your precious eye.

To lose't or give't away were such perdition   65

As nothing else could match.

[handwritten note] ← othello asking for the handkerchief

42–3 *the hearts ... hearts:* Othello appears to be contrasting old customs with newer ones and observing that people once gave hands and hearts at the same time, showing their sincerity, but now the offer of the hand may well be divorced from the feelings of the heart

44 *cannot speak of:* don't understand

45 *chuck:* normally a term of affection

47 *I ... me:* I have a heavy and wretched headcold that is troubling me

55 *She ... charmer:* the Egyptian was a magician or enchantress

57 *amiable:* loveable, beloved

60 *hold her loathly:* regard her with loathing

60–1 *spirits ... fancies:* desires would chase after new loves

62 *wived:* married

63 *her:* my wife

64 *Make ... darling:* cherish it

65 *perdition:* utter loss

DESDEMONA

Is't possible?

OTHELLO

'Tis true, there's magic in the web of it.

A sibyl, that had number'd in the world

The sun to course two hundred compasses,

70 In her prophetic fury sew'd the work;

The worms were hallow'd that did breed the silk;

And it was dyed in mummy, which the skilful

Conserved of maidens' hearts.

DESDEMONA

I' faith, is't true?

OTHELLO

Most veritable, therefore look to't well.

DESDEMONA

75 Then would to God that I had never seen it!

OTHELLO

Ha, wherefore?

DESDEMONA

Why do you speak so startingly and rash?

OTHELLO

Is't lost? Is't gone? Speak, is it out o' the way?

DESDEMONA

Heaven bless us!

OTHELLO

80 Say you?

DESDEMONA

It is not lost, but what an if it were?

OTHELLO

Ha!

DESDEMONA

I say, it is not lost.

OTHELLO

Fetch't, let me see't!

DESDEMONA

Why, so I can, sir, but I will not now,

85 This is a trick to put me from my suit.

I pray let Cassio be receiv'd again.

---

67 *web:* weaving

68–9 *A ... compasses:* a prophetess who had lived long enough to count 200 revolutions of the sun (i.e. she was at least 200 years old)

70 *In ... fury:* inspired by the spirit of prophecy

72 *mummy:* liquid supposedly derived from embalmed bodies and used for medicinal or magical purposes
the skilful: those trained in the magic arts

74 *veritable:* true

76 *wherefore:* why

77 *startingly and rash:* incoherently and rashly

81 *an if:* if

85 *suit:* plea, petition

OTHELLO
Fetch me the handkerchief, my mind misgives.

DESDEMONA
Come, come,
You'll never meet a more sufficient man.

OTHELLO
The handkerchief!

DESDEMONA
            I pray, talk me of Cassio.   90

OTHELLO
The handkerchief!

DESDEMONA
            A man that all his time
Hath founded his good fortunes on your love,
Shar'd dangers with you …

OTHELLO
The handkerchief!

DESDEMONA
            I' faith, you are to blame.

OTHELLO
Zounds!   95

Exit.

EMILIA
Is not this man jealous?

DESDEMONA
I ne'er saw this before.
Sure there's some wonder in this handkerchief.
I am most unhappy in the loss of it.

EMILIA
'Tis not a year or two shows us a man: 100
They are all but stomachs, and we all but food;
They eat us hungerly, and when they are full,
They belch us.

Enter CASSIO and IAGO.
            Look you, Cassio and my husband.

IAGO
There is no other way, 'tis she must do it,
And lo, the happiness! Go and importune her.   105

---

87 *my mind misgives:* I am suspicious

89 *sufficient:* qualified

90 *me:* to me

101–3 The earthy Emilia, the woman of common clay, is characterised through her vulgar imagery
102 *hungerly:* hungrily
103 *belch:* discharge, reject

105 *And … happiness:* and look what a piece of good fortune (here she comes)
      importune: plead with

DESDEMONA

How now, good Cassio, what's the news with you?

CASSIO

Madam, my former suit. I do beseech you

That by your virtuous means I may again

Exist and be a member of his love,

110   Whom I, with all the office of my heart,

Entirely honour. I would not be delay'd.

If my offence be of such mortal kind

That neither service past, nor present sorrows,

Nor purpos'd merit in futurity,

115   Can ransom me into his love again,

But to know so must be my benefit.

So shall I clothe me in a forc'd content,

And shut myself up in some other course

To fortune's alms.

DESDEMONA
                 Alas, thrice-gentle Cassio,

120   My advocation is not now in tune.

My lord is not my lord, nor should I know him,

Were he in favour as in humour alter'd.

So help me every spirit sanctified,

As I have spoken for you all my best,

125   And stood within the blank of his displeasure

For my free speech, you must awhile be patient.

What I can do I will, and more I will

Than for myself I dare. Let that suffice you.

IAGO

Is my lord angry?

EMILIA
                 He went hence but now,

130   And certainly in strange unquietness.

IAGO

Can he be angry? I have seen the cannon

When it hath blown his ranks into the air,

And (like the devil) from his very arm

Puff'd his own brother, and can he be angry?

135   Something of moment then. I will go meet him.

There's matter in't indeed, if he be angry.

---

109   *Exist:* Cassio means that with his loss of position and his estrangement from Othello, his existence has lost its meaning; he is asking Desdemona to assist him to restore meaning to his life

110   *office:* dutiful service

112   *mortal:* deadly, fatal

114   *purpos'd ... futurity:* the good resolutions I make regarding future good conduct

116   *But ... benefit:* Cassio wants to know one way or another how he stands with Othello; he would prefer to hear the worst than to remain any longer in uncertainty

117–19   *So ... alms:* if the news is unfavourable, I shall be obliged to accept my lot, and confine myself to some other means of seeking my fortune

120   *My ... tune:* to plead for you just now would not be appropriate

121–2   *nor should ... alter'd:* I would not recognise him at all if his appearance ('favour') were as changed as his mood ('humour')

125   *within the blank:* as a target for

130   *in strange unquietness:* strangely perturbed

131–6   Iago's point here is that if Othello is angry, there must be a very serious reason indeed for his anger. He recalls an incident from the wars when enemy artillery killed Othello's comrade, who had been standing beside him, and implies that, even in that situation, Othello did not show anger

135   *moment:* importance

DESDEMONA

I prithee do so.

Exit IAGO.

Something, sure, of state,

Either from Venice, or some unhatch'd practice

Made demonstrable here in Cyprus to him,   140

Hath puddled his clear spirit; and in such cases

Men's natures wrangle with inferior things,

Though great ones are their object. 'Tis even so.

For let our finger ache and it endues

Our healthful members even to that sense   145

Of pain. Nay, we must think men are not gods,

Nor of them look for such observancy

As fit the bridal. Beshrew me much, Emilia,

I was — unhandsome warrior as I am —

Arraigning his unkindness with my soul;   150

But now I find I had suborn'd the witness,

And he's indicted falsely.

EMILIA

Pray heaven it be state-matters, as you think,

And no conception nor no jealous toy

Concerning you.   155

DESDEMONA

Alas the day, I never gave him cause!

EMILIA

But jealous souls will not be answer'd so.

They are not ever jealous for the cause,

But jealous for they're jealous. It is a monster

Begot upon itself, born on itself.   160

DESDEMONA

Heaven keep that monster from Othello's mind!

EMILIA

Lady, amen.

DESDEMONA

I will go seek him. Cassio, walk hereabout.

If I do find him fit, I'll move your suit,

And seek to effect it to my uttermost.   165

CASSIO

I humbly thank your ladyship.

Exeunt DESDEMONA and EMILIA.

138 *Something . . . state:* I am sure that some official business

139 *unhatch'd practice:* a plot that has not had a chance to develop

140 *Made demonstrable:* now revealed

141 *puddled ... spirit:* muddied or depressed his cheerful mind

141–3 *in such ... object:* when men are confronted with major problems, they tend to focus their annoyance on lesser ones

144 *endues:* leads

145 *healthful members:* healthy parts

147–8 *Nor ... bridal:* it is futile to expect husbands to keep showing the same level of consideration to their wives as they did on their wedding day

148 *Beshrew me:* a plague on me. This phrase is used playfully here

149 *unhandsome:* inadequate, unskilled

150 *Arraigning:* accusing, calling into question

151 *suborn'd the witness:* caused the witness [Desdemona herself] to give false evidence

152 *indicted:* charged

153–5 *Pray ... you:* I, like you, hope that Othello's change of mood is due to matters of state, and not the result of some trifling jealousy or whim concerning you. Emilia may be beginning to have misgivings about her theft of the handkerchief

159 *for:* because

160 *Begot ... on itself:* jealousy breeds jealousy

164 *fit:* in suitable form

165 *effect ... uttermost:* use all my energy to bring it to a successful conclusion

Enter BIANCA.

BIANCA
Save you, friend Cassio!

CASSIO
                              What make you from home?
How is it with you, my most fair Bianca?
I' faith, sweet love, I was coming to your house.

BIANCA
170 And I was going to your lodging, Cassio.
What, keep a week away? Seven days and nights?
Eight score eight hours? And lovers' absent hours,
More tedious than the dial eight score times?
O weary reckoning!

CASSIO
                              Pardon me, Bianca,
175 I have this while with leaden thoughts been press'd.
But I shall in a more continuate time
Strike off this score of absence. Sweet Bianca,

[giving her DESDEMONA'S handkerchief]

Take me this work out.

BIANCA
                              O Cassio, whence came this?
This is some token from a newer friend.
180 To the felt absence now I feel a cause.
Is't come to this? Well, well.

CASSIO
                              Go to, woman!
Throw your vile guesses in the devil's teeth
From whence you have them. You are jealous now
That this is from some mistress, some remembrance.
185 No, by my faith, Bianca.

BIANCA
                              Why, whose is it?

CASSIO
I know not, sweet. I found it in my chamber.
I like the work well. Ere it be demanded,
As like enough it will, I'd have it copied.
Take it, and do't, and leave me for this time.

---

167 *Save you:* God save you (a greeting)

167 *make:* brings

168 *is it with:* are

172 *Eight score eight:* eight times twenty plus eight (i.e. 168)

172–3 *lovers' ... times:* to Bianca's mind, the time of Cassio's absence has seemed 160 ('eight score') times longer than the time measured by the clock ('dial')

174 *reckoning:* counting up

175 *with leaden ... press'd:* to express his miserable state, Cassio uses a metaphor drawn from the torture chamber, where victims were crushed to death with heavy weights

176 *continuate:* opportune

177 *Strike ... absence:* compensate for this absence

178 *Take ... out:* copy this embroidery for me

178 *whence:* from where

180–1 Bianca's jealousy is a parody of Othello's

187 *Ere ... demanded:* before the person who lost it looks for it

BIANCA

Leave you, wherefore? 190

CASSIO

I do attend here on the general,

And think it no addition, nor my wish,

To have him see me woman'd.

BIANCA

Why, I pray you?

CASSIO

Not that I love you not.

BIANCA

But that you do not love me.

I pray you bring me on the way a little, 195

And say if I shall see you soon at night.

CASSIO

'Tis but a little way that I can bring you,

For I attend here, but I'll see you soon.

BIANCA

'Tis very good. I must be circumstanc'd.

Exeunt.

190 *wherefore:* for what reason

192 *addition:* advantage

193 *woman'd:* with a woman

195 *bring:* accompany

199 *be circumstanc'd:* take things as they are; yield to circumstances

Key points

Everything Desdemona does puts her in danger. For example, she innocently seeks out Cassio and continues to plead his case, which only makes her appear unfaithful in Othello's eyes.

- The message that Desdemona gives to the clown for Cassio is fraught with irony: 'tell him I have moved my lord on his behalf and hope all will be well' (lines 15–16). The implications of 'moved' are particularly disturbing. Othello has already been moved to a murderous rage, partly through her innocent activities on Cassio's behalf. The audience knows this, but she does not.

- The scene is dominated by the unseen handkerchief. Desdemona is fearful about its loss. Emilia will not reveal that she has stolen it. Othello uses it as a test of Desdemona's fidelity, on which her life must depend. Desdemona lies about it, unknowingly making her position more desperate. Cassio admires it and gives it to Bianca to copy. It has become Iago's most deadly weapon.

- For Othello, the handkerchief has ceased to be a commonplace article and become a symbol of married love. Its loss represents the breaking of the bond between Desdemona and himself.

- Emilia has an opportunity to thwart Iago's plans. However, she does not tell the truth about the handkerchief's whereabouts.

- Othello addresses Desdemona in a formal manner and is suspicious of everything. For example, her warm, moist hand has a sinister significance for him, confirming his view that she is too free with her affections.

- The two main strands of Iago's plot come together in this scene to make it unbearably tense and exciting. Desdemona's pathetic pleas on Cassio's behalf, and her failure to satisfy Othello's demand for the missing handkerchief, increase his suspicions and jealousy.

- Othello's desire to have his worst fears confirmed is satisfied, and Desdemona is doomed.

Useful quotes

and but my noble Moor
Is true of mind, and made of no such baseness
As jealous creatures are, it were enough
To put him to ill thinking.

(Desdemona, lines 22–5)

Make it a darling, like your precious eye.
To lose't or give't away were such perdition
As nothing else could match.

(Othello, lines 64–6)

'Tis not a year or two shows us a man:
They are all but stomachs, and we all but food;
They eat us hungerly, and when they are full,
They belch us.

(Emilia, lines 100–3)

? Questions

1 It is often pointed out that Othello and Desdemona do not know each other very well. Is this idea confirmed in this scene?

2 The handkerchief takes on a new significance in this scene. What is this significance?

3 Desdemona's responses during Othello's interrogation (lines 48–95) are unfortunate from her point of view. Why is this so? Mention a similar instance in another scene.

4 What do we learn about Emilia from this scene?

5 Outline some examples of irony in this scene.

6 What is Bianca's function in the play?

7 How might costumes, hair and make-up be used to indicate the differences between the three female characters in the play? What other strategies could be used to inform the audience about these characters?

ACT 3 ⚜ Key moments

Scene 1

- Cassio begins his campaign to win back Othello's favour.
- Iago manipulates events to further his own plans against Cassio, Othello and Desdemona.

Scene 2

- Othello is going to inspect the Cypriot defences. He will therefore be absent when Cassio comes to speak with Desdemona.

Scene 3

- Desdemona agrees to intercede with Othello on Cassio's behalf.
- Iago uses the meeting of Cassio and Desdemona to create a nagging doubt in Othello's mind about their relationship.
- Iago implies that if he told him all he knows (or suspects) it would take away Othello's peace of mind.
- Othello states that he will need proof of Desdemona's guilt, or of her innocence.
- Iago emphasises their differences and suggests that Desdemona may be regretting that she did not marry a Venetian.
- Iago tells Othello that Venetian women hide their affairs from their husbands and reminds him that Desdemona has already deceived her father by eloping.
- Desdemona accidentally drops her handkerchief. Emilia steals it for Iago.
- Iago lies that he overheard Cassio dreaming of Desdemona and talking of their love in his sleep.
- Iago claims that he has seen Cassio with Desdemona's handkerchief. This 'evidence' is the ultimate turning point of the play.
- Othello decides that he will kill Desdemona. Iago will kill Cassio. Othello makes Iago his lieutenant in place of Cassio.

Scene 4

- Desdemona's failure to produce the handkerchief when Othello demands it, and her further pleas for Cassio, infuriate Othello, who departs in a rage.

ACT 3 ⚜ Speaking and listening

1 In groups of three, assign the parts of Othello, Emilia and Desdemona. Imagine that the play has been paused at Act 3, Scene 3, line 293, and set up a freeze-frame of this moment. Think about what your character is thinking and feeling at that point in the play and try to convey that through your frozen action. Write a sentence for each character, describing that character's inner thoughts at that moment.

2 In pairs, look through the various photographs in this book. Then agree which casting decisions, in your opinion, work best for the roles of Othello, Iago and Cassio. Choose your favourite photo for each of these three characters and say what you like about it. Come together as a class and compare your selections.

ACT 4 † Scene 1

Plot summary

IAGO CONTINUES TO FUEL Othello's jealousy, suggesting amorous activity between Cassio and Desdemona, and inventing Cassio's 'confession' of his conquest of Desdemona. This causes Othello to fall to the ground in a fit. When he recovers, Iago has another daring scheme in readiness. Othello stands by, unseen, while Iago engages Cassio in conversation. Othello can see Cassio's gestures, but cannot hear exactly what is being said. He totally misinterprets the conversation, as Iago intends him to do. Othello thinks Iago and Cassio are discussing Desdemona. They are, in fact, talking about Bianca, in grossly unflattering terms. Othello is convinced. Iago persuades him not to poison Desdemona, but to strangle her in her bed. Iago volunteers to arrange the murder of Cassio.

Lodovico arrives from Venice, bringing news that Othello is to be recalled from Cyprus and that Cassio will replace him as governor. Desdemona, telling Lodovico of the breach between Othello and Cassio, frankly and innocently mentions the 'love' she has for Cassio. Othello strikes her publicly and dismisses her from the company. Lodovico thinks Othello must be out of his mind. Remembering the noble Othello of former days, Lodovico laments the change he sees, and turns to Iago, of all people, for an explanation of the cause.

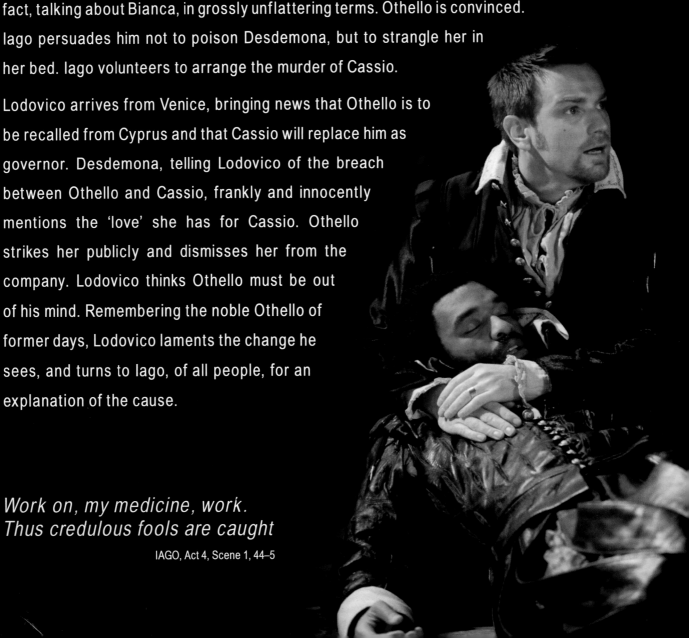

Work on, my medicine, work.
Thus credulous fools are caught

IAGO, Act 4, Scene 1, 44–5

Cyrus. Before the citadel.

Enter OTHELLO and IAGO.

IAGO
Will you think so?

OTHELLO
         Think so, Iago?

IAGO
What, to kiss in private?

OTHELLO
            An unauthoriz'd kiss.

IAGO
Or to be naked with her friend abed
An hour or more, not meaning any harm?

OTHELLO
Naked abed, Iago, and not mean harm?   5
It is hypocrisy against the devil.
They that mean virtuously, and yet do so,
The devil their virtue tempts, and they tempt heaven.

IAGO
So they do nothing, 'tis a venial slip.
But if I give my wife a handkerchief …   10

OTHELLO
What then?

IAGO
Why then 'tis hers, my lord, and being hers,
She may, I think, bestow't on any man.

OTHELLO
She is protectress of her honour, too.
May she give that?   15

IAGO
Her honour is an essence that's not seen,
They have it very oft that have it not.
But for the handkerchief …

OTHELLO
By heaven, I would most gladly have forgot it!
Thou said'st — O, it comes o'er my memory   20
As doth the raven o'er the infected house,
Boding to all! — he had my handkerchief.

---

1 As with almost all scenes in the play, this scene opens in the middle of a conversation

2 *unauthoriz'd:* illicit

6 *hypocrisy … devil:* a false show that cheats the devil's expectation that they will sin

7–8 *They that … heaven:* people who initially intend to do no wrong and yet put themselves in the way of temptation make it difficult even for heaven to save them (or, perhaps, tempt heaven to punish them)

9 *So … slip:* if they do nothing, despite putting themselves at risk, they commit only a minor fault

14 *protectress … honour:* custodian of her reputation (as a virtuous woman)

16 *an essence:* something

17 *They … not:* people who are reputed to be honourable are very often without honour

21–2 *As … all:* the raven is a bird of ill omen, often heralding death, and 'the infected house' is one where plague has occurred, so the raven's visitation is particularly sinister, as is Othello's thought of the handkerchief

IAGO

Ay, what of that?

OTHELLO

That's not so good now.

IAGO

What if I had said I had seen him do you wrong?
25 Or heard him say — as knaves be such abroad,
Who having by their own importunate suit
Or voluntary dotage of some mistress
Convinced or supplied them, cannot choose
But they must blab …

OTHELLO

Hath he said anything?

IAGO

30 He hath, my lord; but be you well assur'd,
No more than he'll unswear.

OTHELLO

What hath he said?

IAGO

Faith that he did — I know not what he did.

OTHELLO

But what?

IAGO

Lie.

OTHELLO

35 With her?

IAGO

With her, on her; what you will.

OTHELLO

Zounds, that's fulsome! Handkerchief — confessions — handkerchief! To confess, and be hanged for his labour. First to be hanged, and then to confess! I
40 tremble at it! Nature would not invest herself in such shadowing passion without some instruction. It is not words that shake me thus. Pish! Noses, ears and lips. Is't possible? — Confess? Handkerchief? O devil!

He falls down.

25–9 *knaves … blab:* there are villains in the world who, through persistence, have seduced a woman or who have gratified the desires of an infatuated woman, and then felt the urge to talk about it

31 *unswear:* deny

37–43 The switch to prose here and the use of disjointed language are signs of Othello's physical and emotional breakdown

37 *fulsome:* disgusting, sickening

40–1 *Nature … instruction:* my nature would not be overwhelmed by this dark passion unless there were some basis for Iago's accusations against Desdemona and Cassio

42–3 *Pish … lips:* Othello is expressing contempt as he thinks of Desdemona and Cassio as lovers

IAGO

Work on,

My medicine, work. Thus credulous fools are caught,   45

And many worthy and chaste dames, even thus

All guiltless, meet reproach. What ho, my lord!

My lord, I say! Othello!

Enter CASSIO.

              How now, Cassio?

CASSIO

What's the matter?

IAGO

My lord is fall'n into an epilepsy.   50

This is his second fit; he had one yesterday.

CASSIO

Rub him about the temples.

IAGO

              No, forbear,

The lethargy must have his quiet course.

If not, he foams at mouth and by and by

Breaks out to savage madness. Look, he stirs.   55

Do you withdraw yourself a little while,

He will recover straight. When he is gone,

I would on great occasion speak with you.

Exit CASSIO.

How is it, general? Have you not hurt your head?

OTHELLO

Dost thou mock me?

IAGO

              I mock you? No, by heaven!   60

Would you would bear your fortune like a man.

OTHELLO

A horned man's a monster, and a beast.

IAGO

There's many a beast then in a populous city,

And many a civil monster.

OTHELLO

Did he confess?   65

47 *meet reproach:* incur shame

48 Iago addresses Othello by his name, only because he is unconscious. This would have been considered inappropriate and disrespectful behaviour in normal circumstances

50 *epilepsy:* epileptic fit

51 *his second fit:* there is no independent evidence in the play for this

52 *forbear:* refrain, leave him alone

53 *lethargy:* coma, unconsciousness

56–8 Iago wants Cassio out of the way; he cannot risk a meeting between Othello and Cassio

57 *straight:* immediately

58 *on great occasion:* on a most important subject

62 *horned man:* cuckold; a man whose wife has been unfaithful

64 *civil monster:* monster resident in a city

66–7 *Think ... with you:* Iago is picturing the marriage bond as a heavy burden drawn by a yoked ox; he associates Othello with all the other men in the world who bear the same burden

68 *unproper:* shared with others

69 *peculiar:* their own exclusively

70–2 *'tis ... chaste:* the devil beholds with supreme and mocking satisfaction the spectacle of a deceived husband totally ignorant of his wife's infidelity

71 *lip ...couch:* kiss a woman of easy virtue, while free from suspicion of wrongdoing

73 *knowing ... shall be:* Shakespeare gives Iago many such mysterious remarks. He may mean: I know what would become of her if I were in your position

75 *Confine ... list:* keep yourself within the bounds of patience

79 *ecstasy:* swoon or trance (his epileptic fit)

80 *anon:* soon

81 *encave:* conceal

82 *mark:* observe
notable: noticeable, obvious

86 *cope:* meet with, copulate with

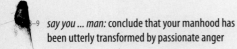

88–9 *say you ... man:* conclude that your manhood has been utterly transformed by passionate anger

92 *keep time:* maintain control, restrain yourself

94 *housewife:* here it means a prostitute

IAGO

                  Good sir, be a man.

Think every bearded fellow that's but yok'd

May draw with you; there's millions now alive

That nightly lie in those unproper beds

Which they dare swear peculiar. Your case is better.

70   O, 'tis the spite of hell, the fiend's arch-mock,

To lip a wanton in a secure couch,

And to suppose her chaste. No, let me know,

And knowing what I am, I know what she shall be.

OTHELLO

O, thou art wise; 'tis certain.

IAGO

                      Stand you awhile apart,

75   Confine yourself but in a patient list.

Whilst you were here, o'erwhelmed with your grief —

A passion most unsuiting such a man —

Cassio came hither. I shifted him away,

And laid good 'scuse upon your ecstasy,

80   Bid him anon return and here speak with me,

The which he promis'd. But encave yourself,

And mark the jeers, the gibes and notable scorns

That dwell in every region of his face.

For I will make him tell the tale anew,

85   Where, how, how oft, how long ago, and when

He has and is again to cope your wife.

I say, but mark his gesture. Marry, patience,

Or I shall say you are all in all in spleen,

And nothing of a man.

OTHELLO

                Dost thou hear, Iago?

90   I will be found most cunning in my patience,

But — dost thou hear? — most bloody.

IAGO

                     That's not amiss,

But yet keep time in all. Will you withdraw?

OTHELLO withdraws.

Now will I question Cassio of Bianca;

A housewife that by selling her desires

Buys herself bread and clothes. It is a creature 95

That dotes on Cassio — as 'tis the strumpet's plague

To beguile many and be beguil'd by one.

He, when he hears of her, cannot refrain

From the excess of laughter.

Enter CASSIO.

                              Here he comes.

As he shall smile, Othello shall go mad, 100

And his unbookish jealousy must conster

Poor Cassio's smiles, gestures and light behaviour

Quite in the wrong. How do you now, lieutenant?

CASSIO

The worser that you give me the addition

Whose want even kills me. 105

IAGO

Ply Desdemona well and you are sure on't.

Now if this suit lay in Bianca's power,

How quickly should you speed!

CASSIO

                              Alas, poor caitiff!

OTHELLO [aside]

Look how he laughs already!

IAGO

I never knew a woman love man so. 110

CASSIO

Alas, poor rogue, I think i' faith, she loves me.

OTHELLO [aside]

Now he denies it faintly, and laughs it out.

IAGO

Do you hear, Cassio?

OTHELLO [aside]

                              Now he importunes him

To tell it o'er. Go to, well said, well said.

IAGO

She gives it out that you shall marry her. 115

Do you intend it?

CASSIO

Ha, ha, ha!

97   *To ... one:* to captivate many but be infatuated with one

101   *unbookish:* ignorant
      conster: construe, interpret
102   *light:* frivolous

104–5 *The ... kills me:* I feel even worse now that you give me the very title [lieutenant] the loss of which is causing me such mortal distress

108   *speed:* succeed

108   *caitiff:* wretch

112   *faintly:* half-heartedly
      laughs it out: laughs it off

113   *importunes:* urges

118 *Roman:* Othello seems to be using 'Roman' as a synonym for anyone who triumphs; there is the suggestion, however, that Cassio's triumph is seen as short-lived

119 *customer:* prostitute

122 *They ... win:* this is a proverbial phrase meaning that the only ones entitled to laugh are those who win in the end; Othello is implying that Cassio will not be one of these

123 *the cry goes:* the common talk is

126 *scor'd:* wounded, injured

127 *the monkey's ... out:* Bianca's own story

128 *flattery:* self-esteem

130 *beckons me:* signals to me; it does not mean calls me

133 *bauble:* plaything

136 *imports it:* carries that meaning

OTHELLO [*aside*]

Do you triumph, Roman, do you triumph?

CASSIO

I marry her? What? A customer?

120   I prithee, bear some charity to my wit,

Do not think it so unwholesome. Ha, ha, ha!

OTHELLO [*aside*]

So, so, so, so. They laugh that win.

IAGO

Faith, the cry goes you shall marry her.

CASSIO

Prithee, say true.

IAGO

125   I am a very villain else.

OTHELLO [*aside*]

Ha' you scor'd me? Well.

CASSIO

This is the monkey's own giving out. She is persuaded I will marry her, out of her own love and flattery, not out of my promise.

OTHELLO [*aside*]

130   Iago beckons me; now he begins the story.

CASSIO

She was here even now, she haunts me in every place. I was t'other day talking on the sea-bank, with certain Venetians, and thither comes this bauble. By this hand, she falls me thus about my neck …

OTHELLO [*aside*]

135   Crying 'O dear Cassio!' as it were; his gesture imports it.

CASSIO

So hangs, and lolls, and weeps upon me. So shakes and pulls me — ha, ha, ha!

OTHELLO [aside]

Now he tells how she pluck'd him to my chamber.
I see that nose of yours, but not that dog I shall
throw't to.

CASSIO

Well, I must leave her company.

Enter BIANCA.

IAGO

Before me! Look, where she comes.

CASSIO

'Tis such another fitchew. Marry, a perfum'd one.
What do you mean by this haunting of me?

BIANCA

Let the devil and his dam haunt you. What did you
mean by that same handkerchief you gave me
even now? I was a fine fool to take it. I must take
out the whole work! A likely piece of work that you
should find it in your chamber and not know who
left it there! This is some minx's token, and I must
take out the work! There, give it your hobby-horse.
Wheresoever you had it, I'll take out no work on't.

CASSIO

How now, my sweet Bianca, how now, how now?

OTHELLO [aside]

By heaven, that should be my handkerchief!

BIANCA

An you'll come to supper to-night, you may. An you
will not, come when you are next prepar'd for.

Exit.

IAGO

After her, after her.

CASSIO

Faith, I must, she'll rail i' the street else.

IAGO

Will you sup there?

CASSIO

Faith, I intend so.

140

145

150

155

160

140–1 *I see … to:* Othello is thinking of punishing Cassio by cutting off his nose and throwing it to a dog. Presumably he cannot see the dog because the time for vengeance is yet to come

143 Iago gets lucky again, this time with the arrival of Bianca and the handkerchief

144 *'Tis … one:* Cassio's contemptuous estimate of Bianca. A 'fitchew' is a polecat, a creature associated with lechery and a foul smell. Cassio is saying, 'Here comes our polecat, her foul smell masked by her perfume'

146 *dam:* mother

151 *minx:* prostitute

152 *hobby-horse:* harlot

155 *should:* must

156 *An:* if

157 *prepar'd for:* expected (i.e. never)

159 *rail:* shout abuse
else: otherwise

160 *sup:* have supper

162 *I would ... fain:* I am very anxious to

167 Iago's remark is perfectly appropriate, and justified. Cassio did laugh at his vice, but not at the one that Iago has deluded Othello into contemplating

171 *prizes:* values

174 *I ... a-killing:* I would spend nine years killing him (i.e. take my time and kill him slowly)

181 *command him tasks:* give him orders

182 *your way:* what you should be thinking of now

IAGO

Well, I may chance to see you, for I would very fain speak with you.

CASSIO

Prithee come, will you?

IAGO

165 Go to; say no more.

Exit CASSIO.

OTHELLO

[advancing] How shall I murder him, Iago?

IAGO

Did you perceive how he laughed at his vice?

OTHELLO

O, Iago!

IAGO

And did you see the handkerchief?

OTHELLO

170 Was that mine?

IAGO

Yours, by this hand, and to see how he prizes the foolish woman your wife! She gave it him, and he hath given it his whore.

OTHELLO

I would have him nine years a-killing. A fine woman,
175 a fair woman, a sweet woman!

IAGO

Nay, you must forget.

OTHELLO

And let her rot, and perish, and be damned to-night, for she shall not live. No, my heart is turn'd to stone; I strike it and it hurts my hand. O, the world has not
180 a sweeter creature; she might lie by an emperor's side and command him tasks.

IAGO

Nay, that's not your way.

OTHELLO

Hang her, I do but say what she is: so delicate with her needle, an admirable musician, O, she will sing the savageness out of a bear! Of so high and plenteous wit and invention!

185

IAGO

She's the worse for all this.

OTHELLO

A thousand, thousand times! And then of so gentle a condition!

IAGO

Ay, too gentle.

190

OTHELLO

Ay, that's certain, but yet the pity of it, Iago.
O Iago, the pity of it, Iago!

IAGO

If you are so fond over her iniquity, give her patent to offend, for if it touches not you, it comes near nobody.

195

OTHELLO

I will chop her into messes — Cuckold me!

IAGO

O, 'tis foul in her.

OTHELLO

With mine officer!

IAGO

That's fouler.

OTHELLO

Get me some poison, Iago, this night. I'll not expostulate with her, lest her body and beauty unprovide my mind again. This night, Iago.

200

IAGO

Do it not with poison. Strangle her in her bed, even the bed she hath contaminated.

OTHELLO

Good, good, the justice of it pleases, very good.

205

186 *invention:* imagination

188–9 *so gentle a condition:* such gentle birth. In the next line Iago interprets 'gentle' to mean submissive to Cassio

193–5 *If ... nobody:* if you want to be so foolishly indulgent towards Desdemona's transgression, why not give her a licence to offend as she pleases, since it does not affect you, or anybody else for that matter

196 *messes:* pieces of food ready for consumption

198 In Othello's mind, Desdemona's imagined transgression is as much against his exalted public position as it is against true love

201 *expostulate:* argue in detail

202 *unprovide my mind:* alter the resolution I have made

206 *his undertaker:* the one who is to deal with him or take him on

IAGO

And for Cassio, let me be his undertaker. You shall hear more by midnight.

OTHELLO

Excellent good. *[a trumpet within]* What trumpet is that same?

IAGO

210 Something from Venice, sure.

Enter LODOVICO, DESDEMONA, and ATTENDANTS.

'Tis Lodovico,

Come from the duke; and see, your wife is with him.

LODOVICO

Save you, worthy general!

OTHELLO

With all my heart, sir.

LODOVICO

The duke and senators of Venice greet you.

Gives him a letter.

OTHELLO

I kiss the instrument of their pleasures.

Opens the letter, and reads.

214 *instrument ... pleasures:* letter setting out their wishes

DESDEMONA

215 And what's the news, good cousin Lodovico?

IAGO

I am very glad to see you, signior.

Welcome to Cyprus.

LODOVICO

I thank you. How does Lieutenant Cassio?

IAGO

Lives, sir.

218 Lodovico's response to Iago's warm welcome may be seen as somewhat dismissive. This would explain Iago's curt reply in the next line

DESDEMONA

220 Cousin, there's fall'n between him and my lord

An unkind breach, but you shall make all well.

221 *unkind breach:* unnatural division

OTHELLO

Are you sure of that?

DESDEMONA

My lord?

OTHELLO

[reads] 'This fail you not to do, as you will ...'

LODOVICO

He did not call, he's busy in the paper.   225

Is there division between my lord and Cassio?

DESDEMONA

A most unhappy one. I would do much·

To atone them, for the love I bear to Cassio.

OTHELLO

Fire and brimstone!

DESDEMONA

      My lord?

OTHELLO

         Are you wise?

DESDEMONA

What, is he angry?

LODOVICO

      Maybe the letter mov'd him,   230

For, as I think, they do command him home,

Deputing Cassio in his government.

DESDEMONA

By my troth, I am glad on't.

OTHELLO

       Indeed!

DESDEMONA

        My lord?

OTHELLO

I am glad to see you mad.

DESDEMONA

      How sweet Othello?

OTHELLO

[striking her] Devil!   235

DESDEMONA

I have not deserv'd this.

---

225 *in the paper:* with the letter

228 *atone them:* reconcile them, bring about unity between them

229 *Are you wise:* are you in your right mind (to declare your love for Cassio)

232 *Deputing ... government:* appointing Cassio in his place as army commander and governor of Cyprus

233 *By ... on't:* in faith, I am glad to hear it. Is she glad to hear that she and Othello have been ordered home to Venice, or that Cassio has not only been reinstated, but given a post of greater authority than he had before? Othello's reaction shows that he takes the latter meaning from her remark

234 *I ... mad:* this is an unfortunate obscurity at this point in the play. It may mean that Othello is making sarcastic reference to Desdemona's excitement at the news of Cassio's promotion ('mad' with delight), or that he is expressing his satisfaction at her public, and thus 'mad', avowal of her love for Cassio

LODOVICO
My lord, this would not be believ'd in Venice,
Though I should swear I saw't. 'Tis very much.
Make her amends, she weeps.

OTHELLO
                                    O devil, devil!
240 If that the earth could teem with women's tears,
Each drop she falls would prove a crocodile.
Out of my sight!

DESDEMONA
                    [going] I will not stay to offend you.

LODOVICO
Truly, an obedient lady.
I do beseech your lordship, call her back.

OTHELLO
245 Mistress!

DESDEMONA
My lord?

OTHELLO
What would you with her, sir?

LODOVICO
                                    Who, I, my lord?

OTHELLO
Ay, you did wish that I would make her turn.
Sir, she can turn, and turn, and yet go on
250 And turn again; and she can weep, sir, weep;
And she's obedient, as you say, obedient,
Very obedient. Proceed you in your tears.
Concerning this, sir — O, well-painted passion! —
I am commanded home — Get you away!
255 I'll send for you anon — Sir, I obey the mandate
And will return to Venice — Hence, avaunt!

Exit DESDEMONA.

Cassio shall have my place; and, sir, to-night
I do entreat that we may sup together.
You are welcome, sir, to Cyprus. Goats and monkeys!

Exit.

LODOVICO

Is this the noble Moor whom our full senate 260

Call all in all sufficient? This the noble nature

Whom passion could not shake? Whose solid virtue

The shot of accident nor dart of chance

Could neither graze nor pierce?

IAGO

He is much chang'd.

LODOVICO

Are his wits safe? Is he not light of brain? 265

IAGO

He's that he is. I may not breathe my censure

What he might be. If, what he might, he is not,

I would to heaven he were!

LODOVICO

What, strike his wife?

IAGO

Faith, that was not so well. Yet would I knew

That stroke would prove the worst!

LODOVICO

Is it his use? 270

Or did the letters work upon his blood

And new-create this fault?

IAGO

Alas, alas!

It is not honesty in me to speak

What I have seen and known. You shall observe him.

And his own courses will denote him so 275

That I may save my speech. Do but go after,

And mark how he continues.

LODOVICO

I am sorry that I am deceiv'd in him.

Exeunt.

---

261 *all in all sufficient:* absolutely capable

265 *light of brain:* insane

266 *He's ... censure:* Othello is what he is. It is not for me to judge him

267–8 *What ... were:* it is difficult to be sure of Iago's meaning here. Perhaps he is expressing the feigned wish that Othello were back to being the man he might be (and once was); or that if Othello's not insane, it would be better if he was (as it would explain his behaviour)

269–70 *Yet ... worst:* I wish I could be sure that she will suffer no worse than a blow at his hands. There is more than one layer of irony here, since Iago has already suggested that Othello strangle her

270–2 *Is ... fault:* Lodovico is wondering if Othello is usually like this or if the letter stirred him up and was the cause of his crazed behaviour

273 *It ... me:* it would not be honourable for me

275 *courses:* habits or actions
denote him: show what he is really like

Key points

Another painful scene showing Othello's further degradation by Iago. This degradation is depicted in three distinct episodes. First, Othello collapses at Iago's feet in a fit, described by the latter as 'an epilepsy' (line 50). His gloating tormentor relishes the triumph of his 'medicine' over both Othello and Desdemona: 'thus credulous fools are caught, and many worthy and chaste dames … meet reproach' (lines 45–7). Then, Iago persuades Othello to eavesdrop on Cassio; and finally, worst of all, Othello publicly strikes Desdemona.

- Iago's merciless cruelty reaches its climax after Cassio has left with Bianca, leaving Othello and Iago alone. Othello is torn between his love for Desdemona and his passionate rage and disillusionment at her supposed infidelity, and the thought that she has corrupted their noble love (lines 174–89). He refers to her, between periods of threats and curses, in terms which imply that he mourns the destruction of his love for Desdemona and of his faith in her because he still retains a sense of the qualities he loved her for.

- The culmination of Othello's tortured utterance is one of the most harrowing lines of the play: 'O Iago, the pity of it, Iago!' (line 192). Here we see a man driven to despair, and crying out for help to the man who deliberately caused his torment, only to be met with a pitiless response: 'If you are so fond over her iniquity, give her patent to offend' (lines 193–4). Iago has changed tactic from incitement to sarcastic advice. If Othello really feels he can tolerate her offence, or be so foolish ('fond') as to put up with it, then he should give her a licence ('patent') to let her go on with her misbehaviour ('iniquity').

- Iago needs to induce Othello to kill Desdemona quickly, since her continued existence must increase the chances that Iago's villainy will be unmasked. His new strategy works. Othello declares: 'I will chop her into messes' (line 196). This is followed by an agreed arrangement, suggested by Iago, that Desdemona will be strangled in her bed (lines 203–4).

- The episode, contrived by Iago, in which Iago questions Cassio about Bianca, while Othello thinks they are talking about Desdemona, is an interesting dramatic device. It is like a miniature play within the main play, with Iago as both actor and producer. Othello is a spectator who does not know what the true subject of the miniature play really is. Othello is also a commentator on what he thinks is happening, drawing all the wrong conclusions. Iago persuades Othello that Cassio has such contempt for Desdemona that he has given the handkerchief she gave him (the same one given to her by Othello) to Bianca (lines 171–3).

- The passage beginning with the opening of the letter from Venice and ending with the striking of Desdemona (lines 214–35) merits comment. The letter does not necessarily mean good news for Othello. We must assume that Othello is conscious of some loss of face in being called suddenly home and being replaced by Cassio. It is in this context that we should consider Desdemona's comment, 'By my troth, I am glad on't' (line 233), and her previous reference to 'the love I bear to Cassio' (line 228). Desdemona is thinking that Othello's return to Venice will be a relief to him. He feels otherwise, and thinks that she is glad to see him humiliated, and Cassio honoured. When he tells her that he is glad to see her 'mad' (line 234), he probably means that he is glad that she has lost her senses, and publicly revealed what she has been feeling all along about Cassio and himself.

Useful quotes

> O, it comes o'er my memory
> As doth the raven o'er the infected house,
> Boding to all! — he had my handkerchief.
>
> (Othello, lines 20–2)

> I would do much
> To atone them, for the love I bear to Cassio.
>
> (Desdemona, lines 227–8)

> My medicine, work. Thus credulous fools are caught,
> And many worthy and chaste dames, even thus
> All guiltless, meet reproach.
>
> (Iago, lines 45–7)

> Is this the noble Moor whom our full senate
> Call all in all sufficient? This the noble nature
> Whom passion could not shake?
>
> (Lodovico, lines 260–2)

> Do it not with poison. Strangle her in her bed, even the
> bed she hath contaminated. ...
> And for Cassio, let me be his undertaker.
>
> (Iago, lines 203–4, 206)

Questions ?

1 Iago's plot is based on very little fact, but a great deal of invention. Comment on this idea.

2 Iago is now totally in control of events. In what sense is this true of this scene?

3 Iago's cruelty is especially evident in this scene. Refer to some examples in support of this idea.

4 What is the evidence in this scene that Othello's love for Desdemona still survives to some degree?

5 Describe Othello's state of mind at the time of his physical collapse (line 43).

6 Why does Iago want Cassio and Desdemona to die?

7 Desdemona makes an unwitting blunder after the arrival of Lodovico. What is this?

8 Why does Othello strike Desdemona? Describe their relationship at this point in the play.

9 Astonished by Othello's behaviour, Lodovico says, 'Is this the noble Moor, whom our full senate call all in all sufficient? This the noble nature, whom passion could not shake?' (lines 260–2). Comment on the significance of these lines.

10 What kind of role does Iago adopt at the end of this scene?

11 Imagine you are Desdemona. Compose a letter to a friend in Venice, updating her on what has happened since you left for Cyprus.

ACT 4 ✝ Scene 2

Plot summary

OTHELLO IS NOW BROUGHT into contact with Emilia, who has it in her power to reveal the truth about Desdemona, particularly in regard to the handkerchief. What she says does nothing to either confirm or dispel Othello's suspicions and he dismisses her defence of Desdemona as mere fabrication. Othello indulges in self-dramatisation and self-pity, casting himself in the role of the betrayed husband. Desdemona's denials of guilt inflame him: he likens her to a prostitute and Emilia to a pimp. Bewildered, Desdemona sends for Iago. When he arrives, Emilia suggests that some rogue must have poisoned Othello's mind against Desdemona: another example of the continuous thread of irony essential to Iago's role. Iago makes excuses for him and urges Desdemona and Emilia to go to the supper being given in honour of the Venetian visitors. Roderigo arrives, and wants to know what has happened to the jewels he gave Iago to deliver to Desdemona. Iago knows he is in real danger when Roderigo threatens to go to Desdemona. He averts the danger, however, by involving Roderigo in the plot to kill Cassio.

I understand a fury in your words,
But not the words.

DESDEMONA, Act 4, Scene 2, 32–3

Cyrus. The citadel.

Enter OTHELLO and EMILIA.

OTHELLO

You have seen nothing then?

EMILIA

Nor ever heard, nor ever did suspect.

OTHELLO

Yes, and you have seen Cassio and she together?

EMILIA

But then I saw no harm, and then I heard

Each syllable that breath made up between 'em.   5

OTHELLO

What, did they never whisper?

EMILIA

                                    Never, my lord.

OTHELLO

Nor send you out o' the way?

EMILIA

Never.

OTHELLO

To fetch her fan, her mask, her gloves, nor nothing?

EMILIA

Never, my lord.   10

OTHELLO

That's strange.

EMILIA

I durst, my lord, to wager she is honest,

Lay down my soul at stake. If you think other,

Remove your thought; it doth abuse your bosom.

If any wretch ha' put this in your head,   15

Let heaven requite it with the serpent's curse,

For if she be not honest, chaste and true,

There's no man happy. The purest of their wives

Is foul as slander.

OTHELLO

                        Bid her come hither, go.

Exit EMILIA.

---

3 *she:* Desdemona

5 *that breath made up:* spoken

12–19 Emilia is coarse-grained and mildly dishonest, but her instincts are sound; she acknowledges true goodness where she finds it

12 *durst:* would dare

13 *Lay ... stake:* would stake my soul on it

14 *abuse your bosom:* corrupt and dishonour your heart

16 *Let ... curse:* may heaven curse the wretch with the same curse that befell the serpent after the fall in Eden. Here, Iago would be Satan to Othello's Adam; one of many 'diabolic' images in the play

20–1 *She ... as much:* Emilia sounds convincing enough, but it would be a dull and unimaginative procuress who couldn't come up with some such invention as this

21 *a subtle whore:* Desdemona

22 *A closet ... key:* a concealer

20   She says enough, yet she's a simple bawd

That cannot say as much. This is a subtle whore,

A closet, lock and key of villainous secrets.

And yet she'll kneel and pray; I ha' seen her do't.

Enter DESDEMONA and EMILIA.

DESDEMONA

My lord, what is your will?

OTHELLO

Pray, chuck, come hither.

DESDEMONA

25   What is your pleasure?

OTHELLO

Let me see your eyes.

Look in my face.

DESDEMONA

What horrible fancy's this?

OTHELLO

[to Emilia] Some of your function, mistress,

27–8 *Some ... alone:* some of those who ply your trade (i.e. pimps) leave copulators (i.e. their customers) alone. Othello is treating Emilia as if she were a bawd

29 *cry hem:* pretend to clear the throat as a warning

30 *mystery:* trade (i.e. as a brothel-keeper or attendant)
dispatch: off you go

Leave procreants alone and shut the door,

Cough or cry hem if anybody come.

30   Your mystery, your mystery — nay, dispatch.

Exit EMILIA.

DESDEMONA

Upon my knees, what doth your speech import?

31 *import:* mean

I understand a fury in your words,

But not the words.

OTHELLO

Why, what art thou?

DESDEMONA

35   Your wife, my lord, your true and loyal wife.

OTHELLO

Come, swear it, damn thyself,

36 *swear it:* swear your innocence

36–8 *damn thyself ... double-damn'd:* the devils might fear to take her into hell because she looks like an angel ('one of heaven'). If Desdemona swears her innocence, she will be twice damned: once for being unfaithful and once for swearing she is not

Lest, being like one of heaven, the devils themselves

Should fear to seize thee, therefore be double-damn'd:

Swear thou art honest.

DESDEMONA

Heaven doth truly know it.

OTHELLO

Heaven truly knows that thou art false as hell.   40

DESDEMONA

To whom, my lord? With whom? How am I false?

OTHELLO

O Desdemona, away! away! away!

DESDEMONA

Alas, the heavy day! Why do you weep?

Am I the motive of those tears, my lord?

If haply you my father do suspect   45

An instrument of this your calling back,

Lay not your blame on me. If you have lost him,

Why, I have lost him too.

OTHELLO

               Had it pleas'd heaven

To try me with affliction, had he rain'd

All kinds of sores and shames on my bare head,   50

Steep'd me in poverty to the very lips,

Given to captivity me and my hopes,

I should have found in some place of my soul

A drop of patience; but, alas, to make me

A fixed figure for the time of scorn   55

To point his slow unmoving finger at.

Yet could I bear that too, well, very well.

But there, where I have garner'd up my heart,

Where either I must live or bear no life,

The fountain from the which my current run,   60

Or else dries up, to be discarded thence,

To keep it as a cistern for foul toads

To knot and gender in! Turn thy complexion there,

Patience, thou young and rose-lipp'd cherubin,

I here look grim as hell!   65

DESDEMONA

I hope my noble lord esteems me honest.

---

43 *heavy:* sad, woeful

44 *motive:* cause

45–8 *If … too:* if, perhaps, Brabantio has had something to do with your recall to Venice, do not blame me. If you have lost his good will (due to our marriage), so have I. This calls to mind Brabantio's parting words to his son-in-law, which suggested a malicious satisfaction in the notion that Desdemona might prove false: 'She has deceived her father, and may thee' (Act 1, Scene 3, line 293)

48–54 Othello is recalling the sufferings of Job, the pattern of all earthly affliction. Job bore his sufferings in patience; Othello, with characteristic hyperbole, finds that he might endure Job's afflictions with some patience, but goes on to suggest that his own are less bearable. Hyperbole is exaggeration for the sake of emphasis

54–6 *but … finger at:* Othello thinks that heaven and Desdemona have made him an object of ridicule, at which the scornful world ('the time of scorn') will long point a finger

58 *garner'd:* stored. Othello entrusted his heart, the seat of his affections, to Desdemona

60–3 *The … gender in:* the source of all my happiness has been utterly contaminated

63 *knot and gender:* twist and engender

63–5 *Turn … hell:* a fully satisfactory explanation of these lines has not, so far, been offered. Othello seems to mean that even Patience would change colour at the sight of Desdemona's misdeed, and that he looks on grim-faced. If it was 'And' or 'Ay' instead of 'I' in the last line, the whole would make more sense

66 *esteems me honest:* considers me chaste

OTHELLO

O, ay, as summer's flies are in the shambles,

That quicken even with blowing.

O thou black weed, why art so lovely fair?

70 Thou smell'st so sweet that the sense aches at thee.

Would thou hadst ne'er been born!

DESDEMONA

Alas, what ignorant sin have I committed?

OTHELLO

Was this fair paper, this most goodly book,

Made to write 'whore' upon? — What committed?

75 Committed! O thou public commoner!

I should make very forges of my cheeks,

That would to cinders burn up modesty,

Did I but speak thy deeds. What committed!

Heaven stops the nose at it, and the moon winks;

80 The bawdy wind that kisses all it meets

Is hush'd within the hollow mine of earth

And will not hear't. What committed?

DESDEMONA

By heaven, you do me wrong.

OTHELLO

Are not you a strumpet?

DESDEMONA

No, as I am a Christian.

85 If to preserve this vessel for my lord

From any hated foul unlawful touch,

Be not to be a strumpet, I am none.

OTHELLO

What, not a whore?

DESDEMONA

No, as I shall be sav'd.

OTHELLO

Is't possible?

DESDEMONA

90 O, heaven, forgiveness.

OTHELLO

I cry you mercy then.

67–8 *flies ... blowing:* [she is as unchaste as] flies in an abattoir ('shambles') in summer, receiving life as they lay their eggs

72 *ignorant sin:* sin I am unaware of

73 *fair ... book:* Desdemona

75 *commoner:* prostitute

76 *make ... cheeks:* blush (so that his cheeks become red hot)

78 *Did ... deeds:* if I only gave an account of your conduct

79–82 *Heaven ... hear't:* the offence smells to heaven, and the moon [symbol of chastity] closes its eyes to avoid seeing your crime; the wind, though itself promiscuous, is repelled by your deed. Othello has now described her conduct as offensive to the senses of smell, sight and hearing

85 *vessel:* body

90 *I ... mercy:* I beg your pardon (Othello's idea of sarcasm)

I took you for that cunning whore of Venice,
That married with Othello. *[calling]* You, mistress,
That have the office opposite to Saint Peter,
And keep the gate of hell …
Enter EMILIA.

                              Ay, you, you, you!
We ha' done our course; there's money for your pains.   95
I pray you, turn the key, and keep our counsel.
Exit.

EMILIA
Alas, what does this gentleman conceive?
How do you, madam? How do you, my good lady?

DESDEMONA
Faith, half asleep.

EMILIA
Good madam, what's the matter with my lord?   100

DESDEMONA
With who?

EMILIA
Why, with my lord, madam.

DESDEMONA
Who is thy lord?

EMILIA
                    He that is yours, sweet lady.

DESDEMONA
I ha' none. Do not talk to me, Emilia;
I cannot weep, nor answer have I none,   105
But what should go by water. Prithee, to-night
Lay on my bed our wedding sheets, remember,
And call thy husband hither.

EMILIA
                    Here is a change indeed!
Exit.

DESDEMONA
'Tis meet I should be us'd so, very meet.
How have I been behav'd that he might stick   110
The smallest opinion on my greatest abuse?
Enter IAGO and EMILIA.

93 *Saint Peter:* keeper of the keys of the kingdom of heaven

95 *done our course:* finished our business

96 *keep our counsel:* keep our business confidential

97 *conceive:* mean, intend by his words, imagine

106 *go by water:* be conveyed by tears

108 Desdemona sends for Iago because she believes he will advise and help her; this is another of the ironies arising from Iago's character and role

109 *meet:* appropriate, fitting (used ironically here)

110–11 *How … abuse:* even my greatest fault has been so small that I do not understand how he could attach an unfavourable opinion to it

IAGO

What is your pleasure, madam? How is't with you?

DESDEMONA

I cannot tell. Those that do teach young babes

Do it with gentle means and easy tasks;

115   He might ha' chid me so, for, in good faith,

I am a child to chiding.

IAGO

What is the matter, lady?

EMILIA

Alas, Iago, my lord hath so bewhor'd her.

Thrown such despite and heavy terms upon her

As true hearts cannot bear.

DESDEMONA

120   Am I that name, Iago?

IAGO

What name, fair lady?

DESDEMONA

Such as she says my lord did say I was?

EMILIA

He call'd her whore; a beggar in his drink

Could not have laid such terms upon his callet.

IAGO

Why did he so?

DESDEMONA

125   I do not know, I am sure I am none such.

IAGO

Do not weep, do not weep. Alas the day!

EMILIA

Has she forsook so many noble matches,

Her father, and her country, and her friends,

To be call'd whore? Would it not make one weep?

DESDEMONA

130   It is my wretched fortune.

IAGO

Beshrew him for it!

How comes this trick upon him?

DESDEMONA

Nay, heaven doth know.

---

115 *chid:* rebuked

116 *I ... chiding:* I become like a child when I am scolded; or, I am not used to being rebuked

117 *bewhor'd her:* called her a whore

118 *despite:* abuse, hatred

123 *laid ... callet:* attributed such wicked names (insults) to his slut

127 *forsook ... matches:* given up the chance to marry one of the many Venetian noblemen who were her suitors

130 *Beshrew:* curse

131 *trick:* delusion, deception

EMILIA

I will be hang'd if some eternal villain,

Some busy and insinuating rogue,

Some cogging, cozening slave, to get some office,

Have not devis'd this slander. I'll be hang'd else.   135

IAGO

Fie, there is no such man, it is impossible.

DESDEMONA

If any such there be, heaven pardon him!

EMILIA

A halter pardon him, and hell gnaw his bones!

Why should he call her whore? Who keeps her company?

What place, what time, what form, what likelihood?   140

The Moor's abus'd by some outrageous knave,

Some base notorious knave, some scurvy fellow.

O heaven, that such companions thou'ldst unfold,

And put in every honest hand a whip

To lash the rascal naked through the world,   145

Even from the east to the west!

IAGO

                            Speak within door.

EMILIA

O, fie upon him! Some such squire he was

That turn'd your wit the seamy side without

And made you to suspect me with the Moor.

IAGO

You are a fool, go to.

DESDEMONA

                        O good Iago,   150

What shall I do to win my lord again?

Good friend, go to him, for, by this light of heaven,

I know not how I lost him. Here I kneel.

If e'er my will did trespass 'gainst his love,

Either in discourse of thought or actual deed,   155

Or that mine eyes, mine ears or any sense

Delight them in any other form,

Or that I do not yet, and ever did

And ever will (though he do shake me off

To beggarly divorcement), love him dearly,   160

132–4 *eternal … slave:* utter villain, some villainous interfering busybody, some cheating, wretched impostor

134 *get some office:* gain a job or position. With Iago present, this passage is a remarkable irony

136 *Fie:* an exclamation of disgust or indignation

138 *A halter pardon him:* may he be hanged. A double irony

142 *Some … fellow:* some dishonourable, out and out scoundrel, some despicable fellow

143 *O … unfold:* Emilia wishes that heaven would reveal such rascals to the eyes of honest men and women

146 *Speak within door:* lower your voice

147 *squire:* a young man; the term is used contemptuously here

148–9 *turn'd … Moor:* turned your judgement the wrong side out and caused you to suspect that I was unfaithful to you with Othello. This confirms that Iago has genuinely entertained suspicions of Othello

150 *go to:* be quiet

155 *discourse of thought:* thinking

157 *Delight … form:* took delight in another person

159–60 *though … divorcement:* even if he divorces me and leaves me a beggar

161	*forswear:* abandon
162	*defeat:* deprive me of

Comfort forswear me! Unkindness may do much;

And his unkindness may defeat my life,

But never taint my love. I cannot say 'whore';

It does abhor me now I speak the word.

165

To do the act that might the addition earn,

Not the world's mass of vanity could make me.

165	*addition:* title
166	*mass of vanity:* luxuries and privileges

IAGO

I pray you, be content, 'tis but his humour.

The business of the state does him offence

And he does chide with you.

168	*does him offence:* troubles his mind

DESDEMONA

170

If 'twere no other, …

IAGO

'Tis but so, I warrant you.

[trumpets within]

Hark, how these instruments summon you to supper,

And the great messengers of Venice stay.

Go in, and weep not, all things shall be well.

Exeunt DESDEMONA and EMILIA.

Enter RODERIGO.

How now, Roderigo?

172	*stay:* await

✗ **RODERIGO** *Bodrigo standing up to Iago*

175

I do not find that thou deal'st justly with me.

IAGO

What in the contrary?

RODERIGO

Every day thou daff'st me with some device, Iago, and rather, as it seems to me, thou keepest from me all conveniency than suppliest me with the least

180

advantage of hope. I will indeed no longer endure it, nor am I yet persuaded to put up in peace what already I have foolishly suffered.

176	*in:* to
177	*thou … device:* you put me off with some scheme
178–80	*rather … hope:* you are depriving me of all my dearest needs instead of furthering my hopes
181	*to put up:* to put up with

IAGO

Will you hear me, Roderigo?

RODERIGO

Faith, I have heard too much, for your words and

185

performances are no kind together.

184–5	*your words … together:* you have completely failed to do what you had promised me (i.e. to help me to win Desdemona)

IAGO

You charge me most unjustly.

RODERIGO

With nought but truth. I have wasted myself out of means: the jewels you have had from me to deliver to Desdemona would half have corrupted a votarist. You have told me she hath receiv'd 'em, and I return'd me expectations and comforts of sudden respect and acquaintance, but I find none.   190

IAGO

Well, go to, very well.

RODERIGO

Very well, go to! I cannot go to, man, 'tis not very well. By this hand, I say 'tis very scurvy, and begin to find myself fopp'd in it.   195

IAGO

Very well.

RODERIGO

I say it is not very well! I will make myself known to Desdemona. If she will return me my jewels, I will give over my suit and repent my unlawful solicitation; if not,   200 assure yourself I seek satisfaction of you.

IAGO

You have said now.

RODERIGO

Ay, and I have said nothing but what I protest intendment of doing.

IAGO

Why, now I see there's mettle in thee, and even from   205 this time do build on thee a better opinion than ever before. Give me thy hand, Roderigo. Thou hast taken against me a most just exception, but yet I protest, I have dealt most directly in thy affairs.

RODERIGO

It hath not appear'd.   210

IAGO

I grant indeed it hath not appeared, and your suspicion is not without wit and judgement. But Roderigo, if thou hast that within thee indeed, which I have greater reason to believe now than ever, I mean purpose, courage and valour, this night show   215 it. If thou the next night following enjoyest not

---

187–8 *wasted … means:* squandered all my money

189 *votarist:* nun

191 *expectations:* hopes
sudden respect: immediate attention

194 *go to:* Roderigo interprets Iago's dismissive 'go to' as meaning 'have sexual relations'
195 *scurvy:* despicable
196 *fopp'd:* fooled, duped

200 *solicitation:* courtship

201 *seek satisfaction:* look for revenge (by fighting a duel with Iago)

202 *You … now:* Iago is pretending to praise Roderigo's determination. 'Well said' is perhaps a modern equivalent

203–4 *protest intendment:* declare my intention

205 *mettle:* spirit, courage

208 *exception:* objection

209 *directly:* straightforwardly

210 *It … appear'd:* I cannot see any evidence of it

OTHELLO **147**

218 *engines for:* scenes against

219 *compass:* possibility

224 *he ... Mauritania:* this is probably an invention of Iago's

225–7 *unless ... Cassio:* unless some accident makes it necessary for him to remain here, and no accident can be as effective in this regard as the removal of Cassio

234 *He ... fortune:* he does not yet know of his appointment as Othello's successor

235 *thence:* from there
fashion: arrange

237 *at your pleasure:* any way you like
second: support

241 *high:* fully

242 *About it:* let's get moving

Desdemona, take me from this world with treachery and devise engines for my life.

RODERIGO

Well, is it within reason and compass?

IAGO

220 Sir, there is especial commission come from Venice to depute Cassio in Othello's place.

RODERIGO

Is that true? Why then Othello and Desdemona return again to Venice.

IAGO

O no, he goes into Mauritania and takes away with 225 him the fair Desdemona, unless his abode be linger'd here by some accident, wherein none can be so determinate as the removing of Cassio.

RODERIGO

How do you mean 'removing' of him?

IAGO

Why, by making him uncapable of Othello's place 230 — knocking out his brains.

RODERIGO

And that you would have me to do?

IAGO

Ay, if you dare do yourself a profit and a right. He sups to-night with a harlot, and thither will I go to him. He knows not yet of his honourable fortune. If you 235 will watch his going thence, which I will fashion to fall out between twelve and one, you may take him at your pleasure. I will be near to second your attempt, and he shall fall between us. Come, stand not amaz'd at it, but go along with me. I will show you such a 240 necessity in his death that you shall think yourself bound to put it on him. It is now high supper-time, and the night grows to waste. About it.

RODERIGO

I will hear further reason for this.

IAGO

And you shall be satisfied.

Exeunt.

Key points

This scene marks an even more extreme stage in the degradation of Othello, who by now is thoroughly corrupted. His corruption is emphasised by his use of ideas and language previously characteristic of Iago. He has taken on Iago's role, as he blackens Desdemona's character.

- Desdemona is reduced to a pitiful, uncomprehending wreck through the vile abuse of her character by the person she loves.

- In the previous scene, Iago enjoyed his triumph over a helpless, suffering Othello. In this scene, he pitilessly enjoys a similar triumph over Desdemona.

- It is a cruel irony that Desdemona pleads with Iago to help her win back her husband's love, only to be met with the same cold, merciless response that greeted Othello when he cried out for understanding from Iago. Her kneeling to heaven (line 153) to confess her fidelity parallels Othello's similar action in Act 3, Scene 3, when his motive was to seek divine sanction for his revenge.

- The irony of this scene is often intense. When, for example, Iago enters to observe the suffering Desdemona, Emilia stumbles on the truth about Othello's behaviour. She is convinced that 'some eternal villain, some busy and insinuating rogue' (lines 132–3) has slandered Desdemona. The irony is that she does not know that this 'rogue' is standing beside her, planning further evil.

- Iago has been lucky so far in his schemes. He has benefited from accident and coincidence (for example, Desdemona's loss of the handkerchief, Emilia finding it and Cassio's giving it to Bianca). He has also made good use of his skills in planning and plotting and his shrewd judgement of the characters of those around him. It now seems inevitable that Desdemona will soon die, and that either Cassio or Roderigo will dispose of the other.

- Iago has not considered that Emilia may prove a problem. His failure to take his wife into account may be due to his low regard for her as a person. Whatever the reason, it will prove to be his undoing. In this scene there are signs that the truth is dawning, however vaguely, on Emilia. Her inkling that Othello's jealousy has been inspired by some self-seeking third party should be a warning to Iago that she might yet arrive at more of the truth. He is not worried. He takes her good will for granted.

O Desdemona, away! away! away!

OTHELLO, Act 4, Scene 2, 42

Useful quotes

Remove your thought; it doth abuse your bosom.
If any wretch ha' put this in your head,
Let heaven requite it with the serpent's curse,
For if she be not honest, chaste and true,
There's no man happy.

(Emilia, lines 14–18)

Some such squire he was
That turn'd your wit the seamy side without
And made you to suspect me with the Moor.

(Emilia, lines 147–9)

O, ay, as summer's flies are in the shambles,
That quicken even with blowing.
O thou black weed, why art so lovely fair?

(Othello, lines 67–9)

O good Iago,
What shall I do to win my lord again?
Good friend, go to him

(Desdemona, lines 150–2)

I will be hang'd if some eternal villain,
Some busy and insinuating rogue,
Some cogging, cozening slave, to get some office,
Have not devis'd this slander.

(Emilia, lines 132–5)

Unkindness may do much;
And his unkindness may defeat my life,
But never taint my love.

(Desdemona, lines 161–3)

? Questions

1 Blindness to reality is one of the characteristics of Shakespeare's tragic heroes. How is this blindness evident in Othello's case?

2 Some commentators have found Othello extremely self-centred. Is there evidence of this quality in this scene?

3 Othello's language and imagery indicate how successful Iago has been in infecting his mind. Give examples of this.

4 Describe Emilia's role in this scene.

5 Desdemona is a changed person by the end of this scene. In what ways is she different from the Desdemona of Act 1?

6 In what ways is Iago's inhumanity stressed in this scene?

7 There is remarkable irony in Emilia's explanation of the reasons for Othello's behaviour (lines 132–49). Examine this statement.

8 Roderigo's new attitude poses problems for Iago. What are these, and how does Iago deal with them?

ACT 4 ✝ Scene 3

THE FORMAL SUPPER IN honour of the Venetian ambassador and his attendants is over. Othello orders Desdemona to go to bed and to dismiss Emilia. Emilia expresses strong disapproval of Othello, but Desdemona defends him. The effects of her ill-treatment by Othello now begin to show. Her mind lingers on thoughts of death and on a far-off song of tragic love like her own, learned from an ill-fated maid who died singing it. She wonders aloud whether there can really be women capable of the kind of infidelity that Othello has accused her of. Emilia tells her that there are, and declares that female infidelity is a response to the inadequacies and misdeeds of husbands. Desdemona cannot see why one evil deed should be repaid with another one.

Dost thou in conscience think — tell me, Emilia —
That there be women do abuse their husbands
In such gross kind?

DESDEMONA, Act 4, Scene 3, 60–2

Cyrus. The citadel.

Enter OTHELLO, DESDEMONA, LODOVICO, EMILIA, and ATTENDANTS.

LODOVICO
I do beseech you, sir, trouble yourself no further.

OTHELLO
O, pardon me, it shall do me good to walk.

LODOVICO
Madam, good night. I humbly thank your ladyship.

DESDEMONA
Your honour is most welcome.

OTHELLO
                                        Will you walk, sir?

5   O, Desdemona!

DESDEMONA
My lord?

OTHELLO
Get you to bed on the instant: I will be return'd forthwith, dismiss your attendant there — look it be done.

DESDEMONA
10   I will, my lord.

Exeunt OTHELLO, LODOVICO, and ATTENDANTS.

EMILIA
How goes it now? He looks gentler than he did.

DESDEMONA
He says he will return incontinent.
He hath commanded me to go to bed,
And bade me to dismiss you.

EMILIA
                                        Dismiss me?

DESDEMONA
15   It was his bidding, therefore, good Emilia,
Give me my nightly wearing, and adieu,
We must not now displease him.

---

4   After her harrowing experience at Othello's hands just before this, Desdemona exhibits admirable self-possession

8   *forthwith:* immediately

11   *He looks gentler:* this suggests that Othello has recovered some of his self-control

12   *incontinent:* straightaway

16   *nightly wearing:* nightgown

EMILIA

I would you had never seen him!

DESDEMONA

So would not I, my love doth so approve him

That even his stubbornness, his checks and frowns — 20

Prithee unpin me — have grace and favour in them.

EMILIA

I have laid those sheets you bade me on the bed.

DESDEMONA

All's one. Good faith, how foolish are our minds!

If I do die before thee, prithee shroud me

In one of those same sheets.

EMILIA

                                        Come, come, you talk.   25

DESDEMONA

My mother had a maid call'd Barbary.

She was in love and he she lov'd prov'd mad

And did forsake her. She had a song of 'willow',

An old thing 'twas, but it express'd her fortune,

And she died singing it. That song to-night   30

Will not go from my mind — I have much to do,

But to go hang my head all at one side

And sing it like poor Barbary. Prithee dispatch.

EMILIA

Shall I go fetch your night-gown?

DESDEMONA

                                No, unpin me here.

This Lodovico is a proper man.   35

EMILIA

A very handsome man.

DESDEMONA

He speaks well.

EMILIA

I know a lady in Venice would have walk'd barefoot to

Palestine for a touch of his nether lip.

19 *approve:* commend him to my eyes

20 *stubbornness:* harshness
   checks: rebukes, snubs

22 *sheets:* the wedding sheets that Desdemona requested in the previous scene

23 *All's one:* all right, no matter

25 *you talk:* this is idle talk

27 *mad:* unfaithful or unstable

28 *forsake:* leave
   willow: a traditional emblem of deserted love

31–3 *I have ... Barbary:* it is all I can do to stop myself singing the song as Barbary did

34 *night-gown:* dressing-gown

35 *proper:* handsome

37 *He speaks well:* Desdemona may be contrasting Lodovico's coherent, well-ordered speech with Othello's disjointed ravings

38–9 *walk'd ... Palestine:* gone on a pilgrimage

39 *nether:* lower

DESDEMONA

40 [sings] *The poor soul sat sighing by a sycamore tree,*

Sing all a green willow;

Her hand on her bosom her head on her knee,

Sing willow, willow, willow.

The fresh streams ran by her, and murmur'd her moans;

45 *Sing willow, willow, willow.*

Her salt tears fell from her, which soften'd the stones; —

Lay by these. —

Sing willow, willow, willow. —

Prithee hie thee. He'll come anon. —

50 *Sing all a green willow must be my garland.*

Let nobody blame him, his scorn I approve, —

Nay, that's not next. Hark, who's that knocks?

EMILIA

It is the wind.

DESDEMONA

I call'd my love false love; but what said he then?

55 *Sing willow, willow, willow.*

If I court moe women, you'll couch with moe men.

Now get thee gone. Good night. Mine eyes do itch,

Does that bode weeping?

EMILIA

'Tis neither here nor there.

DESDEMONA

I have heard it said so. O, these men, these men!

60 Dost thou in conscience think — tell me, Emilia —

That there be women do abuse their husbands

In such gross kind?

EMILIA

There be some such, no question.

DESDEMONA

Wouldst thou do such a deed for all the world?

EMILIA

Why, would not you?

DESDEMONA

No, by this heavenly light!

---

47 *these:* Desdemona's jewels

49 *hie:* hurry
anon: at once

52 *that's not next:* Desdemona is correcting herself, saying that she has got the words of her song in the wrong order

56 *moe:* more

58 *bode:* foretell

58 *'Tis ... there:* it is of no account either one way or the other

60 *in conscience:* really, truly

61–2 *abuse ... kind:* treat their husbands so monstrously (i.e. commit adultery)

62 *no question:* there is no doubt about that

64 *heavenly light:* the moon, whose Roman goddess was also the goddess of chastity

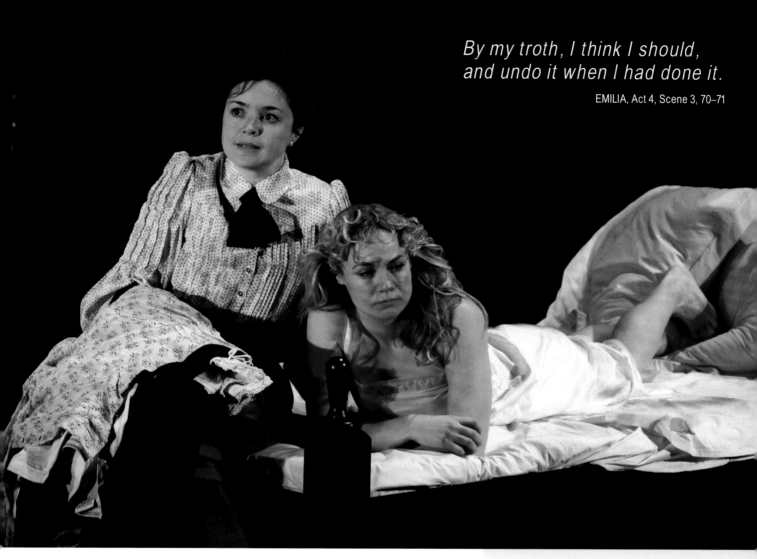

*By my troth, I think I should,
and undo it when I had done it.*

EMILIA, Act 4, Scene 3, 70–71

EMILIA

Nor I neither by this heavenly light.   65

I might do it as well in the dark.

DESDEMONA

Wouldst thou do such a deed for all the world?

EMILIA

The world is a huge thing. It is a great price

For a small vice.

DESDEMONA

               Good troth, I think thou wouldst not.

69   *Good troth:* in good faith

EMILIA

By my troth, I think I should, and undo it when I had   70
done it. Marry, I would not do such a thing for a
joint-ring, or for measures of lawn, nor for gowns or
petticoats, nor caps, nor any such exhibition; but, for
the whole world? Ud's pity, who would not make her

72   *joint-ring:* ring with interlocking halves
      lawn: fine linen
73   *exhibition:* payment or offer
74   *Ud's:* God's

75–6 *I should … it:* Emilia would risk purgatory for being unfaithful to her husband if this unfaithfulness meant making him a monarch. Her mention of purgatory rather than hell suggests that she does not consider this kind of infidelity a mortal sin. Her values are not Desdemona's

79–82 *Why … right:* Emilia is replying that if Desdemona were to get the whole world in exchange for doing wrong, she would then control the world in which she had done the wrong and could easily undo the wrong

84 *to the vantage:* over and above, in addition

85 *Store:* fill, populate

88 *foreign:* other

89 *peevish:* foolish. Emilia may be referring to the jealousies of both Othello and Iago

90 *Throwing … us:* restricting our freedom

91 *Or … despite:* or reduce whatever allowance or provision we previously had, out of spite

92 *galls:* good grounds for resenting the treatment we get

94 *have sense:* have the use of their senses

98 *doth … it:* does it arise from passion or desire?

99 *frailty:* moral weakness; giving in to temptation

103 *The … so:* whatever harm we do has been prompted and inspired by their bad example

104 *uses:* practices

105 *Not … mend:* not to grow worse through bad luck or unfortunate experiences, but to learn from them

---

75 husband a cuckold to make him a monarch? I should venture purgatory for it.

DESDEMONA
Beshrew me if I would do such a wrong
For the whole world.

EMILIA
Why, the wrong is but a wrong i' the world; and
80 having the world for your labour, 'tis a wrong in your own world, and you might quickly make it right.

DESDEMONA
I do not think there is any such woman.

EMILIA
Yes, a dozen, and as many to the vantage as would
85 Store the world they played for.
But I do think it is their husbands' faults
If wives do fall. Say that they slack their duties,
And pour our treasures into foreign laps,
Or else break out in peevish jealousies,
90 Throwing restraint upon us, or say they strike us,
Or scant our former having in despite;
Why, we have galls, and though we have some grace,
Yet have we some revenge. Let husbands know
Their wives have sense like them: they see, and smell,
95 And have their palates both for sweet and sour,
As husbands have. What is it that they do
When they change us for others? Is it sport?
I think it is. And doth affection breed it?
I think it doth. Is't frailty that thus errs?
100 It is so too. And have not we affections,
Desires for sport, and frailty, as men have?
Then let them use us well, else let them know
The ills we do, their ills instruct us so.

DESDEMONA
Good night, good night. Heaven me such uses send
105 Not to pick bad from bad, but by bad mend!
Exeunt.

Key points

This is a pathetic and beautiful scene, sad without ever becoming sentimental. Its most moving feature is Desdemona's absolute loyalty to and unconditional love for Othello, despite the indignity and cruelty he has visited on her.

- Given all that has happened, Emilia's wish, 'I would you had never seen him!' (line 18), is not surprising. Desdemona counters this with an expression of unqualified love for Othello, whose greatest faults, according to her, 'have grace and favour in them' (line 21).

- The scene highlights the differences between the natures and attitudes of the two principal female characters. With the approach of her death, Desdemona's childlike innocence and moral goodness are emphasised in everything she says. These qualities are contrasted with the experience and cynical worldliness of Emilia. Desdemona could never entertain the thought of infidelity, no matter what the provocation. Emilia tends to see marriage as a bargain, to be observed by the wife only as long as the husband remains faithful to it.

- Desdemona's song is sadly appropriate to her situation and Othello's. Its last few words, 'you'll couch with moe men' (line 56), anticipate one of the reasons Othello is to give for killing her: 'else she'll betray more men' (Act 5, Scene 2, line 6). The girl who is the subject of the song is as gentle and inoffensive as Desdemona, and she, too, endures cruelty from the man she loves.

- Desdemona's demeanour and conversation throughout this scene convey her overwhelming sense of impending doom. Her wedding sheets are to be her shroud.

Useful quotes

*If I do die before thee, prithee shroud me
In one of those same sheets.*

(Desdemona, lines 24–5)

*Dost thou in conscience think — tell me, Emilia —
That there be women do abuse their husbands
In such gross kind?*

(Desdemona, lines 60–2)

Questions ?

1 Discuss Shakespeare's presentation of Desdemona as her death approaches.

2 Why, do you think, does Shakespeare include the willow song in the play at this point?

3 Emilia reveals a good deal about herself in this scene. How would you describe her?

4 Contrast Desdemona and Emilia. Describe their relationship.

5 What is the atmosphere in this scene? How might this be conveyed on stage?

ACT 4 ✝ Key moments

Scene 1

- Iago invents lurid details of Desdemona's supposed relationship with Cassio, causing Othello to fall down in a fit.

- Iago offers Othello the apparent opportunity to witness Cassio giving details of his affair with Desdemona. Othello does not know that Cassio is actually discussing Bianca.

- Bianca returns the handkerchief to Cassio, further inflaming Othello's anger.

- Othello repeats his sentence of death on Desdemona. First he wants to chop her up, then he decides to poison her, but finally he accepts Iago's suggestion that he strangle her in bed. Iago promises to deal with Cassio.

- Othello is summoned to return to Venice, and Cassio is appointed in his place. Desdemona angers Othello when she appears to express pleasure at Cassio's promotion. Othello strikes her.

Scene 2

- Emilia does not take the opportunity to tell Othello the truth about the handkerchief.

- Othello is outraged by Desdemona's denials of guilt.

- Desdemona requests Iago's help in understanding what has distressed Othello. Iago makes excuses for Othello's behaviour.

- Iago persuades Roderigo that he should kill Cassio.

Scene 3

- Othello orders Desdemona to dismiss Emilia and go to bed. Desdemona has a strong sense of foreboding but cannot think wrong of Othello.

ACT 4 ✝ Speaking and listening

1 In groups of four, assign the roles of Iago, Cassio, Othello and Bianca. Read through Act 4, Scene 1, lines 93 to 166 together. Pay attention to the rhythm of the lines. Think about how each line should be spoken. Practise delivering the lines in different ways to see what works best. Consider where the characters should be positioned on stage and their appropriate actions and expressions.

2 In groups of three, assign the roles of Desdemona, Emilia and Bianca. Imagine that the three women are discussing their situations. What would each character say about herself and what view might she have on men, given her experiences?

ACT 5 † Scene 1

Plot summary

THE CONSPIRATORIAL ACTIVITY OF Iago and Roderigo in the midnight street takes our minds back to the opening scene of the play. Iago knows that he cannot keep Roderigo at bay much longer. He also knows that Cassio, alive, is a permanent risk to the success of his scheme against Othello and Desdemona. What he now has in mind, a plan in which each should kill the other, would dispose of these problems at a stroke. He almost succeeds. Roderigo is wounded but does not harm Cassio. Iago, however, wounds Cassio, and rushes off. He then returns, in response to Cassio's call for help, and kills Roderigo. Othello comes momentarily on the scene and sees the wounded Cassio; he is deeply impressed by what he takes to be Iago's zeal on his behalf. When Bianca arrives, Iago tries to attribute to her some of the responsibility for what has happened; she is taken away for questioning.

'Tis but a man gone.
Forth my sword, he dies.

RODERIGO, Act 5, Scene 1, 10

Cyprus. A street.

Enter IAGO and RODERIGO.

IAGO

Here, stand behind this bulk. Straight will he come.

Wear thy good rapier bare, and put it home,

Quick, quick. Fear nothing, I'll be at thy elbow.

It makes us or it mars us, think on that,

And fix most firm thy resolution.   5

RODERIGO

Be near at hand, I may miscarry in 't.

IAGO

Here, at thy hand. Be bold and take thy stand.

He retires.

RODERIGO

I have no great devotion to the deed,

And yet he has given me satisfying reasons.

'Tis but a man gone. Forth my sword, he dies.   10

IAGO

I have rubb'd this young quat almost to the sense,

And he grows angry. Now, whether he kill Cassio,

Or Cassio him, or each do kill the other,

Every way makes my gain. Live Roderigo,

He calls me to a restitution large   15

For gold and jewels that I bobb'd from him

As gifts to Desdemona;

It must not be. If Cassio do remain,

He hath a daily beauty in his life

That makes me ugly, and besides, the Moor   20

May unfold me to him; there stand I in peril:

No, he must die. Be 't so. I hear him coming.

Enter CASSIO.

RODERIGO

I know his gait, 'tis he. Villain, thou diest!

Thrusts at CASSIO.

CASSIO

That thrust had been my enemy indeed,

But that my coat is better than thou think'st.   25

---

1 *bulk:* projecting stall of a shop
   Straight: immediately

2 *bare:* unsheathed
   home: into his body

5 *fix ... resolution:* be most determined

6 *miscarry in 't:* fail to do it properly

retires: pulls back or withdraws, perhaps behind a pillar or into a doorway

8–10 Roderigo's lack of moral standards is underlined here. He doesn't particularly want to kill Cassio, but doesn't mind doing so either – he places little or no value on human life. Iago displays much the same attitude when he kills Roderigo

11 *I ... sense:* I have rubbed this pimple or boil until it is irritated

14 *Every ... gain:* I win anyway

14–16 *Live ... from him:* if Roderigo survives, he will ask me to return the large quantity of gold and jewels I swindled him of (Iago did not pass them on to Desdemona)

19–20 *He ... ugly:* Iago is jealous of Cassio's good looks

21 *unfold:* expose

23 *gait:* footstep
   Thrusts: stabs with his sword

24 *had been:* would have been

25 *my coat:* perhaps Cassio is wearing a coat of mail or heavy leather

I will make proof of thine.

Draws, and wounds RODERIGO.

RODERIGO

O, I am slain!

IAGO, from behind, wounds CASSIO in the leg; exit.

CASSIO

I am maim'd for ever. Light ho, murder, murder!

He falls.

Enter OTHELLO.

OTHELLO

The voice of Cassio; Iago keeps his word.

RODERIGO

O villain that I am!

OTHELLO

Hark, 'tis even so.

CASSIO

O, help ho! Light! A surgeon!   30

OTHELLO

'Tis he. O brave Iago, honest and just,

That hast such noble sense of thy friend's wrong,

Thou teachest me. Minion, your dear lies dead

And your fate hies apace. Strumpet, I come.

Forth of my heart those charms, thine eyes, are blotted.   35

Thy bed, lust-stain'd, shall with lust's blood be spotted.

Exit.

Enter LODOVICO and GRATIANO.

CASSIO

What ho, no watch, no passage? Murder, murder!

GRATIANO

'Tis some mischance, the cry is very direful.

CASSIO

O, help!

LODOVICO

Hark!   40

RODERIGO

O wretched villain.

---

26 *make proof of:* test

27 *maim'd for ever:* permanently injured

31–3 Here we have a striking series of ironies

33 *Minion:* darling; used here as a term of abuse for Desdemona

34 *hies apace:* is coming quickly towards you

35 *Forth of:* out of. Othello has wiped the memory of Desdemona's eyes from his mind

37 *no watch, no passage:* no watchmen, no passers-by

38 *mischance:* mishap, calamity
    direful: dreadful

42 *heavy:* dark, dismal

43 *counterfeits:* decoys

44 *come into the cry:* this can mean 'join the pack', but here it probably means go to where the cry is coming from

47 Iago arrives dressed like a man newly risen from his bed, another of his deft touches

48 *noise cries on:* report cries out

54 *spoil'd, undone:* wounded, destroyed

LODOVICO

Two or three groan. It is a heavy night.

These may be counterfeits, let's think't unsafe

To come into the cry without more help.

RODERIGO

45 Nobody come? Then shall I bleed to death.

Enter IAGO, with a light.

LODOVICO

Hark!

GRATIANO

Here's one comes in his shirt, with lights and weapons.

IAGO

Who's there? Whose noise is this that cries on murder?

LODOVICO

I do not know.

IAGO

                    Did not you hear a cry?

CASSIO

50 Here, here, for heaven's sake, help me!

IAGO

                                What's the matter?

GRATIANO

This is Othello's ancient, as I take it.

LODOVICO

The same indeed, a very valiant fellow.

IAGO

What are you here that cry so grievously?

CASSIO

Iago! O, I am spoil'd, undone by villains,

55 Give me some help.

IAGO

O, my lieutenant! What villains have done this?

CASSIO

I think the one of them is hereabout,

And cannot make away.

IAGO

O treacherous villains!

What are you there? Come in and give some help.

59 This line is addressed to Lodovico and Gratiano

RODERIGO

O, help me here! 60

CASSIO

That's one of 'em.

IAGO

O murderous slave! O villain!

Stabs RODERIGO.

RODERIGO

O damn'd Iago! O inhuman dog!

IAGO

Kill him in the dark? Where be those bloody thieves?

How silent is this town! Ho, murder, murder!

What may you be? Are you of good or evil? 65

65 This line is addressed to Lodovico and Gratiano

LODOVICO

As you shall prove us, praise us.

66 *prove us:* find out what we are like

IAGO

Signior Lodovico?

LODOVICO

He, sir.

IAGO

I cry you mercy. Here's Cassio hurt by villains.

69 *I ... mercy:* I beg your pardon

GRATIANO

Cassio! 70

IAGO

How is it, brother?

71 *brother:* a term normally applied to your equal

CASSIO

My leg is cut in two.

72 An example of hyperbole (exaggeration for emphasis)

IAGO

Marry, heaven forbid!

Light! Gentlemen, I'll bind it with my shirt.

Enter BIANCA.

BIANCA

What is the matter, ho? Who is't that cried?

75 lago mockingly repeats Bianca's question in an attempt to cast doubt on her honesty

78 *notable strumpet:* notorious whore

79 *mangled:* wounded

82 *chair:* a sedan chair. The modern equivalent would be a stretcher

83 *hence:* from here

85 *trash:* worthless person (Bianca)

86 *bear a party:* be involved

89 lago's acting skills are to the fore here as he wonders who the dead man is

93 *accidents:* sudden happenings

IAGO

75 Who is't that cried?

BIANCA

O my dear Cassio! O my sweet Cassio!

Cassio, Cassio!

IAGO

O notable strumpet! Cassio, may you suspect

Who they should be that have thus mangled you?

CASSIO

80 No.

GRATIANO

I am sorry to find you thus, I have been to seek you.

IAGO

Lend me a garter. So. O for a chair

To bear him easily hence!

BIANCA

Alas, he faints! O Cassio, Cassio, Cassio!

IAGO

85 Gentlemen all, I do suspect this trash

To bear a party in this. — Patience awhile, good Cassio.

Lend me a light. Know we this face, or no?

Alas, my friend and my dear countryman,

Roderigo? No — yes, sure — O heaven, Roderigo.

GRATIANO

90 What, of Venice?

IAGO

Even he, sir, did you know him?

GRATIANO

          Know him? Ay.

IAGO

Signior Gratiano, I cry you gentle pardon;

These bloody accidents must excuse my manners

That so neglected you.

GRATIANO

          I am glad to see you.

IAGO

95 How do you, Cassio? O, a chair, a chair!

GRATIANO
Roderigo!

IAGO
He, 'tis he.

A chair is brought in.

          O, that's well said, the chair!
Some good man bear him carefully from hence.
I'll fetch the general's surgeon. — For you, mistress,
Save you your labour. — He that lies slain here, Cassio,   100
Was my dear friend. What malice was betwixt you?

CASSIO
None in the world, nor do I know the man.

IAGO
[to Bianca] What, look you pale? — O, bear him out
        o' the air.

CASSIO and RODERIGO are borne off.
Stay you, good gentlemen. Look you pale, mistress?
Do you perceive the gastness of her eye?   105
Nay, if you stare — we shall hear more anon.
Behold her well I pray you, look upon her.
Do you see, gentlemen? Nay, guiltiness
Will speak, though tongues were out of use.

Enter EMILIA.

EMILIA
'Las, what's the matter? What's the matter, husband?   110

IAGO
Cassio has here been set on in the dark
By Roderigo, and fellows that are 'scap'd.
He's almost slain, and Roderigo dead.

EMILIA
Alas, good gentleman! Alas, good Cassio!

IAGO
This is the fruit of whoring. Prithee, Emilia,   115
Go know of Cassio where he supp'd to-night.
What, do you shake at that?

BIANCA
He supp'd at my house, but I therefore shake not.

---

97 *well said:* well done

99 *mistress:* Bianca

100 *Save ... labour:* do not bother tending to Cassio

100–1 *He ... friend:* Iago, although he has just stabbed Roderigo to death, has no problem calling the dead man his friend

101 *malice:* ill feeling, ill will

103–9 Iago is controlling everyone here, speaking separately to Bianca, to some attendants, and to Lodovico and Gratiano

105 *gastness of:* frightened look in

106 *stare:* Iago does not complete his threat to Bianca

110 *'Las:* alas

114 *good gentleman:* Roderigo

116 *know of:* find out from

117 *shake:* tremble. Iago is talking to Bianca

118 *I therefore shake not:* that is not why I tremble

119 *charge you:* order you to

IAGO

O, did he so? I charge you go with me.

EMILIA

120 Fie, fie upon thee, strumpet!

BIANCA

I am no strumpet, but of life as honest

As you that thus abuse me.

EMILIA

As I? Faugh, fie upon thee!

IAGO

Kind gentlemen, let's go see poor Cassio dress'd.

123 *dress'd:* have his wound dressed

124 *Come ... tale:* he is telling Bianca that she will have to come up with a more convincing story

Come, mistress, you must tell's another tale.

125 Emilia, run you to the citadel

And tell my lord and lady what has happ'd.

Will you go on, I pray.

[*aside*] This is the night

128 *fordoes:* undoes, destroys
quite: totally

That either makes me or fordoes me quite.

Exeunt.

Key points

The busy movement of this scene contrasts with the quiet passivity of the previous one.

- Intrigue predominates here, with Iago as the central agent. For the first time, however, he is not totally successful. His overall plan is marred by his narrow failure to dispose of both Cassio and Roderigo. Cassio is not mortally wounded. Iago's astonishing luck has run out.

- There are significant echoes of crucial events in earlier scenes. Othello's few moments at the scene of Cassio's injury remind us of his intervention in the brawl that led to Cassio's dismissal in Act 2, Scene 3. In the earlier scene, however, Othello was a majestic, authoritative figure, lording it over everybody by virtue of his mere presence. Now, he pauses like a thief in the night, degraded to a mere conspirator, remaining concealed from view. He relishes Iago's treacherous attempt on Cassio's life and is inspired by it to hurry off and carry out his act of vengeance on Desdemona.

- Even the noble music of Othello's speeches is no longer in evidence. His few lines foretelling Desdemona's fate are strident and melodramatic.

- Iago, as usual, is fully alive to his own interests. His mind is always busy. He cunningly conceals himself while Roderigo attacks Cassio and soon emerges to play the role of a brave and helpful citizen. He pretends to be shocked by the villainies of others. He wins the admiration of Lodovico, who finds him a very valiant fellow.

- There is even a touch of ironic comedy in Iago's question to Cassio: 'O, my lieutenant! What villains have done this?' (line 56). It is not difficult to imagine the satisfaction the use of 'lieutenant' must give him in this context.

- One of the most suggestive clues to Iago's motivation is perhaps to be found in his characterisation of Cassio at the beginning of the scene. He cannot tolerate Cassio's continued existence because 'he hath a daily beauty in his life that makes me ugly' (lines 19–20). The contemplation of beauty, grace, happiness or nobility in Othello, Desdemona or Cassio destroys Iago's peace of mind. He is compelled to undermine or eradicate such virtues whenever he finds them.

- By the end of the scene, Iago has arrived at the critical point in his fortunes: 'This is the night that either makes me or fordoes me quite' (lines 127–8). Until this moment, Iago has been supremely confident of success and has gloried in his own matchless cunning. The possibility of failure had not occurred to him, but these lines are the first sign of uneasiness and uncertainty.

Useful quotes

I have rubb'd this young quat almost to the sense,
And he grows angry. Now, whether he kill Cassio,
Or Cassio him, or each do kill the other,
Every way makes my gain.

(Iago, lines 11–14)

He hath a daily beauty in his life
That makes me ugly

(Iago, lines 19–20)

O brave Iago, honest and just,
That hast such noble sense of thy friend's wrong,
Thou teachest me.

(Othello, lines 31–3)

O damn'd Iago! O inhuman dog!

(Roderigo, line 62)

He that lies slain here, Cassio,
Was my dear friend. What malice was betwixt you?

(Iago, lines 100–1)

Questions ?

1 Roderigo's moral weaknesses emerge in this scene. Comment on this idea.

2 How does Iago hope to profit by his latest intrigue?

3 Describe the Iago–Roderigo relationship in this scene.

4 Iago gives an important clue to his motives early in the scene. What is this clue?

5 What props are needed for this scene?

6 We learn a good deal about Iago's character from the opening action of this scene. Mention the main things this tells us about the kind of person he is.

7 Iago displays some ingenuity in this scene. Give examples of this.

8 How would you describe Othello's conduct in this scene? Compare it with his behaviour in earlier scenes.

Plot summary

OTHELLO LOOKS AT THE sleeping Desdemona. He is moved by her innocent beauty. He is at the same time troubled by what he sees as the shocking contrast between her heavenly appearance and her sinful soul. The only way he can bring himself to kill her is to convince himself that he is acting for the general good. He sheds involuntary tears, but he feels compelled to set aside his human reaction and kill the one he loves. He tells the awakened Desdemona to pray for her soul. He interrogates her in a legal-style process in which he plays the parts of judge, counsel for the prosecution and jury. The language is that of the courtroom and the confessional. Desdemona meets his charges against her with a straightforward denial. Othello's patience begins to give way. Her grief when he mentions Cassio's supposed death destroys his self-control and seals her fate. He will not now give her time to pray. He kills her in a blind rage.

As Othello strangles Desdemona, Emilia knocks at the door. When, after some delay, Othello lets Emilia in, she gives him the false news that Cassio has killed Roderigo. Desdemona's dying cries attract Emilia's attention. The murdered wife expires with words of love for her husband and a pathetic attempt to free him from responsibility for her death. Emilia courageously defies Othello and curses Iago's villainy. She shouts for help. Montano, Gratiano and Iago arrive. For the first time Iago must face in public someone who knows the truth about his schemes. Emilia presses home her case with convincing urgency. Iago betrays himself in a futile display of murderous violence, stabs Emilia to death, and tries to escape. When he is brought back, Othello wounds him. Lodovico produces evidence implicating both Iago and Roderigo in the attempts on Cassio's life. Othello is relieved of his position in Cyprus, and Cassio is appointed in his place. The truth dawns on Othello and he dies by his own hand. It is left to Cassio to decide the fate of Iago.

Cyprus. The citadel.

DESDEMONA in her bed. Enter OTHELLO, with a light.

OTHELLO

It is the cause, it is the cause, my soul,

Let me not name it to you, you chaste stars.

It is the cause. Yet I'll not shed her blood,

Nor scar that whiter skin of hers than snow,

And smooth as monumental alabaster.   5

Yet she must die, else she'll betray more men.

Put out the light, and then put out the light.

If I quench thee, thou flaming minister,

I can again thy former light restore,

Should I repent me. But once put out thine,   10

Thou cunning pattern of excelling nature,

I know not where is that Promethean heat

That can thy light relume. When I have pluck'd the rose

I cannot give it vital growth again,

It must needs wither. I'll smell it on the tree.   15

[kissing her] A balmy breath that dost almost persuade

Justice herself to break her sword. Once more.

Be thus when thou art dead, and I will kill thee

And love thee after. Once more and this the last.

So sweet was ne'er so fatal. I must weep,   20

But they are cruel tears. This sorrow's heavenly,

It strikes where it doth love. She wakes.

DESDEMONA

Who's there? Othello?

OTHELLO

                   Ay, Desdemona.

DESDEMONA

Will you come to bed, my lord?

OTHELLO

Have you pray'd to-night, Desdemona?

DESDEMONA

                   Ay, my lord.   25

OTHELLO

If you bethink yourself of any crime

Unreconciled as yet to heaven and grace,

Solicit for it straight.

1–3 It … blood: Othello sees himself as an agent of justice. 'Cause', the crucial word here, has various possible layers of meaning: it may mean reason or occasion, or have the legal sense of charge, accusation, or a matter requiring action. The reference to 'chaste stars' makes it clear that it is Desdemona's supposed adultery that Othello has in mind as the subject of his 'cause'

4 that … snow: that skin of hers, which is whiter than snow

5 alabaster: fine white material derived from limestone and used to make tombs

7 the light … the light: the first light is that of the torch he is carrying, the second is Desdemona's life

8 flaming minister: serviceable torch

10 thine: the light of Desdemona's life

11 Thou … nature: he sees Desdemona as a beautifully wrought model of human perfection, which nature excelled even herself in fashioning

12 Promethean: Prometheus was the mythological bringer of fire to men

13 relume: rekindle

14 vital: living

15 on the tree: while the rose (i.e. Desdemona) is still alive

16–17 A … sword: Othello, thinking himself about to perform an act of justice, finds that Desdemona's fragrant breath almost unsettles his resolution

17 sword: one of the emblems of Justice
Once more: he kisses her again

19 Once … last: he gives her a final kiss

20 So … fatal: nothing so sweet as this was ever associated with death

21–2 This … love: a cruel, blasphemous parody of St Paul's 'For whom the Lord loveth, he chasteneth'

25 Othello does not want to be the agent of her eternal damnation

26–8 If … straight: if you can think of any crime of which you have not yet repented, beg heaven's pardon for it immediately

DESDEMONA

Alas, my lord, what may you mean by that?

OTHELLO

30   Well, do it, and be brief. I will walk by.

I would not kill thy unprepared spirit.

No, heaven forfend, I would not kill thy soul.

DESDEMONA

Talk you of killing?

OTHELLO

                            Ay, I do.

DESDEMONA

                                        Then heaven

Have mercy on me!

OTHELLO

                        Amen, with all my heart!

DESDEMONA

35   If you say so, I hope you will not kill me.

OTHELLO

Hum!

DESDEMONA

And yet I fear you, for you are fatal then

When your eyes roll so. Why I should fear I know not,

Since guiltiness I know not, but yet I feel I fear.

OTHELLO

40   Think on thy sins.

DESDEMONA

                                    They are loves I bear to you.

OTHELLO

And for that thou diest.

DESDEMONA

That death's unnatural that kills for loving.

Alas, why gnaw you so your nether lip?

Some bloody passion shakes your very frame.

45   These are portents, but yet I hope, I hope,

They do not point on me.

OTHELLO

                                Peace, and be still!

And yet I fear you, for you are fatal then
When your eyes roll so. Why I should fear I know not,
Since guiltiness I know not, but yet I feel I fear.

DESDEMONA, Act 5, Scene 2, 37–9

DESDEMONA
I will so. What's the matter?

47 *What's the matter:* what are you really concerned about?

OTHELLO
That handkerchief which I so lov'd and gave thee,
Thou gavest to Cassio.

DESDEMONA
            No, by my life and soul,
Send for the man and ask him.   50

OTHELLO
Sweet soul, take heed, take heed of perjury,
Thou art on thy death-bed.

51 *perjury:* lying under oath

DESDEMONA
             Ay, but not yet to die.

OTHELLO
Yes, presently.
Therefore confess thee freely of thy sin,

53 *presently:* at once

55 *article:* item in the charge against her. Othello is acting as judge

56 *choke ... conceit:* suppress the strong belief

57 *withal:* with

60 *Offend:* wrong

61 *warranty:* allowance, approval

62 *token:* sign or gift of love

64 *stone thy heart:* turn your heart to stone

65–6 *makest ... sacrifice:* Desdemona's answer makes Othello feel like taking personal revenge (which would be plain murder) rather than adopting the role of justice (in which case he would view the deed as a necessary and impersonal 'sacrifice')

74 *ta'en order for't:* taken steps to bring it about

75 *my fear interprets:* my anxiety tells me (that Cassio is dead)

---

55 For to deny each article with oath

Cannot remove nor choke the strong conceit

That I do groan withal: thou art to die.

DESDEMONA

Then Lord have mercy on me!

OTHELLO

                              I say amen.

DESDEMONA

And have you mercy, too! I never did

60 Offend you in my life — never lov'd Cassio,

But with such general warranty of heaven

As I might love. I never gave him token.

OTHELLO

By heaven, I saw my handkerchief in his hand.

O perjur'd woman, thou dost stone thy heart

65 And makest me call what I intend to do

A murder, which I thought a sacrifice.

I saw the handkerchief.

DESDEMONA

                         He found it then.

I never gave it him. Send for him hither.

Let him confess a truth.

OTHELLO

                          He hath confess'd.

DESDEMONA

70 What, my lord?

OTHELLO

That he hath used thee.

DESDEMONA

                          How? Unlawfully?

OTHELLO

Ay.

DESDEMONA

He will not say so.

OTHELLO

                    No, his mouth is stopp'd.

Honest Iago hath ta'en order for't.

DESDEMONA

75 O, my fear interprets. What, is he dead?

OTHELLO

Had all his hairs been lives, my great revenge

Had stomach for 'em all.

DESDEMONA

Alas, he is betray'd, and I undone.

OTHELLO

Out strumpet! Weep'st thou for him to my face?

DESDEMONA

O, banish me, my lord, but kill me not.   80

OTHELLO

Down, strumpet!

DESDEMONA

Kill me to-morrow, let me live to-night.

OTHELLO

Nay, and you strive …

DESDEMONA

But half an hour, but while I say one prayer!

OTHELLO

'Tis too late.   85

He smothers her.

DESDEMONA

O Lord, Lord, Lord!

76–7   *Had … all:* if he had had as many lives as he had hairs on his head, my vengeful appetite would have been capable of taking all of them

86   Desdemona tries to pray

Down, strumpet!

OTHELLO, Act 5, Scene 2, 81

87 *[within]:* outside the door
Emilia's words are a weird echo of Desdemona's attempt at prayer

91 *So, so:* the extinction of Desdemona's life, as Othello thinks (some editors suggest that he stabs her here)

92 *I'ld:* I would like to

94 *like:* probable

95 *noise was high:* clamour was loud

100 Othello is already repentant

101–3 *a huge ... alteration:* eclipses and earthquakes (the yawning earth) should accompany such momentous changes as Desdemona's death. In Shakespeare's time an eclipse was seen as an omen of evil and disruption on earth

107 *Soft:* wait a moment
draw: he draws the curtains of the bed to conceal Desdemona's body

109 *yonder's:* there is

EMILIA *[within]*
My lord, my lord! What ho, my lord, my lord!

OTHELLO
What voice is this? Not dead? Not yet quite dead?
I that am cruel, am yet merciful,
90 I would not have thee linger in thy pain —
So, so.

EMILIA *[within]*
    What ho, my lord, my lord!

OTHELLO
                            Who's there?

EMILIA *[within]*
O good my lord, I'ld speak a word with you!

OTHELLO
Yes, 'tis Emilia. — By and by. — She's dead.
'Tis like she comes to speak of Cassio's death;
95 The noise was high. Ha! No more moving?
Still as the grave. Shall she come in? Were't good?
I think she stirs again. No. What's the best?
If she come in, she'll sure speak to my wife.
My wife, my wife: what wife? I ha' no wife.
100 O insupportable, O heavy hour!
Methinks it should be now a huge eclipse
Of sun and moon, and that the affrighted globe
Should yawn at alteration.

EMILIA *[within]*
I do beseech you I may speak with you, —
105 Good my lord!

OTHELLO
I had forgot thee. O, come in, Emilia.
Soft, by and by. Let me the curtains draw.
Where art thou?

He unlocks the door. Enter EMILIA.
                    What's the matter with thee now?

EMILIA
O, my good lord, yonder's foul murders done!

OTHELLO
110 What, now?

EMILIA
        But now, my lord.

OTHELLO

It is the very error of the moon,

She comes more nearer earth than she was wont

And makes men mad.

EMILIA

Cassio, my lord, has kill'd a young Venetian

Call'd Roderigo.

OTHELLO

         Roderigo kill'd!   115

And Cassio kill'd?

EMILIA

        No, Cassio is not kill'd.

OTHELLO

Not Cassio kill'd? Then murder's out of tune,

And sweet revenge grows harsh.

DESDEMONA

O, falsely, falsely murder'd!

EMILIA

            O Lord, what cry is that?

OTHELLO

That? What?   120

EMILIA

Out and alas, it is my lady's voice.

Help, help, ho, help! O lady, speak again.

Sweet Desdemona, O sweet mistress, speak!

DESDEMONA

A guiltless death I die.

EMILIA

O, who hath done this deed?   125

DESDEMONA

Nobody, I myself. Farewell.

Commend me to my kind lord. O, farewell!

She dies.

OTHELLO

Why, how should she be murder'd?

EMILIA

           Alas, who knows?

111–13 *It ... mad:* the moon, wandering or erring from her proper course, is affecting the sanity of mortals. Giving the moon human qualities is an example of personification

117 *out of tune:* not had the appropriate result

118 *sweet ... harsh:* the sweet hopes of revenge entertained by Othello have suddenly been dashed by the news that Cassio is alive

122 Emilia opens the curtains at this point and sees Desdemona

126 *Nobody, I myself:* Desdemona's lie, paradoxically, proves her loyalty to Othello, even in death

128 *how ... murder'd:* who could have killed her?

OTHELLO

You heard her say herself, it was not I.

EMILIA

130   She said so, I must needs report the truth.

OTHELLO

She's like a liar gone to burning hell.

'Twas I that kill'd her.

EMILIA

                              O, the more angel she,

And you the blacker devil!

OTHELLO

She turn'd to folly and she was a whore.

EMILIA

135   Thou dost belie her and thou art a devil.

OTHELLO

She was false as water.

EMILIA

                              Thou art rash as fire

To say that she was false. O, she was heavenly true!

OTHELLO

Cassio did top her, ask thy husband else.

O, I were damn'd beneath all depth in hell,

140   But that I did proceed upon just grounds

To this extremity. Thy husband knew it all.

EMILIA

My husband?

OTHELLO

Thy husband.

EMILIA

                              That she was false to wedlock?

OTHELLO

Ay, with Cassio. Nay, had she been true,

145   If heaven would make me such another world

Of one entire and perfect chrysolite,

I'ld not have sold her for it.

EMILIA

                              My husband?

134   *folly:* wantonness

135   *belie:* lie about

136   *false as water:* Othello is thinking of water as an unstable, unsteady element

138   *else:* if you don't believe me

140   *But ... grounds:* had I not gone about the matter in a spirit of strict justice. From the beginning of the scene, Othello has been thinking of himself as an instrument of heavenly justice
141   *extremity:* last violent act (i.e. the killing of Desdemona)

146   *entire:* pure
      chrysolite: topaz (a semi-precious stone)
147   *I'ld:* I would

OTHELLO

Ay, 'twas he that told me first.

An honest man he is, and hates the slime

That sticks on filthy deeds.

EMILIA

My husband?　　　　　　　　　　　150

OTHELLO

What needs this iteration? Woman, I say thy husband.

EMILIA

O mistress, villainy hath made mocks with love!

My husband say that she was false?

OTHELLO

He, woman.

I say thy husband: dost understand the word?

My friend, thy husband: honest, honest Iago.　　155

EMILIA

If he say so, may his pernicious soul

Rot half a grain a day! He lies to the heart.

She was too fond of her most filthy bargain.

OTHELLO

Ha!

EMILIA

Do thy worst,　　　　　　　　　　　160

This deed of thine is no more worthy heaven

Than thou wast worthy her.

OTHELLO

Peace, you were best.

EMILIA

Thou hast not half that power to do me harm

As I have to be hurt. O gull, O dolt,

As ignorant as dirt. Thou hast done a deed —　　165

I care not for thy sword. I'll make thee known

Though I lost twenty lives. Help, help, O help!

The Moor has kill'd my mistress. Murder, murder!

Enter MONTANO, GRATIANO, IAGO, and others.

MONTANO

What is the matter? How now, general?

EMILIA

O, are you come, Iago? You have done well　　170

That men must lay their murders on your neck.

151 *iteration:* repetition

152 *villainy ... love:* villainy [in the person of Iago] has made a mockery of love

156 *pernicious:* destructive

158 *her ... bargain:* Othello. Emilia shows rare courage here

159 Othello is making a threatening gesture towards Emilia

160 *Do thy worst:* do what you like to me (I'm not afraid of you)

162 *Peace ... best:* you had better hold your tongue

163–4 *Thou ... hurt:* the new Emilia reveals an unexpected sensitivity when she points out that her suffering and anguish at what has happened to Desdemona are so extreme that no harm which Othello can inflict on her can cause her greater distress than she already feels

164 *gull:* dupe, fool

171 *lay ... neck:* blame you for the murders they commit

ALL

What is the matter?

EMILIA

Disprove this villain if thou be'st a man.

He says thou told'st him that his wife was false.

175   I know thou didst not, thou'rt not such a villain.

Speak, for my heart is full.

IAGO

I told him what I thought, and told no more

Than what he found himself was apt and true.

178   *apt:* in accordance with the facts

EMILIA

But did you ever tell him she was false?

IAGO

180   I did.

EMILIA

You told a lie, an odious damned lie.

Upon my soul, a lie, a wicked lie!

She false with Cassio? Did you say with Cassio?

IAGO

With Cassio, mistress. Go to, charm your tongue.

184   *charm your tongue:* be silent

EMILIA

185   I will not charm my tongue, I am bound to speak.

My mistress here lies murder'd in her bed.

ALL

O heavens forfend!

187   *forfend:* forbid

EMILIA

And your reports have set the murder on.

OTHELLO

Nay, stare not, masters, it is true indeed.

GRATIANO

190   'Tis a strange truth.

MONTANO

O monstrous act!

EMILIA

            Villainy, villainy, villainy!

I think upon't, I think I smell't. O villainy!

I thought so then. I'll kill myself for grief.

O villainy, villainy!

193   *I thought so then:* Emilia has already suspected Iago of underhand dealings, if not of villainy. The 'then' of this line may refer to Iago's desire to have the handkerchief, or to her suspicion that 'some eternal villain' had slandered Desdemona in order 'to get some office' (Act 4, Scene 2, lines 132–5)

IAGO

What, are you mad? I charge you get you home. 195

EMILIA

Good gentlemen, let me have leave to speak.

'Tis proper I obey him, but not now.

Perchance, Iago, I will ne'er go home.

OTHELLO

[falling on the bed] O! O! O!

EMILIA

Nay, lay thee down and roar,

For thou hast kill'd the sweetest innocent 200

That e'er did lift up eye.

OTHELLO

[rising] O, she was foul.

I scarce did know you, uncle; there lies your niece,

Whose breath indeed these hands have newly stopp'd.

I know this act shows horrible and grim.

GRATIANO

Poor Desdemona, I am glad thy father's dead. 205

Thy match was mortal to him and pure grief

Shore his old thread atwain. Did he live now,

This sight would make him do a desperate turn.

Yea, curse his better angel from his side

And fall to reprobation. 210

OTHELLO

'Tis pitiful, but yet Iago knows

That she with Cassio hath the act of shame

A thousand times committed. Cassio confess'd it.

And she did gratify his amorous works

With that recognizance and pledge of love 215

Which I first gave her; I saw it in his hand.

It was a handkerchief, an antique token

My father gave my mother.

EMILIA

O God! O heavenly God!

IAGO

Zounds, hold your peace.

197 *proper:* right

198 *Perchance:* perhaps, or by good fortune

202 *uncle:* Gratiano, being Desdemona's uncle, would have been regarded by Othello as his also

206 *mortal:* lethal, murderous

207 *Shore ... atwain:* cut the thread of his life in two. The reference is to the Greek myth of Atropos, one of the three Fates, whose task it was to sever the thread of life with her shears
Did he live: if he were alive

208 *do ... turn:* take a desperate course of action (i.e. suicide)

209–10 *curse ... reprobation:* he would banish his guardian angel and incur damnation ('reprobation')

214 *gratify ... works:* reward his acts of love

215 *recognizance:* token

218 *father:* in Act 3, Scene 4 Othello told Desdemona that the handkerchief was given to his mother by an Egyptian enchantress

219 *hold your peace:* be silent

EMILIA

220 'Twill out, it will. I hold my peace sir? No.

I'll be in speaking liberal as an air.

Let heaven and men, and devils, let 'em all,

All, all cry shame against me, yet I'll speak.

IAGO

Be wise, and get you home.

EMILIA

                        I will not.

IAGO goes to stab EMILIA.

GRATIANO

                             Fie,

225 Your sword upon a woman?

EMILIA

O thou dull Moor, that handkerchief thou speak'st on,

I found by fortune and did give my husband;

For often with a solemn earnestness,

More than indeed belong'd to such a trifle,

230 He begg'd of me to steal it.

IAGO

                      Villainous whore!

EMILIA

She give it Cassio? No, alas, I found it,

And I did give't my husband.

IAGO

                   Filth, thou liest!

EMILIA

By heaven, I do not. I do not, gentlemen.

O murderous coxcomb! What should such a fool

235 Do with so good a wife?

OTHELLO

                  Are there no stones in heaven

But what serves for the thunder? Precious villain!

He runs at IAGO. IAGO stabs EMILIA.

GRATIANO

The woman falls, sure he has kill'd his wife.

EMILIA

Ay, ay. O lay me by my mistress' side.

Exit IAGO.

GRATIANO
He's gone, but his wife's kill'd.

MONTANO
'Tis a notorious villain. Take you this weapon,   240
Which I have here recover'd from the Moor.
Come, guard the door without. Let him not pass,
But kill him rather. I'll after that same villain,
For 'tis a damned slave.

Exeunt MONTANO and GRATIANO.

OTHELLO
                    I am not valiant neither,
But every puny whipster gets my sword.   245
But why should honour outlive honesty?
Let it go all.

EMILIA
                What did thy song bode, lady?
Hark, canst thou hear me? I will play the swan
And die in music. *[sings] Willow, willow, willow.*
Moor, she was chaste; she lov'd thee, cruel Moor.   250
So come my soul to bliss, as I speak true;
So speaking as I think, I die. I die.

She dies.

OTHELLO
I have another weapon in this chamber,
It is a sword of Spain, the ice-brook's temper.
O, here it is. Uncle, I must come forth.   255

GRATIANO *[within]*
If thou attempt it, it will cost thee dear.
Thou hast no weapon, and perforce must suffer.

OTHELLO
Look in upon me then, and speak with me,
Or, naked as I am, I will assault thee.

Enter GRATIANO.

GRATIANO
What is the matter?

OTHELLO
                    Behold, I have a weapon,   260
A better never did itself sustain
Upon a soldier's thigh. I have seen the day

240 *notorious:* absolute, outstanding

245 *whipster:* contemptible individual (Montano)
246 *why ... honesty:* as my title to true merit has been lost, why should I care for mere reputation?

248 *swan:* swans were reputed to sing just before their death

251 *bliss:* heaven

254 *ice-brook's temper:* made of steel tempered in ice-cold water

257 *perforce:* inevitably

259 *naked:* unarmed

265 *your stop:* your power to stop me

266 *'Tis ... now:* Othello can no longer overcome opposition

268 *butt:* end, goal, destination

269 *sea-mark ... sail:* beacon marking the limit of my farthest journey

270 *lost:* idle

271 *Man ... rush:* attack with nothing but a reed

272 *retires:* withdraws

273 *wench:* used here as a term of endearment for Desdemona

274 *compt:* Judgement Day

276 *fiends:* devils

280–1 Othello's vision of his own final damnation

287 *I look ... fable:* Othello is referring to the belief that the devil has cloven feet. He cannot see these on Iago, but, as the next line makes clear, this does not mean that Iago is not a devil

291 *For ... die:* in my present state, I see death as a happy release

---

That with this little arm, and this good sword,

I have made my way through more impediments

265 Than twenty times your stop. But, O vain boast,

Who can control his fate? 'Tis not so now.

Be not afraid, though you do see me weapon'd.

Here is my journey's end, here is my butt,

And very sea-mark of my utmost sail.

270 Do you go back dismay'd? 'Tis a lost fear.

Man but a rush against Othello's breast

And he retires. Where should Othello go?

Now, how dost thou look now? O ill-starr'd wench!

Pale as thy smock. When we shall meet at compt,

275 This look of thine will hurl my soul from heaven

And fiends will snatch at it. Cold, cold, my girl,

Even like thy chastity. O cursed slave!

Whip me, ye devils,

From the possession of this heavenly sight.

280 Blow me about in winds, roast me in sulphur,

Wash me in steep-down gulfs of liquid fire!

O Desdemona! Desdemona dead!

Oh, oh, oh!

Enter LODOVICO, MONTANO, and OFFICERS, with IAGO (prisoner), and CASSIO in a chair.

LODOVICO

Where is this rash and most unfortunate man?

OTHELLO

285 That's he that was Othello. Here I am.

LODOVICO

Where is this viper? Bring the villain forth.

OTHELLO

I look down toward his feet, but that's a fable.

If that thou be'st a devil I cannot kill thee.

Wounds IAGO.

LODOVICO

Wring his sword from him.

IAGO

                                        I bleed, sir; but not kill'd.

OTHELLO

290 I am not sorry neither, I'ld have thee live,

For in my sense 'tis happiness to die.

LODOVICO

O thou, Othello, that wert once so good,

Fall'n in the practice of a damn'd slave.

What shall be said to thee?

OTHELLO

                        Why, anything;

An honourable murderer, if you will,   295

For nought did I in hate, but all in honour.

LODOVICO

This wretch hath part confess'd his villainy.

Did you and he consent in Cassio's death?

OTHELLO

Ay.

CASSIO

Dear general, I never gave you cause.   300

OTHELLO

I do believe it, and I ask your pardon.

Will you, I pray, demand that demi-devil

Why he hath thus ensnar'd my soul and body?

IAGO

Demand me nothing. What you know, you know.

From this time forth I never will speak word.   305

LODOVICO

What, not to pray?

GRATIANO

                    Torments will ope your lips.

OTHELLO

Well, thou dost best.

LODOVICO

Sir, you shall understand what hath befall'n,

Which, as I think, you know not. Here is a letter

Found in the pocket of the slain Roderigo.   310

And here another. The one of them imports

The death of Cassio, to be undertook

By Roderigo.

OTHELLO

O villain!

CASSIO

                  Most heathenish and most gross!

---

293 *practice:* stratagem, plot
     slave: villain

298 *consent in:* agree to

302 *demand:* ask

306 *Torments:* tortures
     ope: open

307 *thou dost best:* you are wise to stay silent

311 *imports:* concerns, involves as a consequence

314 *gross:* monstrous

315 *discontented paper:* page full of unhappy thoughts

318–19 *belike ... him:* probably, Iago, just in time, intervened and gave him an explanation that satisfied him

319 *pernicious caitiff:* evil wretch

322–4 Iago has admitted his deed, but has been deliberately vague about his motivation

326 *upbraids:* condemns, rebukes

327 *Brave:* provoke, defy
whereon it came: as a result of which it happened

328 *cast:* dismissed

331–8 Lodovico is speaking to Othello

333 *For this slave:* with regard to Iago

335 *That ... long:* that can torture him greatly, but not kill him for a long time

336 *close prisoner rest:* remain a confined prisoner

339 *Soft you:* one moment

342 *unlucky:* unfortunate

343 *extenuate:* mitigate, lessen

LODOVICO

315 Now here's another discontented paper,

Found in his pocket too, and this, it seems,

Roderigo meant to have sent this damned villain,

But that, belike, Iago in the nick

Came in and satisfied him.

OTHELLO

O the pernicious caitiff!

320 How came you, Cassio, by a handkerchief

That was my wife's?

CASSIO

I found it in my chamber,

And he himself confess'd it, even now,

That there he dropp'd it, for a special purpose

Which wrought to his desire.

OTHELLO

O fool, fool, fool!

CASSIO

325 There is besides in Roderigo's letter,

How he upbraids Iago that he made him

Brave me upon the watch, whereon it came

That I was cast; and even but now he spake,

After long seeming dead, Iago hurt him,

330 Iago set him on.

LODOVICO

You must forsake this room and go with us,

Your power and your command is taken off,

And Cassio rules in Cyprus. For this slave,

If there be any cunning cruelty

335 That can torment him much, and hold him long,

It shall be his. You shall close prisoner rest,

Till that the nature of your fault be known

To the Venetian state. Come, bring him away.

OTHELLO

Soft you, a word or two before you go.

340 I have done the state some service, and they know't;

No more of that. I pray you in your letters,

When you shall these unlucky deeds relate,

Speak of me as I am; nothing extenuate,

Nor set down aught in malice. Then must you speak

Of one that lov'd not wisely, but too well; 345

Of one not easily jealous, but being wrought,

Perplex'd in the extreme; of one whose hand,

Like the base Judean, threw a pearl away,

Richer than all his tribe; of one whose subdued eyes,

Albeit unused to the melting mood, 350

Drop tears as fast as the Arabian trees

Their med'cinable gum. Set you down this.

And say besides, that in Aleppo once,

Where a malignant and a turban'd Turk

Beat a Venetian and traduc'd the state, 355

I took by the throat the circumcised dog,

And smote him thus.

Stabs himself.

LODOVICO

O bloody period!

GRATIANO

          All that's spoke is marr'd.

OTHELLO

I kiss'd thee ere I kill'd thee, no way but this,

Killing myself, to die upon a kiss. 360

Falls on the bed, and dies.

CASSIO

This did I fear, but thought he had no weapon,

For he was great of heart.

LODOVICO

              [to Iago] O Spartan dog,

More fell than anguish, hunger or the sea,

Look on the tragic lodging on this bed.

This is thy work. The object poisons sight, 365

Let it be hid. Gratiano, keep the house

And seize upon the fortunes of the Moor,

For they succeed on you. To you, lord governor,

Remains the censure of this hellish villain:

The time, the place, the torture. O, enforce it! 370

Myself will straight aboard and to the state

This heavy act with heavy heart relate.

Exeunt.

344 *aught:* anything

345–7 *Of ... extreme:* Othello's verdict on himself has met with the disapproval of many commentators

346 *wrought:* provoked

347 *Perplex'd:* distracted, bewildered

348 *base Judean:* this is the First Folio reading; the Quartos have 'Indian'. The 'base Judean' is Judas Iscariot, and a reference to him fits in with the general religious imagery of the play. S. I. Bethell has pointed out that 'Othello, like Judas Iscariot, has cast away the pearl of great price, he has rejected Desdemona, and in doing so has rejected heaven. Like Judas, he fell through loss of faith'

349 *subdued eyes:* tearful eyes, subdued by grief

350 *Albeit:* although

352 *med'cinable gum:* myrrh, one of the gifts of the Magi or Three Wise Men, associated with atonement and sacrifice

353 *Aleppo:* a Syrian city where it was a capital crime for a Christian, such as Othello, to strike a Turk

355 *traduc'd:* slandered, dishonoured

357 *smote:* struck (here, stabbed)

358 *period:* ending

358 *marr'd:* ruined (by his actions)

359–60 Othello addresses these words to Desdemona's corpse

362 *Spartan dog:* the term addressed to Iago presumably denotes ferocity

363 *fell:* cruel, deadly

365 *The object poisons sight:* the sight before our eyes is so terrible it does not bear looking at

366 *keep:* guard

367 *seize upon:* confiscate

368 *they succeed on you:* you inherit them
lord governor: Cassio

369 *censure ... villain:* the sentencing of Iago. Here, too late, poetic justice is in some minor sense satisfied

Key points

This is one of the finest and most moving scenes in all Shakespearean tragedy.

- Up to this final scene, the principal focus of attention has been on Iago, who has dictated the course of the action and its pace. Most of the other characters have been largely passive victims of his activities.

- In the first part of this scene, Othello becomes the active agent. Everything now depends on what he will do. The tensions leading up to the first of the two great climaxes, the murder of Desdemona, are generated by our hopes, fears and expectations concerning her fate.

- Emilia's role takes on a vital interest and significance. Her heroic, self-forgetful defiance of Othello, and her exposure of Iago's treachery, are the dominant features up to the time of her murder. Her conduct here reflects her transformation, under Desdemona's influence, from cynical worldliness to heroism.

- Iago is also transformed, from a self-assured, supremely confident manipulator of everybody else's destiny to a fatuous criminal, who hits and runs away.

- The Othello who murders Desdemona is a deluded creature, moving towards and through his deed in a pose of self-sacrificing duty. He commits the murder in a blind rage, not, as he suggests, as an agent of justice, but as a provoked husband taking a purely personal revenge. Iago has led him to this absurd end, having suggested even the manner of Desdemona's death.

- Othello's nightmare is followed by an even more terrible awakening. Emilia makes him face the fact that he has been fatally deceived, and forces him to see the real Iago for the first time. He finally confronts the appalling truth about himself and his deed.

- In death, Othello recovers some of his old nobility and dignity.

- Shakespeare brings the play to a second climax with a brilliant piece of technical skill. In his final speech, Othello summarises his career in the service of Venice, and the main issues of the tragic action. He looks to posterity for a fair and objective verdict on his life and deeds. His tears imply healing and penance. With his account of his slaying of the Turk, the past startlingly merges into the present, as he acts out the deed he describes.

- Othello also wants to be remembered by the people of Venice as the Moor who turned Christian, and who, in a war between Christians and Turks, defended the Christian cause by killing 'a malignant and a turban'd Turk' (line 354). He demonstrates how he killed that Turk by stabbing himself to death with his own weapon. The way in which he brings about his own death shows that, in a symbolic way, he has now become the Turk. By murdering Desdemona, he abandoned his Christian values and damned himself.

- The Othello who dies by his own hand is the double of the Turk he once killed. This Turk had 'beat a Venetian and traduc'd the state' (line 355). Othello, too, has beaten a Venetian (Desdemona) and thereby dishonoured the Venetian state. In a symbolic sense, it is therefore fitting that Othello should suffer the punishment he inflicted on the Turk for the same offence.

Useful quotes

O perjur'd woman, thou dost stone thy heart
And makest me call what I intend to do
A murder, which I thought a sacrifice.

(Othello, lines 64–6)

Nobody, I myself. Farewell.
Commend me to my kind lord. O, farewell!

(Desdemona, lines 126–7)

I will not charm my tongue, I am bound to speak.
My mistress here lies murder'd in her bed.

(Emilia, lines 185–6)

Nay, lay thee down and roar,
For thou hast kill'd the sweetest innocent
That e'er did lift up eye.

(Emilia, lines 199–201)

Blow me about in winds, roast me in sulphur,
Wash me in steep-down gulfs of liquid fire!
O Desdemona! Desdemona dead!

(Othello, lines 280–2)

I look down toward his feet, but that's a fable.
If that thou be'st a devil I cannot kill thee.

(Othello, lines 287–8)

Will you, I pray, demand that demi-devil
Why he hath thus ensnar'd my soul and body?

(Othello, lines 302–3)

Then must you speak
Of one that lov'd not wisely, but too well;
Of one not easily jealous, but being wrought,
Perplex'd in the extreme

(Othello, lines 344–7)

For he was great of heart.

(Cassio, line 362)

Questions ?

1 In what frame of mind does Othello approach the murder of Desdemona?

2 What is his frame of mind as he commits the murder?

3 How does Shakespeare make us feel about Othello at this point in the play? Does he want us to pity him, to despise him, to condemn him or to find excuses for him?

4 Does Othello show any pity for Desdemona, or has he any feeling at all for her? Can you account for his behaviour in this scene?

5 'Desdemona helps to bring about her own destruction.' Would you agree with this statement?

6 Emilia has a vital role in this scene. What is her importance?

7 The scene reveals a new Emilia. What changes does she undergo, and why?

8 'Iago is destroyed by his oversights and by accidental circumstances.' Comment on this statement.

9 Images of heaven and hell are prominent in this scene. Mention some of these images. What do they signify in the context of the play?

10 As the end approaches, Othello becomes more like his earlier self. What are the indications of this?

ACT 5 ⸸ Key moments

Scene 1

- Iago reveals his contempt for Roderigo and would like to see him dead so that he cannot demand the return of the gold and jewels that Iago has stolen from him. Iago also wants to get rid of Cassio in case Othello confronts him and discovers the truth. His preference, therefore, is for Cassio and Roderigo to kill each other.

- Iago doesn't quite pull off this plan: Roderigo dies, but Cassio survives. So far, however, Iago has managed to avoid attracting suspicion.

Scene 2

- Othello makes it clear that he is not going to kill Desdemona as an act of personal revenge, since that would be murder. Instead, the killing will be an act of justice, as if he were ridding the world of a criminal.

- Othello's order to have Cassio killed, however, is an act of personal revenge. He tells Desdemona that if Cassio had as many lives as he has hairs on his head, he would want to take all of them.

- Desdemona, almost with her final breath, undermines Othello's claim that her death is an act of justice.

- Emilia exposes Iago's lies to Othello about Desdemona and Cassio. Iago kills Emilia.

- Othello acknowledges his guilt, foreseeing Desdemona in heaven and himself in hell, but persists in regarding himself as an honourable killer.

- A letter in Roderigo's pocket confirms Iago's complicity in the attack on Cassio.

- Iago runs off but is captured and brought back. Othello wounds him.

- Othello takes his own life.

- Cassio takes over in Cyprus.

ACT 5 ⸸ Speaking and listening

1 In small groups, select a significant moment in Act 5 and discuss how it might be interpreted on stage. Assign the roles and portray your chosen moment in a freeze-frame. Consider what your character may be thinking and feeling at that point in the play and try to convey that through your frozen action. The other members of the class must identify the moment and explain its significance.

2 The class is divided into five groups, each representing a particular character: Othello, Desdemona, Emilia, Cassio or Roderigo. Each group must come up with (a) a short 'victim impact statement' setting out the impact that Iago has had on his or her life, and (b) a list of four questions that they would like Iago to answer. Your teacher will assume the part of Iago. Each character group reads out its statement and questions. Unlike Iago's refusal to speak at the end of the play, this 'Iago' will attempt to answer each question.

*O*THELLO IS A tragedy. In tragedies we see the random interaction of external forces (such as fate, chance or accident) and human weakness (such as vice, lack of awareness or stupidity). The result threatens the well-being of the individual and of society.

The tragic aspect of *Othello* arises from what happens within Othello as the events unfold. It is the development of Othello's understanding of himself and his plight, and his sharing of this with the audience, that lifts the play to a higher plane.

one whose hand,
Like the base Judean, threw a pearl away,
Richer than all his tribe

OTHELLO, Act 5, Scene 2, 347–9

To be truly **tragic**, a **play** must satisfy a number of **criteria**:

External factors also have a part to play. In Shakespearean tragedy it is difficult to avoid the impression that **fate** is working against the hero from the beginning. Whatever Othello may do, he is in some sense a doomed man. The influence of order, justice and reason is extremely limited.

The tragic hero's situation and world are organised in such a way that he has **no chance of a happy outcome**. If Iago repented and admitted the truth to Othello, thus saving Desdemona's life and preventing Othello's suicide, the necessary tragic ending would be absent.

Tragic drama focuses on a single individual, whom we call the **tragic hero**. The tragic hero must enjoy the audience's earnest good will. The tragic hero in this play is Othello.

The **audience must identify with the tragic hero** in his sufferings. He must remind us strongly of our humanity, so that we can see him as in some way standing for us. He must be vulnerable to extreme suffering, as Othello clearly is, and we should feel some degree of **pity and fear** for him.

In Shakespearean tragedy the hero is invariably **a man of status** and noble personality, an eminent individual who is engaged in great events. Othello is a respected and successful military leader.

For the hero, **recognition** is the essential tragic experience. It occurs when he finally understands his character and situation. For Othello, it involves recognising his blindness to Iago's villainy and to the reality of Desdemona's love for him. This understanding brings a profound and cruel sense of loss.

The tragic hero must be motivated by a serious purpose or undertake a **serious course of action**. In Othello's case this action is his elopement with Desdemona, a young Venetian noblewoman.

The tragic hero ends up **isolated** from those who loved and admired him, but grows in stature, and in the audience's estimation, as he **faces up to his destiny** and confronts it. Othello's final words reflect a greater self-awareness; and his former blindness and ignorance die with him.

Through that purpose or action, the tragic hero inevitably meets with grave physical and/or spiritual **suffering**. The direction of his career in the play is always **from prosperity to adversity**. Othello starts out as a happily married and much admired war hero but has lost everything by the end of the play.

Shakespearean tragedy depicts the **violation and restoration of order** and health in society. Iago, as the agent of social disorder and sickness, involves good characters (Cassio and Desdemona) and less good ones (Roderigo and Emilia) in his corrupt schemes. As the play reaches its climax, order is restored: Iago's villainy is exposed and Cassio is made governor. This comes at a terrible price: the innocent Desdemona is murdered, Emilia dies for revealing the truth about Iago, and Othello kills himself.

This passage from good to bad fortune is the result of some initial and fundamental **human 'error'**. This may be a false step, a miscalculation or a defect of character. Such a defect is generally described as the hero's **tragic flaw**. (See Hero, heroine and villain: Othello, p. 219.)

Iago's plot

A S THE TITLE OF the play suggests, Othello is its central character and the play is his tragedy. In an important sense, however, Iago has the key role. The other characters mostly react to what he says and does, and move according to his plans. Even those events that he is not responsible for, accidental circumstances such as Desdemona's loss of the handkerchief or Bianca's timely arrival in Act 4, Scene 1, are put to clever use by Iago, and become part of his plot.

In terms of the percentage of lines spoken by the characters, Iago has the major part, with 31 per cent of the lines. Othello has 25 per cent and Desdemona 11 per cent. Iago also has approximately the same number of speeches as Othello and exactly the same number of scenes on stage.

Although everyone's destiny is in his hands, two important unplanned events bring Iago down. These are Emilia's revelations and the discovery of incriminating evidence in Roderigo's pocket. Iago plans and foresees the ruin of others, but his own downfall is unplanned and unforeseen.

To set out the stages in Iago's intrigue is also to summarise the action of *Othello*.

Act 1 Scene 3

- In Iago's soliloquy at the end of this scene, it is clear that the outlines of his intrigue are vague. He has nothing more definite in mind than getting Cassio's place as Othello's lieutenant. Then something occurs to him: he will 'abuse Othello's ear' with the suggestion that Cassio 'is too familiar' with Desdemona (lines 391–2). This represents the 'monstrous birth' of Iago's plot against Othello and Cassio (line 400).

Act 2 Scene 1

- Iago observes Cassio's elaborate show of courtesy to Desdemona, remarking that 'as little a web as this will ensnare as great a fly as Cassio' (lines 168–9).

- Iago encourages Roderigo to 'find some occasion to anger Cassio' (lines 262–3). His idea here is that Cassio will respond by striking Roderigo, and Iago will cause the Cypriots to mutiny. Iago hopes that this will result in the removal of Cassio from his post.

- Iago plans to put Othello 'into a jealousy so strong that judgement cannot cure' (lines 296–7) by suggesting that Desdemona and Cassio are lovers. Iago expects to be loved and rewarded by Othello in return.

Act 2 Scene 3

- Iago gets Cassio drunk, and sends Roderigo to provoke him and then to 'cry a mutiny' (line 148). Othello dismisses Cassio.

- Iago urges Cassio to ask Desdemona to plead his case with Othello: 'Confess yourself freely to her, importune her' (line 309). Iago knows that the harder she tries to restore Cassio to favour, the more likely it is that 'She shall undo her credit with the Moor' (line 349).

- Iago plans to bring Othello to where he will find Cassio 'soliciting his wife' (line 376).

Act 3 Scene 3

- Iago begins to undermine Othello's faith in Desdemona when he claims that Cassio is sneaking away 'guilty-like' from her (line 40). He implies that Cassio may not be 'honest' (line 105).

- Iago insinuates that Othello may have cause for jealousy by warning him solemnly against it (line 169). He then advises Othello to watch Desdemona carefully, pointing out that she has already deceived her father (line 210).

- Othello falls into Iago's trap and asks that Emilia spy on Desdemona: 'Set on thy wife to observe' (lines 243–4). This is a major step in Othello's degradation.

- An accident now helps Iago's scheme. Desdemona drops the handkerchief Othello has given her as a gift. Emilia picks it up and gives it to Iago. Iago intends to turn it into a piece of incriminating circumstantial evidence against Cassio and Desdemona (lines 326–9).

- Iago manufactures further 'evidence' by giving a graphic account of Cassio's imaginary dream (lines 419–32). This persuades Othello that Desdemona has been unfaithful.

- Iago introduces the 'evidence' of the handkerchief, claiming that he saw Cassio wipe his beard with it (line 446). Othello orders Iago to have Cassio killed; he will kill Desdemona himself.

- Othello appoints Iago in Cassio's place: 'Now art thou my lieutenant' (line 485). With Cassio dismissed and sentenced to death, Iago has already achieved more than he first planned.

Act 4 Scene 1

- Iago reduces Othello to raving incoherence and physical collapse (line 43).

- Iago arranges for Othello to overhear Cassio boasting about his supposed conquest of Desdemona. Cassio is actually talking about Bianca, but Othello does not know this (lines 93–142).

- In another lucky break for Iago, Bianca arrives (line 143) and Othello sees the handkerchief in her hand. This convinces Othello of Desdemona's guilt. On Iago's advice, he decides to strangle Desdemona in her bed (lines 203–4).

- Iago's strategy is working. Othello strikes Desdemona in public (line 235). He is unable to control his feelings even in the presence of the Venetian ambassadors, and leaves their company a raving, broken man, with his public reputation completely shattered.

Act 4 Scene 2

- Iago enjoys a further triumph when Desdemona kneels to beg his intercession with Othello on her behalf: 'Good friend, go to him' (line 152). This is one of the cruellest ironies in a play remarkable for irony.

- Iago has reached the peak of his good fortune. He has displaced Cassio as Othello's lieutenant; inflicted intense mental suffering on Othello, whose faith in Desdemona he has totally undermined; and arranged with Othello for the killing of both Cassio and Desdemona.

- A shadow is cast over Iago's triumphs when Roderigo threatens to go to Desdemona (lines 198–201). Instead, Iago persuades Roderigo to make an attempt on Cassio's life (lines 224–42).

Act 5 Scene 1

- Iago's fortunes suffer a serious decline when Roderigo fails to kill Cassio (lines 24–6). But he puts on a show of honesty that convinces Cassio, Lodovico and Gratiano of his good intentions.

- Iago stabs Roderigo, intending to remove a major threat to his own safety (line 61).

Act 5 Scene 2

- Iago's plans seem to prosper when Othello smothers Desdemona (line 85).

- The fatal turning point in Iago's fortunes comes in a manner that he, for all his cunning, failed to foresee. His wife, Emilia, proves his undoing. Othello tells her that it was Iago who informed him that Desdemona had been false. Emilia's eyes are at last opened to the villainy of her husband. She reveals the truth about the handkerchief (lines 231–2).

- Iago kills Emilia, but the damage has been done and he runs away (line 238).

- Iago is brought back a prisoner and is wounded by Othello (line 288). He refuses to give reasons for his actions.

- A final revelation makes it clear that Iago would have been ruined even without Emilia's intervention. He has killed Roderigo, but correspondence found in the dead man's pocket implicates Iago in the plot against Cassio and reveals the intrigue between Iago and Roderigo (lines 309–19).

Characters

ALL ACCOUNTS OF DRAMATIC characters and their relationships, including those given here, should be received with caution. It is not possible to give a definite account of any character or relationship in *Othello* or any other Shakespearean play. For a start, all such interpretations are culturally conditioned.

It is important to recognise that Shakespeare's first audiences would have responded to some of the characters and events of *Othello* in ways that differ fundamentally from what might be expected from a modern audience. For example, the conventions of the time would have deemed Desdemona's elopement and her treatment of Brabantio to be a serious violation of social propriety and parental rights.

A brief consideration of the differing ways in which the characters and their relationships have been seen over the centuries shows how strongly interpretations are influenced by prejudices of many kinds: cultural, social and racial, for example, as well as differing world-views. There are almost as many interpretations of Othello, Iago, Desdemona and other characters as there are readers.

Portrayals on stage

Faced as they are with a rich variety of possibilities, actors and directors will choose one aspect of a character to focus on in their stage production. The result can be some startling contrasts in interpretations of *Othello*, for example:

Othello

- noble Othello
- Othello jealous by nature
- Othello not jealous by nature
- barbarous Othello
- courtly Othello
- self-centred Othello
- magnanimous Othello
- Othello who loves Desdemona too much
- Othello who never really loves Desdemona
- Othello the ignorant fool
- trusting Othello
- suspicious Othello

Iago

- Iago the genius, with remarkable powers of intellect, insight and versatility
- stupid Iago, who misjudges Emilia and fails to take account of Desdemona's influence on her
- attractive Iago, who, for all his wickedness, contributes much liveliness and energy to the plot
- motiveless Iago, enjoying evil for its own sake like some sort of devil
- Iago who acts as he does out of a pathological jealousy of his wife, a suspicion that she is unfaithful, a hatred of Othello for passing him over for promotion in favour of Cassio, and a hatred of Cassio for accepting a position that he is less qualified for than Iago is

Theatrical and cinematic productions exploit the possible combinations of these and other qualities. The various images in this book illustrate some recent casting choices.

There was a time when actors and producers did not dare to present a black Othello on stage. This was particularly the case in the nineteenth century, when one commentator claimed that Shakespeare would not have depicted a white Venetian girl falling in love with a black foreigner, since this would have suggested a lack of balance in Desdemona!

In such a climate of opinion, actors portrayed Othello as a tawny, turbaned North African Arab. The play, however, supplies clear evidence that Shakespeare visualised Othello as black, not tawny. The most telling piece of evidence is supplied by Othello himself: 'for I am black' (Act 3, Scene 3, line 267). Other physical descriptions are provided by Iago and Roderigo in Act 1, Scene 1, not to mention Brabantio's reference to Othello's 'sooty bosom' (Act 1, Scene 2, line 70).

In Shakespeare's day all the actors were white and male. Boy actors played the female roles.

Othello

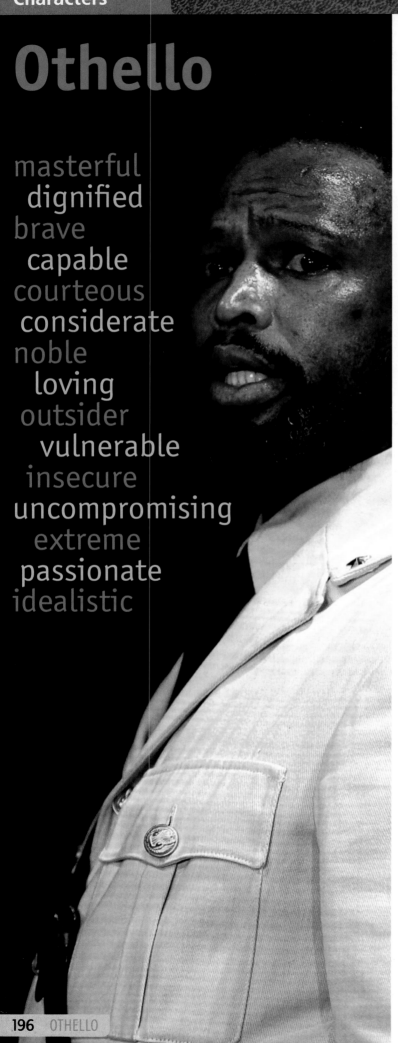

masterful
dignified
brave
capable
courteous
considerate
noble
loving
outsider
vulnerable
insecure
uncompromising
extreme
passionate
idealistic

In the closing moments of the play, Lodovico asks:

O thou, Othello, that wert once so good,
Fall'n in the practice of a damn'd slave.
What shall be said to thee?

(Act 5, Scene 2, lines 292–4)

In a few words, Lodovico gives the essential facts of Othello's tragic career. Othello is a man who had the good will of those who knew how to value virtue, achievement and nobility, but he was corrupted and acted out his corruption, and therefore fell.

It is useful to consider the different phases of Othello's character and career.

The noble hero

We are left in no doubt, from Othello's first appearance to his last, that we are to see him as a distinguished and virtuous man. When Othello, in a towering rage, publicly strikes Desdemona and banishes her from his sight, Lodovico remembers an earlier Othello, who would never have acted like this.

Lodovico's 'noble Moor' (Act 4, Scene 1, line 260), masterful and in full control of every situation, is the Othello we meet in Act 1. He is an admirable figure. It is true that the earliest things said about Othello are unflattering, but the speakers are Iago and Roderigo, and we are expected to take their remarks as the envious reflections of low-minded, foul-mouthed enemies.

When Othello first appears on stage, he impresses us at once with the force of his personality and his air of easy command. Confronted by a very hostile Brabantio, he masters a potentially dangerous situation with graceful diplomacy.

Othello enjoys recalling warlike feats, but he is a soldier with a difference, one who knows when forceful methods are not appropriate. He chooses to deal with Brabantio with words, not weapons, making it clear at the same time that his conciliatory attitude is not due to any weakness on his part. He is reasonable, civil and dignified when he defends himself before the Duke.

The early Othello is therefore the master of his own emotions, self-controlled and not easily moved to passion, even where his deepest interests are concerned.

The complete man

Lodovico's claim that Othello is 'all in all sufficient' (Act 4, Scene 1, line 261) suggests that he is the complete man. His concern for the wounded Montano – 'Sir, for your hurts, myself will be your surgeon' (Act 2, Scene 3, line 245) – shows him at his best in his public role, while his delicate concern for Desdemona – 'Look, if my gentle love be not rais'd up' (Act 2, Scene 3, line 241) – indicates his sensitivity in private relationships.

In his final speech, Othello remembers with proper pride his public service to Venice. Even Iago had to admit that Venice needs his military leadership in the Cyprus wars: 'Another of his fathom they have not to lead their business' (Act 1, Scene 1, lines 152–3).

Before the onset of his jealousy, Desdemona has no cause to find Othello to be anything but balanced and reasonable. Nothing she knows about him gives her cause to think him prone to jealousy or suspicion. On the contrary, she is sure that Othello 'is true of mind, and made of no such baseness as jealous creatures are' (Act 3, Scene 4, lines 23–4).

In soliloquy, where we must presume Iago speaks the truth as he sees it, Iago refers to Othello's 'constant, noble, loving nature' and expects that he would 'prove to Desdemona a most dear husband' (Act 2, Scene 1, lines 284–6).

His degradation

The play's main tragic action concerns the degradation of this great and noble character. The destruction of Othello's admirable self-control is recorded with satisfied malice by Iago, the man who engineered it: 'I see, sir, you are eaten up with passion' (Act 3, Scene 3, line 397).

The radiant, exotic images and the dignified music of his earlier speeches (such as 'of antres vast and deserts idle, rough quarries, rocks and hills, whose heads touch heaven'; Act 1, Scene 3, lines 140–1) give way to disordered and disgusting modes of expression, until his mind becomes like 'a cistern for foul toads to knot and gender in' (Act 4, Scene 2, lines 62–3).

His delicate care for Desdemona's feelings and wishes is soon replaced by a cruelty that leaves her helpless, humiliated and baffled. In Act 2 Desdemona is his 'soul's joy', the source of his absolute content (Scene 1, line 184). Early in Act 4 he is determined to 'chop her into messes' (Scene 1, line 196).

Iago's influence alone cannot explain Othello's fall. Iago displays remarkable determination, cunning and ingenuity, and enjoys astonishing luck, but he could not make Othello believe in Desdemona's 'infidelity' without being able to work on insecurities and weaknesses in his victim's character.

Some commentators accept Iago's verdict that Othello is 'egregiously an ass' (Act 2, Scene 1, line 304) for thinking his wife unfaithful on what appears to be absurdly flimsy 'evidence'. However, if Othello is seen as an ignorant fool, he cannot command the active good will and sympathy one extends to a tragic hero, and the play degenerates into farce.

If Othello is simply stupid and gullible, what are we to think of Iago's other victims? Roderigo remains more or less convinced until the moment of his death that Iago has his interests at heart. Desdemona and Cassio think of Iago as a sympathetic friend. Emilia does not suspect that her husband hates Othello and does not discover until it is too late what he has in mind for Desdemona.

The outsider

Othello's sense of insecurity in relation to Desdemona makes Iago's task much easier. This insecurity has a great deal to do with the fact that he is an outsider in Venetian society. The inhabitants of Venice, as the play often reminds us, have a reputation for sophistication and subtlety.

The fact that Othello is racially distinct in a very obvious way from his wife, and ignorant of the ways of Venetian women, is also important. Iago uses this to cruel effect when he tells Othello that Venetian wives are notorious for being unfaithful to their husbands and when he suggests that Desdemona's marriage to him was unnatural in the first place (since she should have married a Venetian).

Iago's assertion that the moral code of Venice sanctions adultery on condition that it is not found out would have corresponded with the general view of Shakespeare's contemporary audience that Venetian society was morally corrupt. Given this climate of opinion, Othello's readiness to succumb to Iago's suggestions would not have been considered incredible or indicative of crass stupidity.

At first Othello appears every bit as civilised as the most polished Venetian. However, when Iago raises spurious doubts in his mind about Desdemona, he plunges quickly into verbal and physical cruelty and violence. The nature and swiftness of his degradation might be seen as evidence that he is, essentially, a barbarian, albeit a noble and even kingly one.

Shakespeare gives us an outstanding representative of upper-class Venetian society: the Duke of Venice. When Brabantio falsely alleges that Othello has used magic spells to win Desdemona, the Duke adopts a rational approach to his testimony, pointing out that accusations and assertions are not the same as proofs, and neither are suspicions (Act 1, Scene 3, lines 106–9).

When Iago drives Othello insane with jealousy and doubt, Othello does not stop to ask for firm evidence. Either he has forgotten the Duke's admirable example or he is unable to follow it. He lacks balance, poise and moderation. Instead, he jumps straight into the contemplation of violent and cruel revenge.

Iago knows that Othello needs certainty at all costs. He learned this about him during the brawl scene when Othello took instant action, without sifting and reflecting on the evidence. Iago manipulates this character flaw.

'one that lov'd not wisely, but too well'

In his final speech, Othello asks those who are to report on his case to speak:

> Of one that lov'd not wisely, but too well:
> Of one not easily jealous, but being wrought,
> Perplex'd in the extreme

(Act 5, Scene 2, lines 345–7)

What he is telling us, and telling himself, is that he centred his life too exclusively on Desdemona, and when his trust in her collapsed, his world collapsed with it. Earlier he remarked that with the loss of her love, his public career was at an end: 'Othello's occupation's gone' (Act 3, Scene 3, line 363).

It is clear that whatever Othello undertakes has to involve his whole being. When he loves Desdemona, she is all his life and thought and joy. When he believes she has been unfaithful, his jealousy and disillusionment are as absolute as his love was and his vocation is to devise a fitting punishment.

Othello's claim that he was not easily jealous has been hotly contested. Some commentators regard it as a typical piece of self-deception. However, a case can be made for Othello's view of the matter. He may well be said to fall not through jealousy but through the deception of a cunning rogue. This deception arouses in him an uncontrollable passion, making him act without reflection or delay.

There is an egotistical element in Othello, as there is in all Shakespeare's tragic heroes. Othello tends to judge situations by reference to himself. His grief at Desdemona's supposed offence involves a strong sense of outrage at his loss of dignity and public standing. To his mind, infidelity is bad enough, but Desdemona's 'infidelity' with Cassio, 'mine officer', implies an added humiliation and loss of reputation (Act 4, Scene 1, line 198).

Othello's promptness in responding to Iago's suggestions and his anxiety that Iago elaborate on them indicate a thoroughly suspicious nature, along with a lack of faith in Desdemona and in the virtue of Venetian women in general. After all, he believes Iago, whom he has no obvious reason to trust, and disbelieves Desdemona, whom he has every reason to love and trust.

Iago

convincing
inventive
evildoing
hate-filled
slanderer
cunning
hypocritical
coarse
vulgar
self-centred
destructive
deceiver
dishonest
envious
racist
insecure
cynical
disloyal
amoral
ingenious
intelligent
subtle
intriguer
diabolical
inhuman

Iago is the chief problem-character of the play. He is a villain who not only confesses his villainy with the utmost frankness, but also pays generous tribute to the noblest qualities of his victims while in the very act of planning their ruin.

Although he is a sinister artist in evil, Iago is able to impress everybody around him with his absolute reliability and virtuous intent. 'Honest' and 'honesty' are the first words that occur to most other characters when they refer to him. (See Themes: Tragic irony, p. 211.)

Then there is the question of Iago's motivation. The main problem is not the number of motives Iago mentions, but the fact that most of them, once mentioned, do not come to light again. This has caused some commentators to suggest that Iago is merely hunting for spurious motives to justify his evil intentions and acts.

The stage villain

To Shakespeare's contemporary audience, Iago was a familiar and perfectly comprehensible villain. They were used to villains who required no motivation, who did evil things because they embodied evil principles, and who were driven by a single-minded hatred of whatever was good. They were familiar with the slanderer whose evil reports were always believed, no matter how incredible they sounded. They also recognised the villain of genius, a figure associated with the devil and whose function it was to initiate and complicate the action. This kind of villain, much like Iago, was a vital piece of dramatic machinery.

It is wrong, however, to treat *Othello* as a museum-piece or historical curiosity. The conventions of Shakespeare's theatre are not ours. We need to be able to read and watch Shakespeare in terms of our own expectations and understanding of character and motive. When viewed with modern eyes, although he remains a puzzling character, Iago is by no means incredible.

The devil's agent

Many critics are content to accept Iago as a Satanic figure on the strength of his explicit commitment of his cause to the devil:

> *Divinity of hell!*
> *When devils will their blackest sins put on,*
> *They do suggest at first with heavenly shows,*
> *As I do now.* (Act 2, Scene 3, lines 340–3)

The 'Divinity of hell' refers to the teaching of the devil, which from that point will direct Iago's conduct. Satanic evil, of course, needs no motive; it is a self-starting principle.

It is certainly possible to argue a case for a diabolic Iago, possessed by an evil force that sweeps all before it and is detected too late.

The avenger

A case can also be made that Shakespeare provides convincing motives for everything Iago does. For example, Iago considers himself a talented, practical soldier, but Othello has recently passed him over for promotion in favour of Cassio, a better-educated but less experienced officer. Iago is also facing the prospect of getting no further money from Roderigo, another situation for which he can partly blame Othello.

A clear impression is given that these grievances are not the cause of Iago's hatred of Othello, but are simply reinforcements of it. This hatred, one of the three radical emotions of the play (the others being Desdemona's love and Othello's jealousy) is not fully accounted for.

There is, however, a strong undercurrent of crude cultural and racial prejudice in Iago's attitudes. Envy, too, plays its part: envy that a foreigner such as Othello has attained so central a role in Venice, while Iago must be content with a relatively humble status.

Iago draws attention to a number of other motives in his soliloquies. For example, he wants to get Cassio's place, and so he will engineer Cassio's dismissal. Furthermore, Cassio's life irritates him, since it makes his own appear ugly.

Iago is disturbed by rumours that his wife, Emilia, and Othello are lovers. The imagery he uses to convey his feelings – the thought of it 'doth like a poisonous mineral gnaw my inwards' (Act 2, Scene 1, line 292) – carries the stamp of genuine feeling. Iago seems pathologically insecure in his marriage, since he also suspects Cassio of being Emilia's lover.

The oddest and most grotesque of all Iago's avowed motives is his thwarted love of Desdemona: 'I do love her too' (Act 2, Scene 1, line 286). This 'love' is partly entertained as a means of getting even with Othello, 'wife for wife' (Act 2, Scene 1, line 294).

Further possible motives and explanations for Iago's schemes may be deduced from his predicament. He is, by training, a professional soldier, and military service is his only hope of advancement. When he fails in this, his self-love and self-respect are naturally outraged and he wants to teach those responsible a lesson.

The psychopath

Iago's motives, like everything else about him, reflect his extreme egotism. He is a totally godless creature, amoral, without ideals or allegiances, and moved only by appetite and self-interest.

Iago conceals a destructive hatred of everything outside himself. He knows nothing of love or friendship. He sees his wife as a useful means of achieving his villainous ends. When she threatens his survival, he kills her. He cynically uses Roderigo to enrich himself, and as a weapon against Cassio, and gives nothing in return. When Roderigo becomes dangerous to his plans, Iago disposes of him without emotion.

Iago enjoys contemplating the suffering that he will inflict on others and he revels in the agonies of Othello and Desdemona, seeing it as a pleasurable sport. After one of his intrigues, Cyprus is in a state of riot, Montano is wounded, Cassio is dismissed in disgrace, and Othello has been angered. Iago is profoundly pleased. For him, it was a night of delightful adventure: 'By the mass, 'tis morning; pleasure and action make the hours seem short' (Act 2, Scene 3, lines 367–8).

The masterful manipulator

Iago shows remarkable ingenuity. His heart may be cold and callous, but his intelligence is always alive and active. He can improvise with great skill, is highly inventive and makes clever use of circumstances as they present themselves.

Iago is an astute judge of the weak points of all those he plans to destroy. He enjoys exercising his talent for intrigue and deception, while always wearing the mask of honesty. He revels in being able to impose his will on the very people who failed to recognise his abilities.

Iago is often compared to a dramatist. He manipulates people in the same fashion as a dramatist controls his or her characters and he enjoys exerting his power over others from behind the scenes. Iago's cast of characters, however, is drawn from among those he lives and works with. He assigns parts to all of them in accordance with the fate he has arranged for each.

Iago also contrives the plot of his drama, and directs its development. This plot goes according to plan for four of the five Acts, but unravels when Emilia fails to play the part assigned to her, as do Roderigo and Cassio.

Iago has a degraded view of human nature and his supreme error is to assume that other people share his outlook. He is destroyed by the power of love, which he cannot comprehend because it is not in his nature. He fails to realise that Emilia, for love of Desdemona, is likely to risk death rather than allow Desdemona's reputation to be destroyed. This failure leads to Iago's demise.

Desdemona

unselfish
honest
loving
faithful

devoted
loyal
innocent
kind
generous
childlike
sympathetic
persistent
gentle
virtuous
pathetic

In the symbolic pattern of the play, Desdemona is a heavenly force, the polar opposite to the devilish Iago. She is the innocent victim of Othello's misdirected passion. She is the representative of enduring, selfless love in a world of hatred and destructive selfishness. In addition, Shakespeare gives her some distinctive human qualities.

The divine lady

Recurring images underline her heavenly goodness. For example, she is welcomed to Cyprus by Cassio with a salutation carrying decided religious overtones and a prayer:

Hail to thee, lady, and the grace of heaven,
Before, behind thee, and on every hand,
Enwheel thee round!

(Act 2, Scene 1, lines 85–7)

In moments of crisis and danger her appeals are to heaven, and her pleas of innocence are expressed in religious terms: 'By heaven, you do me wrong', 'No, as I am a Christian', 'No, as I shall be sav'd' (Act 4, Scene 2, lines 83, 84, 88).

Othello, looking at her dead body, has a vision of being hurled from heaven by her innocent look, and of being whipped by devils from his 'possession of this heavenly sight' (Act 5, Scene 2, line 279).

The loving wife

Desdemona's love for Othello is the noblest and most precious emotion in the play. She loves Othello for what he is and her love is never in question. Her acceptance of him is undiscriminating and unchanging, even after she has been cruelly abused by him.

Whatever the outcome, she will remain steadfast: 'Unkindness may do much; and his unkindness may defeat my life, but never taint my love' (Act 4, Scene 2, lines 161–3).

On her deathbed, she commends herself to Othello, her 'kind lord' (Act 5, Scene 2, line 127), and makes a pathetic effort to deflect responsibility from him.

Inner strength

Desdemona is not always a passive sufferer. The newly-wed who addresses the senators and outfaces her father is a very positive presence. Her defence of her marriage reveals a quiet determination. She sees no need to find excuses for what she has done, and she puts her father firmly, though respectfully, in his place.

Her strength of character again shines through after Othello has humiliated her in public and banished her from the company. Although reduced to a state of bewildered anguish, she continues to perform her ceremonial duties with dignified composure in the presence of those who have just witnessed her humiliation.

Innocence personified

Innocence is the quality emphasised in all Desdemona's important relationships. The painful scenes in which Othello accuses her of infidelity show her total innocence and purity of heart. She is baffled by his accusations and, as we learn from her discussion of the subject with Emilia, the very notion of infidelity is almost impossible for her to grasp.

It is from Iago that we learn of some of Desdemona's noblest qualities, particularly her kindness and generosity (the very qualities he uses to destroy her). For example, Iago tells Cassio that she is of 'so free, so kind, so apt, so blessed a disposition that she holds it a vice in her goodness not to do more than she is requested' (Act 2, Scene 3, lines 310–13).

Desdemona does, indeed, work hard on Cassio's behalf, but in the grotesque moral universe created and controlled by Iago, her acts of innocent good will, pursued with childlike persistence, become dangerous incitements to Othello's jealousy. The worst that can be said of this is that her repeated insistence on getting a hearing is somewhat irritating.

In tragic drama, the innocent and the guilty suffer alike. Desdemona's fate illustrates this ideal. She is innocent and cannot comprehend why Othello is putting her to death, or why she has lost his favour.

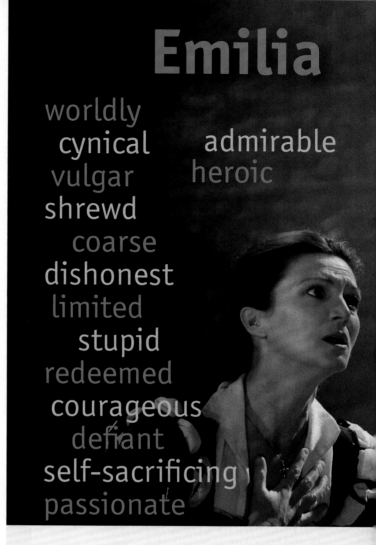

Emilia

worldly
cynical   admirable
vulgar   heroic
shrewd
coarse
dishonest
limited
stupid
redeemed
courageous
defiant
self-sacrificing
passionate

Emilia plays a necessary part in the development of the intrigue. She encourages Desdemona to plead with Othello on Cassio's behalf, which has disastrous consequences for Iago's victims, and her theft of the handkerchief seals the success of Iago's plot.

Human shortcomings

Although she steals the handkerchief without full awareness of the significance of what she is doing, Emilia emerges from this episode without much credit. She knows how much the handkerchief's loss will distress Desdemona.

Furthermore, she fails to mention the theft to Othello at a time when a word of explanation from her might have averted disaster. This silence may be due to her failure to notice the connection between Othello's jealousy and the loss of the handkerchief. If so, Emilia clearly lacks awareness of what is happening around her.

Shakespeare's presentation of Emilia is realistic. Unlike her husband, and unlike Desdemona, she has no symbolic significance. Like Cassio, however, she has moral strengths and weaknesses in good measure. She combines an obvious worldliness and proneness to moral lapses with a basic loyalty and sense of service.

Emilia has a shrewd, sometimes cynical, view of life and humanity, which she expresses with a coarseness and vulgarity all her own. For example:

> 'Tis not a year or two shows us a man:
> They are all but stomachs, and we all but food;
> They eat us hungerly, and when they are full,
> They belch us.

(Act 3, Scene 4, lines 100–3)

Emilia may have no illusions about the fidelity of husbands or the durability of their love, but, almost to the very end, she is blind to the utter depravity of her husband. Nowhere is her limited awareness better shown than in the closing minutes of the play when, even though she knows that Iago has contrived Desdemona's death, she is slow to make the connection with the stolen handkerchief.

Brave heroine

Although Emilia plays an ignoble role for the greater part of the play, she is much redeemed by her courageous defiance of both Othello and Iago in the end. Her change from a coarse, dishonest and worldly creature to a passionate champion of common humanity is one of the finest things in the play.

Emilia's transformation underlines the subtle interplay between Emilia and Desdemona. Desdemona has deeply influenced Emilia in ways that Iago, with his limited conception of human decency, cannot begin to comprehend.

It is left to Emilia to express the passionate indignation that every audience member must feel in the final movement of the play. Her grief over Desdemona's fate overwhelms all thoughts of her own safety.

Cassio

loyal
gallant
chivalrous
attractive
good-mannered
gentlemanly
honourable
idealistic
easy-going
pleasant
weak-willed
capable
trusted
generous
forgiving

Othello is a drama of intrigue as well as of character, and Cassio is central to the intrigue. The plot against Othello could not succeed without him. Iago realises that Cassio will be convincing in the role of Desdemona's supposed lover. His gallantry to her on the quayside in Cyprus (Act 2, Scene 1) gives colour to his reputation as a man likely to be attractive to women. The Florentines, of whom Cassio is one, were noted for their excellent manners and courteous behaviour.

Attractive qualities

Iago supplies an early indication of Cassio's appeal to women, or perhaps their appeal to him, when he describes him as 'a fellow almost damn'd in a fair wife' (Act 1, Scene 1, line 21). In this context, 'wife', as it often does in Shakespeare, must mean 'woman', since Cassio is not married; thus Iago seems to be saying that Cassio's fondness for pretty ('fair') women may lead him into trouble.

Several characters refer to Cassio's personal attractiveness. Iago, for example, notes the 'daily beauty in his life' (Act 5, Scene 1, line 19). Othello feels that Cassio is to be envied for the qualities he himself lacks: sophistication, worldliness, experience in dealing with women of good birth such as Desdemona, and, above all, the Italian background Cassio shares with Desdemona.

It is significant that in the First Folio list of characters, Cassio is described as 'an honourable gentleman'. The refined side of his nature is often demonstrated in his encounters with Iago. One has only to observe the tone of his conversation with Iago on the subject of Desdemona in Act 2, Scene 3 to appreciate the contrast between his idealistic appraisal of her worth and Iago's crude attempts to degrade and vulgarise her.

Cassio responds to Iago's coarse pleasantries with propriety and has no time for his ribald line of talk. He recognises Desdemona's excellence and celebrates it in moving language. His noblest instincts, his idealism and his sense of goodness and gentleness are called forth by her presence.

Cassio's reverence for Desdemona, love for Othello and exemplary loyalty are appealing and admirable characteristics. Even after he discovers that Othello has consented to his death, giving him every reason for resentment, if not hatred, he offers only a hesitant rebuke, 'Dear general, I never gave you cause', and, with true generosity, pronounces Othello's epitaph: 'For he was great of heart' (Act 5, Scene 2, lines 300, 362).

Cassio's status as a capable officer is also clearly established. Othello's choice of him as his second-in-command may not be conclusive evidence of Cassio's worthiness, and he does disappoint expectations by getting drunk while on duty. However, his appointment as Othello's replacement indicates his high standing in Venice.

Human shortcomings

Cassio also has very real human weaknesses. He likes to please and finds it difficult to say no. This aspect of his character is cleverly exploited by Iago, who gets Cassio very drunk, without undue difficulty, on the one occasion when it is most necessary for him to remain sober.

Cassio's relationship with Bianca, who 'by selling her desires buys herself bread and clothes' (Act 4, Scene 1, lines 94–5), underlines the truth of Iago's earlier suggestion that he is susceptible to the charms of pretty women. The critical manner in which he discusses Bianca with Iago (Act 4, Scene 1, lines 104–44) reveals to modern audiences an unpleasant side of his character.

Cassio pays dearly for his errors and flaws of character. His drunken bout, undertaken out of good nature under moral pressure and out of a desire to satisfy the claims of hospitality, results in his curt dismissal as Othello's lieutenant. His liaison with Bianca almost leads to his death.

Roderigo

Roderigo is described as 'a gull'd gentleman' in the First Folio's list of characters. In this, at any rate, he resembles Othello and Cassio: all three are Iago's duped victims.

Roderigo's career has something in common with Emilia's. Iago uses both to further his plans. Both die by his hand, and each contributes something to his eventual undoing: Emilia with her direct testimony and Roderigo through damning letters found in his pocket.

Roderigo's conversations with Iago tell us most of what we need to know about Iago and his plot. Without Roderigo, Iago would be able to communicate his villainy to the audience only through soliloquies. As such, Roderigo is a technical device for projecting Iago's baseness and vulgarity.

When Roderigo had previously pursued Desdemona's affections, he was told by her father 'not to haunt about my doors' (Act 1, Scene 1, line 96). When he informs Brabantio that his daughter has chosen Othello, the father who presumably had good reasons for finding Roderigo unacceptable as a prospective son-in-law regrets his earlier rejection, saying 'O that you had her!' (Act 1, Scene 1, line 176). The motive underlying Brabantio's new regard for Roderigo is dishonourable: their shared prejudice against Othello's colour.

Roderigo and Othello have some similarities. Both men, as Iago puts it, 'will as tenderly be led by the nose … as asses are' (Act 1, Scene 3, lines 397–8). Both are blind as to the direction in which Iago is leading them, and to the true character and motives of their manipulator. Both find Iago out when it is too late.

They respond to Iago's exposure in much the same way: the baffled Othello wondering why Iago 'hath thus ensnar'd my soul and body' (Act 5, Scene 2, line 303); the horrified Roderigo supplying Iago's best epitaph: 'O damn'd Iago! O inhuman dog!' (Act 5, Scene 1, line 62).

It is possible to feel some pity for Roderigo, faintly reflecting the pity one feels for Iago's nobler victims. His helpless nature and confused mind make him a pathetic victim. He is reluctant to take part in Iago's plan to ruin Cassio and has to be pushed into action: 'I have no great devotion to the deed, and yet he has given me satisfying reasons' (Act 5, Scene 1, lines 8–9). This highlights Iago's ability to degrade his victims and paralyse their judgement.

It has been said that Roderigo spends his time trying to swim in a sea that is much too rough for him. He meets a cruel and absurd death at Iago's hands, and his final confession – 'O villain that I am!' (Act 5, Scene 1, line 29) – is a faint and slightly touching anticipation of Othello's awakened sense of guilt in the closing scene.

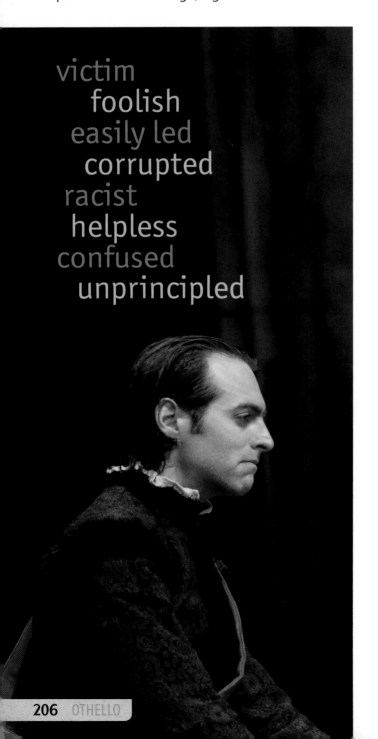

victim
foolish
easily led
corrupted
racist
helpless
confused
unprincipled

Summary

The following diagram illustrates the interactions between the characters in *Othello*.

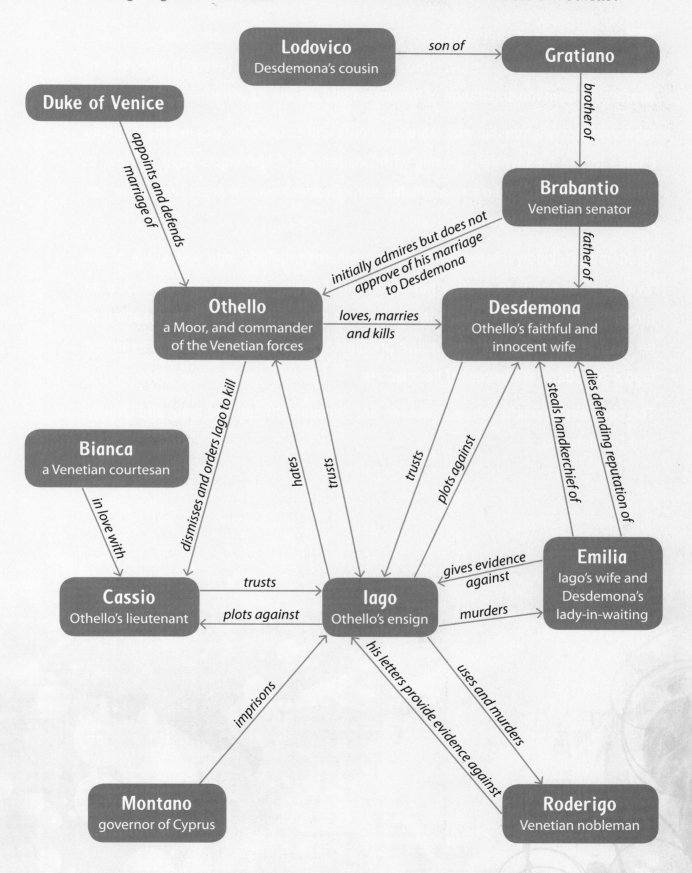

Lodovico
Desdemona's cousin

son of

Gratiano

brother of

Duke of Venice

Brabantio
Venetian senator

appoints and defends
marriage of

initially admires but does not
approve of his marriage
to Desdemona

father of

Othello
a Moor, and commander
of the Venetian forces

loves, marries
and kills

Desdemona
Othello's faithful and
innocent wife

dismisses and orders Iago to kill

hates

trusts

trusts

plots against

steals handkerchief of

dies defending reputation of

Bianca
a Venetian courtesan

in love with

Cassio
Othello's lieutenant

trusts

plots against

Iago
Othello's ensign

gives evidence
against

murders

Emilia
Iago's wife and
Desdemona's
lady-in-waiting

imprisons

his letters provide evidence against

uses and murders

Montano
governor of Cyprus

Roderigo
Venetian nobleman

Relationships

THE SIGNIFICANT RELATIONSHIPS IN the play involve Othello, Iago, Cassio, Desdemona and Emilia. The complex interactions between these five characters form the substance of the action and dictate its progress.

Iago's sinister relationship with Othello colours and distorts the way in which Othello comes to see his own relationship with Desdemona. From Iago's point of view, in order to destroy Othello's relationship with Desdemona, he must first sever the bonds that unite Othello and Cassio.

Desdemona's kindly interest in Cassio's problems provides Iago with some of the 'evidence' he needs to destroy her credit with Othello. Desdemona's influence on Emilia has a profound effect on the way in which she comes to see the world and may be seen as the inspiration for Emilia's principled, self-sacrificing action in exposing Iago's evil deeds at the cost of her own life.

The two central relationships, however, are between Othello and Iago, and Othello and Desdemona.

Othello and Iago

From every point of view, the Othello–Iago relationship is the most vital one in the play. Its progress determines the fate of all the major characters. Iago's attitude to his side of this relationship is expressed in the opening scene. He intends to use Othello for his own purposes: 'I follow him to serve my turn upon him' (Act 1, Scene 1, line 42).

There are many perspectives on the Othello–Iago relationship. For example, some see it as the exploitation of a simple, honest foreigner by a cunning, devilish insider with an astonishing capacity for mind control and successful deception. Some view the play as a version of a bullfight, with Othello, like some noble bull, repeatedly charging the handkerchief waved in his face by the skilled and dominant matador, Iago.

Others refuse to see the relationship as a conflict between Iago's diabolic intellect and Othello's trusting nobility. One reason for this might be that Othello seems to accept Iago's hints at Desdemona's 'infidelity' as if he were already harbouring doubts about her.

If we explain Iago's success not as the triumph of his diabolic intellect, but as the result of Othello's readiness to respond to his insinuations, we may then conclude that Iago has a particularly deep understanding of Othello's character. This enables him to play successfully on Othello's fundamental weaknesses: his proneness to jealousy, his insecurities in relation to Desdemona and as an outsider in Venice, and his impatience.

If we think of Othello as the essentially 'noble Moor', we have to attribute almost superhuman powers to Iago for undermining such nobility so readily and turning it to hatred and savagery. If we think of Othello as simply a credulous fool, all we have to see in Iago is a skilled pathological liar and a convincing hypocrite.

Yet another way of viewing the Iago–Othello relationship is to imagine Iago as the director, writer and actor in a drama of intrigue in which the other characters are obliged to perform the roles he has assigned to them. As his plot develops, he is able to improvise all kinds of variations, and cause his cast of characters to act in new ways. He even manages to change the nature of their relationships with each other (such as Othello's dismissal of Cassio and his adoption of Iago as his soul mate).

It is plausible to argue that Iago functions as an instrument for bringing to the surface of Othello's consciousness the dark and evil impulses lurking beneath. This aspect of Iago's role is made most obvious in Act 3, Scene 3, where Othello is ready to take up Iago's promptings with uncommon enthusiasm: 'By heaven, I'll know thy thoughts!' (line 166).

It does not take long for the monstrous evil in Iago's thoughts to become part of Othello's mindset. It is a matter for debate whether Iago is the sole creator of this monster, or merely causes it to emerge from the depths of Othello's mind.

Othello and Desdemona

The Othello–Desdemona relationship is an unequal, one-sided affair. It is often said that Desdemona's love for her husband is all-embracing and more important to her than her life. This observation is true to the facts of the play.

Even after Othello has abused her as 'that cunning whore of Venice' (Act 4, Scene 2, line 91) and publicly assaulted her, her love for him remains constant. As she tells Iago, she 'ever will (though he do shake me off to beggarly divorcement) love him dearly' (Act 4, Scene 2, lines 159–60).

Othello's account of their early relationship reveals that his feelings for Desdemona were prompted by her willingness to take an interest in his doings and past sufferings. He points out to the senators how fascinated she was with his personal history (Act 1, Scene 3, lines 145–68). It appears that part of the love he feels for her represents his self-satisfaction at being admired by a beautiful, noble, young woman. If his love for her is built on such shallow foundations, it is not difficult to understand Iago's success in undermining it.

Othello is prepared to accept Iago's slanderous insinuations against Desdemona without making the slightest effort to discover whether they have any basis in fact. During the temptation scene, his trust, if he does trust, is in Iago, whom he regards as being 'full of love and honesty' and to whom he is prepared to bind himself 'for ever' (Act 3, Scene 3, lines 122, 217).

Othello's attitude to love, and to Desdemona, is self-regarding and self-serving. He loves her for his own sake, for the happiness she can bring him. There is little evidence of Othello's devotion to Desdemona as a person, as someone to be valued and considered in her own right.

It appears that Othello and Desdemona do not know each other very well. This is significant in the context of Othello's temptation and fall, because when he is confronted by Iago's insinuations, he cannot call on any deep and intimate knowledge of his wife's character to enable him to repel them.

It takes only a few unfounded suggestions from Iago for Othello to distrust Desdemona. A little further manipulation and he is prepared to murder her.

Tragic irony

Irony is a strong feature in *Othello*. It takes two main forms:

- **Irony of situation:** involves taking a course of action that leads to an unexpected outcome.

- **Verbal irony:** involves a contradiction between what is being said, implied or suggested, and what is actually the case.

Irony of situation

In all Shakespearean tragedies, the tragic hero meets with final disaster due to an unforeseen or undeserved failure. He consciously takes a false step, but without any intention of bringing about the evil result that follows. Othello is a victim of this kind of irony of situation.

Othello intends to punish an apparent wrong (Desdemona's 'infidelity') but in doing so he commits a much greater wrong (her murder). He is in a much worse position as a result of his action than if he had taken no action at all.

The knowing spectator is bound to find irony in every confident assertion made by Othello, and in every expression of his faith in Iago, the man working hard to destroy his happiness.

Othello is sure that his marriage to Desdemona will not impede his military career. He declares that if his domestic life interferes with his military one, he is prepared to face public ridicule as a punishment for such a shameful lapse. However, Othello soon becomes a domesticated warrior and his military career suffers fatally.

There is obvious irony in Othello's relationships with Iago and Desdemona. Othello accepts and trusts Iago, although Iago is the person who hates him most; whereas he distrusts and rejects Desdemona, who loves him most.

Irony of situation involves other characters besides Othello. For example, Desdemona's attempt to have Cassio restored to his lieutenancy and to Othello's favour is one of the factors leading to her death.

Cassio is the first person whose death is formally planned (the planners being Othello, Iago and Roderigo). Fate ironically ordains, however, that Cassio will be the chief survivor of the action, and that two of the three plotters of his death will themselves die, while the third, Iago, will be left facing a similar fate. It is a further irony that Cassio succeeds the commander who dismissed him.

Human hope and happiness are often ironically mocked in the play. For example, when Cassio rejoices at Desdemona's safe and speedy arrival in Cyprus, he does not know that the faster she arrives, the faster fate is conducting her to her doom.

Verbal irony

The nature of the Othello–Iago relationship enables Shakespeare to exploit the possibilities of verbal irony with an exceptional fullness. Iago maintains a convincing show of honesty and, until the very end, Othello remains totally unaware of the contrast between Iago's outward show and the villainy beneath.

The commonest example of verbal irony in *Othello* is the consistent reference by other characters to Iago as 'honest Iago', when the opposite is the case. Othello repeatedly uses the words 'honest' and 'honesty' in relation to Iago. Cassio and Desdemona are prone to pay innocent tribute to Iago's sincerity. Indeed, 'honest' and 'honesty' are used over fifty times in the play, almost always with ironic overtones and always so when applied to Iago.

Some examples of irony

The following passages, chosen from a very large number of possible examples, give an idea of the range of ironies in the play.

> *A man he is of honesty and trust,*
> *To his conveyance I assign my wife*
>
> (Act 1, Scene 3, lines 284–5)

Othello is discussing his arrangements with the Duke for the journey to Cyprus and chooses Iago to be Desdemona's escort. There are two kinds of irony here, and Othello is the victim of both. He is unaware of the kind of man to whom he is entrusting his wife and his faith in Iago's honesty is misplaced.

> *My life upon her faith.* (Act 1, Scene 3, line 294)

Othello's faith in Desdemona, who merits it so fully, is to prove short-lived (unlike his faith in Iago, who is at this point plotting to destroy him, which proves more durable). He is prepared to gamble his life on her faith, and both terms come true in a way he cannot foresee: she is to prove faithful in the face of his later doubt, and he is to pay with his life for doubting her.

> *For I have lost him on a dangerous sea.*
>
> (Act 2, Scene 1, line 46)

This is Cassio's reference to the separation of Othello's ship from his own during the stormy journey to Cyprus. His words, in addition to their intended meaning, have a second, much more ominous significance of which he is unaware, and are therefore ironic. He has lost Othello in one storm. He will soon lose him in the storm of violence and passion that marks the brawl scene.

> *For thy solicitor shall rather die*
> *Than give thy cause away.*
>
> (Act 3, Scene 3, lines 27–8)

Desdemona is assuring Cassio of her effectiveness as his advocate ('solicitor'), but she is unknowingly foretelling her own destiny. She sees it as hyperbole – a heightened and exaggerated way of making a point – but it will turn out to be a true statement: her support for Cassio will be a major factor causing her death.

> *I see, sir, you are eaten up with passion.*
>
> (Act 3, Scene 3, line 397)

The Iago–Othello relationship involves many ironies such as this one. Iago has convinced Othello that Desdemona is unfaithful, and Othello's response grows more and more impassioned. Here, Iago pretends to be sorry that Othello should be carried away by the very passion that Iago himself has worked so cleverly to stimulate.

> *The Moor's abus'd by some outrageous knave,*
> *Some base notorious knave, some scurvy fellow.*
>
> (Act 4, Scene 2, lines 141–2)

Emilia, without at all realising it, stumbles on the cause of Othello's disturbed state of mind. The irony lies in Emilia speaking more truly than she knows, and in the fact that as she speaks, Iago, the 'outrageous knave', is standing beside her, casting doubt on what she is saying and telling her not to say it too loudly.

> *O good Iago,*
> *What shall I do to win my lord again?*
>
> (Act 4, Scene 2, lines 150–1)

> *O brave Iago, honest and just,*
> *That hast such noble sense of thy friend's wrong,*
> *Thou teachest me.*   (Act 5, Scene 1, lines 31–3)

Desdemona's heartfelt plea to Iago is one of the cruellest ironies of the play. The irony lies in her absolute unawareness of what her question really means. She is expecting the cause of her misery to become its cure, asking the man who is separating her from Othello's love to help her to regain it. Iago's enjoyment of this kind of irony can readily be imagined.

Othello mistakenly believes that Iago has killed Cassio. His interpretation of character and event here is a source of irony. His deluded belief in Iago's honesty and justice is another. In the light of what we know of Iago's part in this particular enterprise, 'O brave Iago' is another instance of Othello being deceived, and marks him yet again as a victim of irony. Far from being brave, Iago lurks in the background. It is only when Roderigo fails that Iago wounds Cassio from behind and runs away. It is ironic that Othello should thus take Iago's 'brave' activity as an inspiration to act against Desdemona.

Deceitful appearance

The contradiction between appearance and reality is a major theme of the play and is intimately linked to the use of irony. All the characters deceive or confound expectation in one way or another. For example, Emilia, coarse, cynical and materialistic as she appears on the outside, proves to be fundamentally good-natured.

There is a wealth of significance in the Duke's comment to Brabantio that Othello 'is far more fair than black' (Act 1, Scene 3, line 290). Moors in Shakespeare's time had a particularly unsavoury reputation. They were popularly associated with cruelty, witchcraft and lust. The stage-Moor was a demi-devil, Satan in human form. Shakespeare allows Iago, Roderigo and Brabantio to put forward this idea fairly strongly.

It is important to bear in mind, however, that the spirit of the play positively contradicts the popular prejudice against the ethnic type represented by Othello. The demi-devil of the play is not the black Othello but the white Iago, who is able to combine a hidden diabolism with the outward look of an honest fellow.

Instead of conforming to expectations based on outward appearances, and portraying Othello as a pagan, Shakespeare makes him a baptised Christian. Furthermore, Othello bears no resemblance to the lustful Moor of Elizabethan literature. Instead of inspiring fear and distrust, he is a respected leader who inspires confidence and good will.

Othello and Iago agree that 'men should be what they seem' (Act 3, Scene 3, line 130). The irony here is that these two central characters have natures that contradict the expectations associated with their appearances. If appearance reflected character, Iago should be the kind of man Othello is, and vice versa.

Desdemona, too, takes her place in the pattern of deceitful appearance, since she largely deceives the expectations that Shakespeare's audience had of Venetian women: that she would be a fickle courtesan, one of those who 'let God see the pranks they dare not show their husbands' (Act 3, Scene 3, lines 206–7). In contrast, Desdemona is constant in her love for Othello, almost to the point of being a martyr when she tries, from her deathbed, to save him. She does practise some deception, but it is of the most innocent kind.

Love

In essence, *Othello* is a love story that is perverted, with the lovers brought to ruin largely through the intervention of Iago, the supremely cunning villain. This statement might be qualified by saying that Othello must share some of the blame for helping to give this love story a tragic outcome.

An important question about the love between Othello and Desdemona is whether it is equal. Does the depth of Othello's love for Desdemona match that of her love for him? (See also Relationships: Othello and Desdemona, p. 210.)

There can be no doubt, on the evidence supplied by the play, that Desdemona's love for Othello is absolute, unconditional and unchanging. It is the one constant value in the play. Even her dying words, which are a pathetic attempt to deflect blame from Othello, affirm her enduring love for him (Act 5, Scene 2, lines 126–7).

Othello's love for Desdemona is a more complex matter. He views his wife as a newly acquired treasure of great price. Although nobly expressed, his love is not as absolute, unconditional and self-forgetful as Desdemona's love for him. If it were, Iago's temptation, no matter how cleverly contrived, could not succeed in converting it into savage hatred.

It should be remembered that in Shakespeare's time Venice was a great commercial power, a city dominated by trade and money. It may not be surprising then that even love and marriage were seen in terms of ownership. Othello's use of images of commerce and ownership betray his view of her as a beautiful commodity that he has acquired. She is a 'purchase made' that will yield a 'profit' (Act 2, Scene 3, lines 9, 10).

For Desdemona, love for Othello is a gift freely and unconditionally given; and once given, it is proof against anything that fate or chance can bring. For Othello, Desdemona's love for him is a gift to be received, treasured and guarded. It can be argued that he is too self-centred a man to love Desdemona unreservedly.

Perhaps the most revealing and disturbing of Othello's comments on married love is made to Iago:

> *O curse of marriage,*
> *That we can call these delicate creatures ours*
> *And not their appetites! I had rather be a toad,*
> *And live upon the vapour of a dungeon,*
> *Than keep a corner in the thing I love*
> *For others' uses.*
> (Act 3, Scene 3, lines 272–7)

The sentiments expressed here (with the emphasis on 'ours' and 'others' uses') throw light on the insecurity of Othello's love for Desdemona. The possessiveness revealed in this speech, and elsewhere, is of the kind that lies at the heart of all jealousy.

In his final agonised speeches, Othello's emphasis is less on the loving woman he has killed than on the loss *he* has suffered. If he mainly valued Desdemona because she enhanced his self-esteem, the terrible suggestion planted in his imagination by Iago that she has been unfaithful to him, with his lieutenant, removed the main basis for his devotion to her, since it shattered his self-esteem.

It is one of the most profound ironies in a play full of ironies that Othello's absolute need for Desdemona's absolute love for him is fulfilled in reality, since Desdemona's total love for him never varies, and is undermined only in the disgusting web of fantasy woven for him by Iago.

It is also ironic that the man who talks so feelingly of the imagined betrayal of his love for Desdemona should never be able to match the depth, sincerity and stability of her love for him.

Jealousy

The most famous passage in *Othello*, and one of the most controversial, is found in Othello's final speech, where he declares that if his listeners are to judge his character accurately, and transmit this judgement to the people of Venice, then they must speak:

> *Of one that lov'd not wisely, but too well;*
> *Of one not easily jealous, but being wrought,*
> *Perplex'd in the extreme*

(Act 5, Scene 2, lines 345–7)

Othello is saying that his love for Desdemona was without balance or moderation and that he was not easily made jealous, but when he was provoked to jealousy he was liable to work himself into a frenzy.

What do the terms 'jealous' and 'jealousy' mean in Othello's case, and what does he understand them to mean? The answer to such questions is to be found in the various exchanges between Othello and Iago in Act 3, Scene 3.

Iago, who is seeking to make Othello jealous, explains the condition and, while warning against it, cruelly outlines what it will be like when Othello experiences its full force. He describes a man eaten up by extreme jealousy: from minute to minute he endures the pains of hellish suffering and his mind is tormented by the conflicting emotions of love and of suspicion.

Iago seems to be a jealous type, even suspecting that Othello may be having an affair with Emilia. He reflects in one of his soliloquies that 'Trifles light as air are, to the jealous, confirmations strong as proofs of Holy Writ' (Act 3, Scene 3, lines 327–9). In other words, experience tells Iago that a jealous person will be prepared to believe even the most trivial allegations against the object of his jealousy, and give the same credit to such allegations as he would to the word of the Bible. Iago knows what he is talking about. Once he has aroused Othello's suspicions that Desdemona and Cassio are lovers, Othello soon comes to believe any piece of 'evidence' Iago puts before him, and the 'trifles light as air' become 'proofs' of Desdemona's guilt.

How can we reconcile Othello's claim that he is 'not easily jealous' with Iago's success in making him so jealous that he loses all self-control?

One defence of Othello's self-evaluation argues that his nature is not the kind to engender jealousy from within, but is extremely open to outside influence and deception. In addition, the deceiver in this case, Iago, has a remarkable ability to make him believe what he wants him to.

If we accept this, we have also to accept that the tragic flaw that leads to his downfall does not originate within Othello, but that it is the result of an evil process external to Othello. This is the cunning plot against him fabricated and executed by Iago.

If Othello's fate depends mainly on Iago's cunning, malice, intellectual superiority and good luck, we are also driven to consider Othello's remarkable trust in Iago as a decisive factor in his downfall. This trust is frequently emphasised in the play.

The notion that Othello's tragic fate is the outcome of external forces, and that he is trusting and naturally free of jealousy, runs into serious difficulties when it is tested against the action in the temptation scene (Act 3, Scene 3). This scene exposes Othello's distressing readiness to respond to Iago's insidious hints. It is a chronicle of his repeated demands to be allowed to have his jealous insecurities confirmed and reinforced.

If Othello is not to be seen as naturally jealous, naturally inclined to suspicion and possessiveness or both, it is difficult to account for his morbid willingness to get Iago to elaborate on his insinuations, first about Cassio and then about Desdemona. Othello's anxiety to hear the foulest things about both, to share Iago's images of their supposed lust, is almost pathological. He actively facilitates his tempter's efforts to undermine whatever trust he has in Cassio and Desdemona.

If it is true, as Act 3, Scene 3 suggests it is, that Othello is prone to extreme jealousy, then his judgement of himself as 'not easily jealous' conflicts with what the action of the play demonstrates. It thus confirms the common view that Othello, alone among the heroes of Shakespeare's great tragedies, exhibits only limited tragic self-discovery.

Race, colour and alienation

The racial difference between Othello and the other characters assumes a central importance in the plot. The sub-title of the play, *The Moor of Venice*, suggests both Othello's alienation from the rest of the characters, and the part played by race and colour in this alienation.

The prejudices against Othello do not arise simply from the fact that he is a foreigner. Venetians of the late sixteenth century, the period in which the play is set, would not have found it odd that their military forces should be commanded by a foreign general. On the contrary, it was a Venetian custom that the territories of the state were defended by foreign mercenaries, whose general was always a foreigner.

The attitude of Brabantio to Othello is highly significant, and the remarkable change in this attitude helps us to understand the real meaning of the racial prejudice with which Othello is confronted at an early stage in the play.

Othello informs us that Brabantio frequently entertained him at his home and was pleased to have him as a guest:

> Her father lov'd me, oft invited me,
> Still question'd me the story of my life,
> From year to year, the battles, sieges, fortunes,
> That I have pass'd.
>
> (Act 1, Scene 3, lines 128–31)

How then do we account for Brabantio's racially motivated abuse of Othello in Act 1, Scene 2, and particularly his bewilderment that Desdemona could find solace in 'the sooty bosom of such a thing as' Othello (lines 70–1)?

There can be only one answer to this question. A Moor, however black and 'sooty' he may be, is perfectly acceptable at the highest levels of Venetian society as long as he does not want to marry the daughter of a nobleman. This unthinkable prospect drives Brabantio to distraction.

The Venetians clearly regard Othello's race, colour and appearance as sufficient to set him apart radically from themselves. He does not conform to their standards of acceptable appearance. This Venetian outlook would have been largely shared by playgoers in Shakespeare's time.

Most characters who comment on Othello are repelled, or at least claim to be, by his appearance. Roderigo calls him 'thicklips' (Act 1, Scene 1, line 66); Emilia thinks of a devil when she contemplates his blackness; Iago pictures him as 'an old black ram' (Act 1, Scene 1, line 88).

Desdemona, by implication, finds Othello's appearance less than attractive. She accounts for her choice of him as her husband by claiming that she had the good judgement to see 'Othello's visage in his mind' (Act 1, Scene 3, line 252). This can be regarded as an admission on her part that his appearance had to be ignored or overlooked by her if she was to find him attractive.

Brabantio wonders how his daughter could 'fall in love with what she fear'd to look on' (Act 1, Scene 3, line 98). Iago is similarly perplexed, as we discover when he tells Othello how strange he finds Desdemona's love for so terrifying and unattractive a person as him: 'And when she seem'd to shake and fear your looks, she lov'd them most' (Act 3, Scene 3, lines 211–12).

Indeed, Iago argues, and Othello agrees with him, that a woman like Desdemona turning down marriage proposals from eligible men of Venice, men 'of her own clime, complexion and degree', suggests that she harboured 'thoughts unnatural' in choosing a black husband (Act 3, Scene 3, lines 234, 237).

The admiration that Venetians feel for Othello has to do with everything except his colour and appearance. He has earned their respect for his formidable military leadership, experience, judgement and professionalism. They expect him to be content with that esteemed position in society.

When Othello decides to fill the role of husband to an upper-class Venetian woman, their approval quickly turns to revulsion. For example, Othello's marriage to Desdemona releases a cluster of alarming associations in her father's mind: the black man as repulsive, cruel, dangerous, lustful, diabolical, a practitioner of black magic and a dispenser of hypnotic drugs.

Not all Venetians agree. The Duke regards Othello as an admirable human being and a fit husband for Desdemona. He reverses the significance of the black and white imagery at the heart of the play when he tells Brabantio that his new 'son-in-law is far more fair than black' (Act 1, Scene 3, line 290). In this context, fairness represents the Venetian idea of beauty, while blackness represents ugliness. In turn, fairness represents good and blackness represents evil.

Othello is all too conscious of some of the social disadvantages that attach to his race and colour. He even imagines that it may be a cause of Desdemona's 'adultery'. He wonders whether she would feel more sympathetic to him if he had the social graces and refinements of Venetian courtiers: 'those soft parts of conversation that chamberers have' (Act 3, Scene 3, lines 268–9).

Othello's colour is the visible reminder of his alien status. This is the status that Iago exploits with such deadly effect to undermine Othello's faith in Desdemona's fidelity to him. His insecurity and self-confessed ignorance of Venetian manners and customs lead him to believe even the most outrageous suggestions of the 'insider' Iago.

Shakespeare's contemporary audiences would have been acutely conscious of the dramatic clash of cultures depicted in the play. Seeing Othello as a nomadic savage and Desdemona as a refined member of a civilised society would have made their marriage an extraordinary and shocking union. They may have believed that the tragedy was precipitated by irreconcilable differences of race, belief, heritage and social background between the two main victims.

A telling instance of this is provided by Shakespeare's imaginative use of the handkerchief. It is a means of suggesting that Othello belongs to a world utterly remote from anything within the range of Desdemona's experience. The superstitious Othello attaches a magical significance to the handkerchief and believes that its loss would portend disaster, ideas that are incomprehensible to Desdemona.

General vision and viewpoint

Tragic drama necessarily takes a bleak view of the human condition, and of the possibility of human happiness. It is therefore natural to expect *Othello* to reflect such an outlook. In some respects, however, the play is more **painful and dismal** in its effect than tragedies such as *Hamlet* or *King Lear,* where the tragic burden is relieved by sustained passages of comedy.

In *Othello*, Shakespeare focuses, almost without remission, on the frightening success of an evil and clever man in absorbing all those around him in his **depraved vision** of life and human nature. Iago's mental torture of Othello, and the revolting humiliation inflicted in turn by him on Desdemona, culminating in the murder scene, make *Othello* the most **depressing** of Shakespeare's tragedies.

The **claustrophobic** atmosphere of the play, the dense concentration of the action on the activities of a few characters being gradually ensnared and tormented by an actively wicked one, with no prospect of escape, suggest that the play is a cruel sport directed by a sadist.

The play depicts an **unequal struggle between good and evil**, with evil in possession of all the effective weapons, and good almost always unarmed or disarmed. The agent of evil, Iago, has impressive qualifications for his terrible task.

There is a notable contrast between Iago's fiendish ingenuity and the innocent trustfulness of those he destroys. Goodness is allied to blind credulity, even stupidity, while evil is supported by cunning, skill and good fortune.

The play's **pessimism** is heightened by the fact that Iago easily manipulates Cassio, Desdemona, Othello, Roderigo and Emilia, bending them to his evil designs. He is free to pursue these designs because he is protected, until it is too late, by the impenetrable disguise of honesty.

One secret of Iago's success is his total **amorality**. He has no attachment to principles or values of any kind. This gives him the freedom to destroy the lives of others without experiencing inconvenient doubts or twinges of conscience.

Iago's outlook is summed up in a lesson he gives to Roderigo in Act 1, Scene 3: virtue is a worthless thing ('a fig'; line 319), and what some call love is merely 'a lust of the blood' (line 334).

It is hard to accept that nature can create a character of such **absolute evil** as Iago. The essential features of this evil, as Shakespeare projects them through Iago, are twofold:

- Perfectly sane people, with ample gifts of reason and logic, who appear to have no feeling of any kind for other people, exist.
- Such monsters of egotism can thrive only at the expense of others (deriving enjoyment from ruining other people's lives). They avoid detection until their evil work is done.

The comparative ease with which Iago's plot works in *Othello*, and the pathetic vulnerability of goodness and innocence in the case of a character such as Desdemona, suggest a **bleak, hopeless vision** of the human condition.

Through Desdemona, however, Shakespeare suggests that **human nature is redeemable**. There is a symbolic contrast between the visions of life represented by Iago and by Desdemona, with Othello moving between the two. Their opposition mirrors the conflict at the heart of Shakespearean tragedy: between communal values and social anarchy, selfless devotion and crass individualism, benevolence and hatred.

A positive, optimistic feature of the action of *Othello* is that, although his perverse schemes achieve their principal aim, **Iago is not allowed to triumph**. He is brought to destruction by the operation of a good impulse, where his cynical, rational mind never expected to find it: in his wife, Emilia. Emilia's exposure of Iago's wickedness is **evidence of ordinary human decency**. This is a valuable quality in a play that oscillates between extremes of goodness (Desdemona) and depravity (Iago).

Othello

It may seem odd to apply the term 'hero' to a man who is easily misled into thinking his wife is unfaithful and who responds by smothering her to death in their bedroom. Othello is, however, the official hero of the play, which is *his* tragedy.

There would be no tragedy if Othello was not a heroic figure. If he was, for example, corrupt and evil in his ways, he would not be a tragic hero. The central character in a tragedy must inspire good will in the audience and must have some flaw or fault that can be exploited to bring about his downfall.

The exact nature of Othello's flaw, or weakness, is much debated. His own account of it is given in his final speech in Act 5, Scene 2, in which, in modern idiom, he says: I am not jealous by nature, but when I was worked on, my mind was disturbed, and pulled this way and that.

Discussion of Othello the hero must focus on his virtues. It is important to note that all the characters we respect, for example Desdemona, the Duke, Lodovico and Cassio, admire or love Othello; whereas those for whom we feel contempt, namely Iago and Roderigo, hate him.

When we are judging or evaluating a character, it is a sound principle to give serious thought to the quality of his or her friends and enemies. If enemies are evil or repulsive, it says much about the way we regard those they hate.

The hatred felt by Iago for Othello may reasonably be interpreted as an inverted tribute to Othello. An impressive testimony to Othello's moral worth is also provided in Iago's grudging acknowledgement that Othello has 'a free and open nature' (Act 1, Scene 3, line 395).

The play leaves us in little doubt that the essential Othello, the man admired by Lodovico after his tragic fall as 'once so good' (Act 5, Scene 2, line 292), is to be seen as a noble and heroic figure.

Othello's heroic capacity as a Venetian general is acknowledged even by Iago, who points out that he is the indispensable leader of the state's forces. His success in the wars and his heroic capacities are also saluted by Montano, who notes that 'the man commands like a full soldier' (Act 2, Scene 1, lines 35–6).

Desdemona makes a tragically ironic comment after Othello, unknown to her, has decided to kill her. It shows what she (and everybody else apart from Iago) thinks about Othello's disposition at this point: 'my noble Moor is true of mind, and made of no such baseness as jealous creatures are' (Act 3, Scene 4, lines 22–4).

The tragedy lies in the conversion of Othello's dignity and command of his feelings into murderous jealousy. Those who do not like Othello might say that he could not so quickly descend into barbarous savagery of thought and action unless these were already part of his character.

Desdemona and Emilia

There are heroic qualities, as well as flaws, in the two principal female characters.

Desdemona's love for Othello, which remains true and constant to the end, has a heroic dimension, and is one of the great fixed points of the play. In spite of this, she has her critics, some of them within the play, who find her relationship with Othello unnatural and disturbing. Her treatment of her father is another source of reservation about her character. Brabantio believes that Desdemona deceived him and her elopement appears to cause his early death (Act 5, Scene 2, line 206).

A good argument might be made for the claim that Emilia is the moral heroine of the play. Like Othello, she undergoes a remarkable change, but her transformation is for the better. She starts her life in the play as a worldly, faintly corruptible woman. She becomes an agent of Desdemona's destruction when she steals the handkerchief and gives it to Iago. Then, at the climax of the play, she sacrifices her life, in the interests of truth and justice, by betraying Iago's plot.

Iago

It is possible to discuss the 'good' characters in terms of motivation and personality, but the chief villain, Iago, defies understanding. This is because there appears to be more than a human aspect to his desire and ability to do evil to innocent people.

The mysterious depth of Iago's evil behaviour is recognised by Othello in the closing scene, when he wonders if Iago is a devil in human form. Like everyone else, he is at a loss to discover the origins of Iago's evildoing. He asks Cassio, 'Will you, I pray, demand that demi-devil why he hath thus ensnar'd my soul and body?' (Act 5, Scene 2, lines 302–3).

The only character in a position to reveal the secret of Iago's evildoing is Iago himself. However, he refuses to open his mind, and the mystery remains. 'Demand me nothing. What you know, you know. From this time forth I never will speak word' (Act 5, Scene 2, lines 304–5).

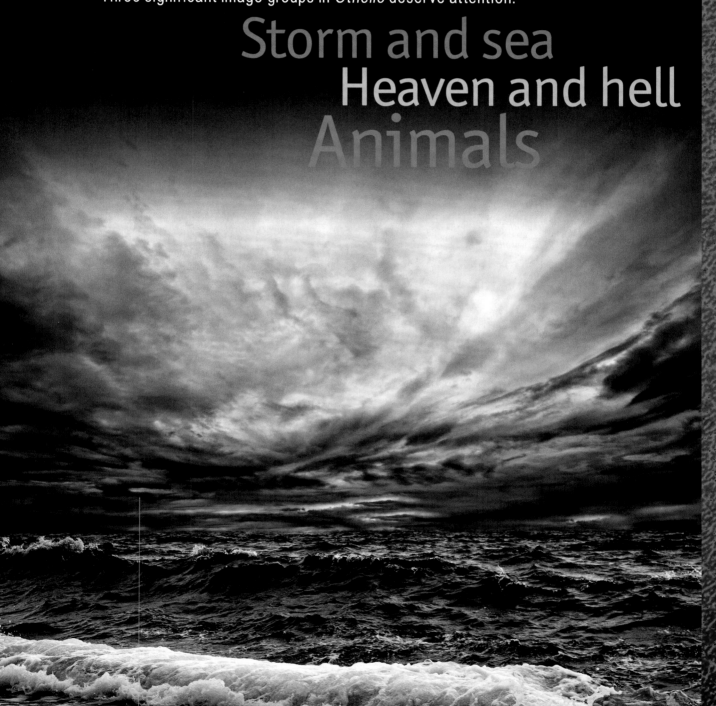

Imagery and symbolism

A careful study of the imagery in *Othello* yields some interesting and rewarding results. Two main functions of the imagery can be distinguished:

- Recurring images help to convey major themes.
- Imagery associated with particular characters helps to establish their attitudes and personal qualities.

Three significant image-groups in *Othello* deserve attention:

Storm and sea
Heaven and hell
Animals

Storm and sea

In Act 2, Scene 1 the Venetian ships and their Turkish enemies are at the mercy of a violent storm at sea. The storm has a **practical function**: it disposes of the Turkish menace, and thus of the political theme, and leaves Shakespeare free to concentrate on the domestic tragedy. However, the main significance of the storm is symbolic.

In Shakespeare's plays, storms are **symbols of human discord**, of massive disruption in the affairs of men. The highly descriptive dialogue in Act 2, Scene 1 creates the atmosphere of the storm at sea. There is a continuous emphasis on the triumphs of Othello and Desdemona over high seas and roaring winds. The storm is presented in all its potential menace and destructive power: 'The chiding billow seems to pelt the clouds, the wind-shak'd surge, with high and monstrous main' (lines 12–13).

The storm is symbolic of the **violent emotion and chaos** soon to engulf Othello's soul. The storm-poetry combines symbolism with irony. This is Cassio on how the storm treats Desdemona:

Tempests themselves, high seas and howling winds,
The gutter'd rocks and congregated sands,
Traitors ensteep'd to clog the guiltless keel,
As having sense of beauty do omit
Their common natures, letting go safely by
The divine Desdemona.

(Act 2, Scene 1, lines 68–73)

Cassio is suggesting that the **dangerous forces of nature** – winds, seas, submerged rocks and sands – choose not to harm Desdemona, whose 'divine' qualities tame nature and hold back its power to destroy. These forces are a symbolic foretaste of what lies in wait for her ashore.

The key terms in the quoted passage are 'traitors ensteep'd' and 'go safely by'. The 'traitors ensteep'd' at sea are treacherous submerged rocks, all the more deadly because they are hidden. The human equivalent on land will be the **destructive power of Iago**, which will be all the more effective because it will be concealed. His victims, whom he will not let 'go safely by', will not detect his treachery until it is too late.

Many of Cassio's comments here have both symbolic and ironic overtones. He prays for Othello's safe arrival: 'and let the heavens give him defence against the elements, for I have lost him on a dangerous sea' (Act 2, Scene 1, lines 44–6). Soon after this he notes that 'The great contention of the sea and skies parted our fellowship' (lines 92–3).

Again, these images of raging storm and violent sea symbolise the **overwhelming human passions** Iago will soon release in Othello. Although Cassio does not know it, he will indeed lose Othello on a dangerous sea, but it is the stormy sea of Othello's anger that ultimately parts their fellowship.

A further passage, this time from Othello, takes up the storm imagery:

O my soul's joy!
If after every tempest come such calms,
May the winds blow till they have waken'd death,
And let the labouring bark climb hills of seas,
Olympus-high, and duck again as low
As hell's from heaven!

(Act 2, Scene 1, lines 184–9)

The storm symbolism creates moving effects here. 'May the winds blow' is cruelly ironic, as is the reference to the power of the winds to waken death. The winds of Othello's passion will soon blow, bringing death in their trail. Othello's 'labouring bark' has now reached its Olympus, the peak of its happiness; it will soon 'duck' to the hellish depths of misery, diving from heaven to hell.

Later, the symbolic identification of sea imagery with the overwhelming force of human passion is beautifully exemplified when the surge of Othello's bloody thoughts, carrying him forward irresistibly, is likened to the movement of:

the Pontic sea,
Whose icy current and compulsive course
Ne'er feels retiring ebb, but keeps due on
To the Propontic and the Hellespont

(Act 3, Scene 3, lines 460–3)

Heaven and hell

Images of heaven and hell are pervasive and have a vital influence on the imaginative effect of the play. There are so many examples of heaven–hell imagery that it is clearly one of the major themes of the play, involving the three main characters: Desdemona, Iago and Othello.

Desdemona

Desdemona is frequently invoked in terms of heavenly images:

- To Cassio she is 'divine Desdemona' (Act 2, Scene 1, line 73). He prays that the 'grace of heaven' (Act 2, Scene 1, line 85) may protect her.

- She makes her own appeals in times of trouble to heaven, such as 'By heaven, you do me wrong' (Act 4, Scene 2, line 83).

- After discovering her murder, Emilia cries 'O, the more angel she' (Act 5, Scene 2, line 132) and calls her 'heavenly true' in response to Othello's accusations (line 137).

- Othello thinks of her eternal destiny as a heavenly one (Act 5, Scene 2, lines 275, 279).

- Even Iago talks of her as 'blessed' (Act 2, Scene 3, line 311).

Iago

Diabolic imagery is used mainly to characterise Iago and his activities. The imagery of hell applied to him, and employed by him, is not simply a conventional device to remind us that he is a villain. Sometimes it takes on a deeper significance.

Some of the diabolic images occur at turning points in the play and are heavily emphasised:

- Iago expects infernal help with his plot against Othello and Cassio: 'Hell and night must bring this monstrous birth to the world's light' (Act 1, Scene 3, lines 399–400).

- 'Diablo [Devil], ho!' is his cry as the bell rings and Cassio's disgrace is imminent (Act 2, Scene 3, line 152).

- He sees himself under the patronage of the 'Divinity of hell', and his hypocrisy as typically infernal: 'When devils will their blackest sins put on, they do suggest at first with heavenly shows' (Act 2, Scene 3, lines 340–2).

When Iago's mask is off, the truth about his nature is emphasised in diabolic images. Othello, at a total loss to understand Iago's motivation, wonders whether he has been dealing with a mortal human or a devil: 'I look down toward his feet, but that's a fable. If that thou be'st a devil I cannot kill thee' (Act 5, Scene 2, lines 287–8). He looks at Iago's feet to see if he has cloven hooves, which devils were supposed to have according to the fable mentioned and dismissed by Othello. A little later, Othello asks Cassio to find out from 'that demi-devil', or half-devil, Iago, why he 'ensnar'd my soul and body' (lines 302–3).

Even when Iago speaks in a lighter vein, hellish images come naturally to him:

- 'If thou wilt needs damn thyself, do it a more delicate way than drowning', he tells Roderigo (Act 1, Scene 3, lines 352–3).

- Iago's own wits, with 'all the tribe of hell' to help them, will, he thinks, make it possible for Roderigo to win Desdemona (Act 1, Scene 3, lines 356–7).

Othello

The diabolic imagery originates with Iago, the Satanic tempter, but as his temptation succeeds and as he gains an ascendancy over Othello's mind, such diabolic imagery becomes a distinctive feature of Othello's speech:

- Othello begins to apply images of hell and damnation to Desdemona. He wants 'some swift means of death for the fair devil' (Act 3, Scene 3, lines 484–5). He finds 'a young and sweating devil' in the palm of her hand (Act 3, Scene 4, line 38).

- He is possessed by the vision of her damnation: 'And let her rot, and perish, and be damned to-night' (Act 4, Scene 1, line 177).

- In the presence of Lodovico, with Desdemona's fate in mind, diabolic images best express Othello's feelings about Desdemona: 'Fire and brimstone!', 'Devil!', 'O devil, devil!' (Act 4, Scene 1, lines 229, 235, 239).

- Later he calls on her to swear she is innocent, so as to destroy her soul and 'therefore be double-damn'd' (Act 4, Scene 2, line 38).

After Desdemona's death, there is a significant change in the way in which diabolic imagery is applied:

- Othello continues for a while with his false identification of Desdemona as a devil 'gone to burning hell' (Act 5, Scene 2, line 131).

- Then Emilia, in possession of the truth, applies the diabolic imagery to Othello, to whom, for the moment at least, it seems appropriate: 'O, the more angel she, and you the blacker devil!' (Act 5, Scene 2, lines 132–3).

- Othello, still convinced his murder of Desdemona was an act of justice, sees himself as being 'damn'd beneath all depth in hell' if he has acted unjustly (Act 5, Scene 2, line 139).

- As realisation dawns, Othello's vision of his own final destiny, eternal separation from Desdemona, is of his soul being hurled on Judgement Day from heaven, by a look from her, to hell, where devils or 'fiends will snatch at it' (Act 5, Scene 2, lines 274–6).

- In his last tormented moments, Othello foresees an eternity of suffering for himself in hell: 'Blow me about in winds, roast me in sulphur, wash me in steep-down gulfs of liquid fire' (Act 5, Scene 2, lines 280–1).

Animals

There are multiple images of animals in *Othello*. The great majority of these are associated with unpleasant, cruel or painful sensations. These images originate with Iago, and are reflections of his mind and outlook. Part of the function of the animal imagery, then, is to characterise Iago.

Iago has a degraded view of human nature. He finds no essential difference between men and beasts. Love for him is a matter of animal instinct, it is 'merely a lust of the blood and a permission of the will' (Act 1, Scene 3, lines 334–5). He visualises Othello and Desdemona's love as nothing better than the union of 'an old black ram' and a 'white ewe' (Act 1, Scene 1, lines 88–9).

Iago's typical presentation of almost any human quality or activity is in terms of some related, and generally repulsive or disturbing, animal one. Hence his references to bird-snaring, asses being led by the nose (Othello's gullibility), a spider catching a fly (Cassio's undoing), wild cats, wolves, goats and monkeys (the last two being emblems of uncontrolled passion).

It is significant that from Act 3, Scene 3 onwards Othello adopts the animal imagery previously employed almost exclusively by Iago. This coarsening of Othello's imagery is an obvious sign that Iago's attempts to poison and corrupt his mind in relation to human relationships are having the desired effect.

When, for example, Othello declares that he would 'rather be a toad, and live upon the vapour of a dungeon' (Act 3, Scene 3, lines 274–5) than share Desdemona with others, we know that Iago has been successful. Indeed, he has been only too successful. Othello's animal imagery in the second half of the play is, if anything, more repulsive than Iago's.

Othello employs animal imagery to degrade both himself and Desdemona, who is the chief subject of his bestial fantasies. His once 'fair warrior' and his 'soul's joy' is now esteemed by Othello as a 'lewd minx' (Act 3, Scene 3, line 482).

The direct impression made on Othello's imagination by Iago's use of animal imagery is conveyed by his repetition of the same terms employed by Iago. For example, Iago depicts the imagined love of Desdemona and Cassio in terms of gross animality: 'as prime as goats, as hot as monkeys' (Act 3, Scene 3, line 409), and later Othello, almost deranged by passionate jealousy, leaves the Venetian emissaries with the cry, 'Goats and monkeys!' (Act 4, Scene 1, line 259).

Exam tips

Read all the questions carefully, making sure that you understand what is being asked in each, then choose the one that you are best prepared to answer. Underline the key words in the question.

Prepare a brief list of the points you want to make and determine the structure of your answer. Make sure that you deal equally with all the elements in the question.

It is essential that you support your answer with suitable reference to the play. In order to do this you must be thoroughly familiar with the details of the plot, as well as with the characters and their actions.

Good answers include brief, relevant quotations to enhance your analysis of the play. There is no need for lengthy quotations; short ones can make the point just as well and leave more space and time for making further points.

From the beginning to the end of your answer it is essential to stay with the exact terms of the question you are dealing with. Remember that marks are awarded for making relevant points clearly and economically, with the support of reference and quotation.

A good way to ensure that you stick to the question is to mention the key term(s) of the question in your introduction, conclusion and at suitable intervals throughout your answer. This reminds the examiner, and yourself, that you are dealing consistently with the issue you have been asked to address.

Students occasionally provide long summaries of the plot or accounts of characters that may, or may not, touch on the issues raised in the question. Other students write long introductions dealing with matters that they are not being asked to discuss. These ramblings will not earn marks.

Know in advance how much time you will give to each question and stick to this plan.

Bring your answer to a clear conclusion, perhaps referring back to the question and summarising your main argument.

Higher Level exam questions on *Othello* may:

- Deal with a major theme or issue in the play, for example jealousy, poor judgement or the clash of good and evil.

- Involve discussion of one character or a particular scene.

- Require a discussion of imagery and/or symbolism, such as storm and tempest, diabolic versus heavenly or white versus black.

- Ask for your response to the play and reasons for enjoying or not enjoying it.

Two of these topics will appear on the paper and you will be asked to deal with one of them.

Ordinary Level exam questions on *Othello* comprise three shorter and one longer question (see examples below). Questions may deal with:

- Significant scenes and what happens in these.

- The motives of characters for behaving as they do.

- Your opinion of individual characters.

- Reasons for what happens to the characters.

- Choosing a character you would like to play and giving reasons for your choice.

- Assessing the play's merits as an exciting, moving drama, or its drawbacks as a painful, agonising experience for audiences and readers.

- How a particular scene might be staged.

- Imagining yourself interviewing one of the characters on his or her conduct at some moment in the play.

Suppose you are asked to choose a character you would like to play and to explain your choice, and you choose Iago. All you have to do is give a number of reasons for wanting to play Iago. What you must not do is set about summarising Iago's character. That is not what the examiner wants to know. Instead, he or she wants to know why you have chosen to play Iago.

Start your answer by giving your first reason for wanting to play Iago. For example: *My first reason for wanting to play Iago is that it is the most enjoyable role for an actor as it is full of variety, action and excitement*. You might support this point by adding an appropriate quotation from the play, such as: *As Iago says himself, 'Pleasure and action make the hours seem short.'*

Remember that the highest marks are obtained by students who deal directly with the question asked and who make their points in a logical sequence. They make a series of clear points, backed up with suitable references to the text and with brief and appropriate quotations.

It is desirable to devote a separate paragraph to each new point you make. This makes it easier for you to structure your answer properly and for the examiner to follow your argument.

Past papers

It is worth looking at past exam papers to familiarise yourself with the types of questions asked. The following specific questions on *Othello* were part of the 2008 Leaving Certificate exam.

Higher Level Paper 2

Answer one of these questions:

(i) 'Othello's foolishness rather than Iago's cleverness leads to the tragedy of Shakespeare's *Othello*.'
Discuss this statement supporting your answer with the aid of suitable reference to the text. (60)

OR

(ii) 'Shakespeare's play *Othello* demonstrates the weakness of human judgement.'
Discuss this statement supporting your answer with the aid of suitable reference to the text. (60)

Note that if you are asked to discuss a statement of opinion, you are not necessarily expected to agree with the opinion quoted. In question (i) the word 'tragedy' refers to the tragic events resulting from Othello's belief in Iago's slanderous suggestions about Desdemona and Cassio. You may decide to argue that the emphasis on Othello's foolishness rather than Iago's cleverness is correct, or that Iago's cleverness is more important than Othello's foolishness, or that it is a combination of both. Each of these options can be argued using supporting evidence from the play.

For a possible answer to question (ii), see Sample essays, pp. 233–4.

Ordinary Level Paper 2

Answer question 1, question 2 and **one** part of question 3:

1 (a) Do you feel sorry for Brabantio, Desdemona's father, when he learns that she has married Othello? Explain your answer. (10)

(b) From your reading of the play, why do you think Desdemona falls in love with Othello? Explain your answer. (10)

2 'Yet she must die, else she'll betray more men.'
Describe the murder of Desdemona by Othello in Act 5, scene 2. (10)

→

3 Answer **ONE** of the following: [Each part carries 30 marks]

(i) At the very end of the play, Lodovico describes Iago as a 'hellish villain'. Do you think this is a fair description of Iago? Support your answer with reference to the play.

OR

(ii) You have been invited to play the part of a character in a production of the play *Othello*. Describe the qualities of your chosen character which you would wish to make clear to your audience. Support your answer with reference to the text.

OR

(iii) Write a report putting forward the view that *Othello* is, **or** is not, a suitable text for Leaving Certificate candidates.

Examination-based questions

The following lists give examples of the type of questions that could be asked about *Othello* in the Leaving Certificate exam.

Suitable for Ordinary Level

1 In *Othello*, a noble, admired general murders his wife. Basing your answer on evidence from the play, explain why he does this.

2 The relationship between Othello and Desdemona changes during the course of the play. How and why does this happen?

3 Why does Othello dismiss Cassio from his post as his lieutenant? In your opinion, does Cassio deserve to be dismissed? Explain your answers.

4 Write an account of the relationship between Iago and Roderigo. What is this relationship based on? On the evidence in the play how does Iago feel about Roderigo, and how does Roderigo feel about Iago?

5 In Act 1, Scene 1 of the play, we learn that Iago hates Othello. Why does he hate him? Give reasons for your answer.

6 How does Iago fool Othello into believing that Desdemona is having an affair with Cassio?

7 With which character in the play do you feel most sympathy? Give reasons for your answer.

8 Describe the scene in which Desdemona dies.

9 What are Othello's motives for killing Desdemona?

10 Mention the scene in the play that you consider the most impressive. Give reasons for your choice.

11 What is your opinion of Emilia? Explain your answer.

12 Describe what happens during the encounter between Iago, Roderigo and Brabantio at the beginning of the play.

13 Does Brabantio deserve (a) sympathy; (b) blame; or (c) both of these for his behaviour during the play? Give reasons for your answer.

14 In the final scene, Emilia addresses Othello in these words: 'O gull, O dolt, as ignorant as dirt.' Does Othello deserve to be spoken to like this? Explain your answer.

15 In your opinion, what are the things that destroy Othello? Base your answer on evidence from the play.

16 Is Desdemona responsible in some ways for what happens to her in the play? Give reasons for your answer.

17 The episodes involving the handkerchief have an important influence on the outcome of the play. Explain why this is so.

18 From the following statements, choose one which, in your opinion, best describes what the play is about and give reasons for your answer: (a) It is a play about evil. (b) It is a play about stupidity. (c) It is a play about love.

19 Based on your reading of the play, write a piece beginning as follows: This is a play about cruelty, violence and suffering.

20 Give your opinion of the behaviour of Cassio throughout the play. Refer to the text in support of the points you make.

21 You have been asked to give a brief talk to your class on your response to *Othello* as a text suitable for study at Leaving Certificate level. Outline some of the points you would make in the course of your talk.

22 It is sometimes claimed that *Othello* should not be performed because some aspects of the story it tells are too disgusting, too evil and too violent. Give your opinion of this statement. You should support your opinion by referring to the text of the play.

23 Choose one episode from *Othello* and describe how you think this episode should be presented on stage or on film. Give your reasons for presenting the episode in this way, and point out the effect you would like your presentation to have on the audience.

24 Your school is putting on a performance of *Othello*. Name the character you would like to play and give reasons for wanting to play this character. These reasons should be based on your knowledge of the play.

25 Imagine you are a sixteenth-century newspaper reporter assigned to visit either Venice or Cyprus with the purpose of interviewing one of the following characters: Othello, Iago, Cassio or Desdemona. Write out your report.

26 'The play raises important questions about honesty and trust.' Write a response to this statement supporting your point of view by reference to *Othello*.

27 You have been appointed to direct a stage performance of *Othello*. Describe the way in which you would use some of the following: scenery, lighting, sound effects, costumes,

and the voices and gestures of actors, to create the atmosphere of the opening scene of the play.

28 Imagine you are Brabantio, and that you keep a diary of the events recorded in the play as they affect you. Write out some of the more important entries in this diary.

29 Describe the part played by Emilia in the story, writing as if you are Emilia.

30 'Act 5 of *Othello* is filled with suspense and excitement.' Briefly describe some features of Act 5 in support of this statement.

31 Briefly describe some of the principal things that help to destroy Othello.

32 Which character in the play do you dislike most? Refer to the text in support of your answer.

33 Which character in the play do you like best? Explain your answer by referring to the play.

34 'Othello is easily deceived.' Agree or disagree with this opinion, supporting your answer by referring to events in the play.

35 There are important conflicts between characters in the play. Describe one conflict that you consider particularly important.

36 What, in your opinion, is the most important moment or event in the play? Give reasons for your choice.

37 'Iago has no real motive for acting as he does, except that he is purely and simply evil, and enjoys doing evil for its own sake.' Give your response to this statement, based on your study of the play.

38 When Brabantio learns that Desdemona has married Othello, he becomes extremely angry. Why, do you think, does he react like this? Explain your answer.

39 In your opinion, why does Desdemona fall in love with Othello? Base your answer on your study of the play.

40 In the final scene of the play, Lodovico describes Iago as a 'hellish villain'. Is this a proper description of Iago? Support your answer with evidence from the text.

Suitable for Higher Level

1 What features of *Othello* impressed you? Refer to the text in support of your answer.

2 'Reading or seeing the play is a horrifying experience.' Write a response to this statement, supporting the points you make by reference to the text.

3 'It is difficult to decide whether the tragic events with which the play closes are more the result of Othello's foolishness than of Iago's cunning.' Give your views on this statement, with the support of suitable reference to the text.

4 'If the play has a lesson to convey, it is that human judgement is unreliable.' Discuss this statement, supporting your discussion with suitable reference to the text.

5 *Othello* has some powerfully dramatic scenes. Choose one scene from the play that you find particularly compelling and say why you find it so. Refer to the text of the play in support of your answer.

6 When we are discussing Iago, which of the following qualities do you think should be emphasised more: his evil nature or his intellect? Your answer should be supported by reference to the text.

7 'In Shakespeare's *Othello*, we are allowed to look into the mind of a hero who is tortured first by suspicion and jealousy, and finally by vain regret.' Write a response to this view of the play, referring to the text in support of your points.

8 Discuss the relationship between Othello and Desdemona through the course of the play, supporting your answer with reference to the text.

9 'Our experience of Shakespeare's *Othello* is enriched by a variety of recurring images.' Write your response to this statement based on your study of the text and/or a performance of the play on stage or in the cinema.

10 'Cassio has a very important role in the development of the action in *Othello*.' Discuss this role, supporting your answer by reference to the text.

11 'Shakespeare's *Othello* offers a number of contrasting views of human nature, ranging from nobility and goodness at one extreme to baseness and sheer evil at another.' Discuss this statement, with the aid of suitable reference to the play.

12 'In many works of fiction, the villains are much more interesting than the heroes and heroines. Shakespeare's *Othello* is no exception.' Discuss this statement, referring to at least one villainous character and one virtuous character. Support your answer with reference to the text.

13 'The three female characters in *Othello* are contrasted in interesting ways.' Discuss this idea, with reference to the text.

14 'Racial and cultural differences play an important part in the development of Iago's intrigue.' Write a response to this statement based on your study of the text.

15 'Iago and Othello have one significant characteristic in common: they are both self-centred.' Discuss this statement, with the aid of suitable reference to the play.

16 'Othello is a character of extremes. He has no middle range.' Write a response to this statement, supporting your answer with suitable reference to the text.

17 'Iago's views on Othello's character are contradicted at several points in the play, but Iago is not always wrong about Othello.' Discuss this statement, with the aid of suitable reference to the text.

18 'In *Othello*, Shakespeare presents a deeply pessimistic view of human nature.' Give your views on this statement, supporting these views with suitable reference to the text.

19 'Iago's stated motives are convincing as far as they go, but they cannot account for the terrible things he does.' Write a response to this statement, with suitable reference to the text.

20 'Iago does not set out with a definite plan in mind, but works out the details as he goes along.' Discuss this statement, with suitable reference to the text.

21 '*Othello* is a tragedy, but from Iago's point of view the action is always liable to appear entertaining.' Discuss this idea, making suitable reference to the text.

22 'Othello's biggest problem, and the one that leads to his tragic fall, is that, being a foreigner, he does not understand the people among whom he lives.' Write a response to this view, supporting your comments with evidence from the text.

23 'Iago is Desdemona's opposite in every way.' Discuss this view, referring to the text in support of your answer.

24 'Irony is a key element in *Othello*.' Discuss the use of irony in the play, making suitable reference to the text.

25 'Iago exists in order to play with the lives of others, and his manipulation of these lives forms the substance of *Othello*, the play.' Write a response to this view, using the text to support your points.

26 'The play is one in which all the major characters make serious errors which combine to bring about fatal results.' Explore this view of *Othello*, making suitable reference to the text.

27 'Chance, accident and coincidence play an important part in the development of events in *Othello*.' Discuss this statement. Your answer should be supported by appropriate reference to the text.

28 'Iago has one big advantage over Othello. He knows Othello's nature, his sense of insecurity and his vulnerability. Othello, on the other hand, has no understanding of Iago's true nature.' Discuss the impact of this contrast on what happens in the play, supporting your points by reference to the text.

29 'Othello begins his career in the play as the focus of attention and admiration on every side. As the action proceeds, he gradually loses this privileged position, until, by the end of the play, he is isolated from the other characters, and his status in his society has been suspended.' Trace the process of Othello's isolation, referring to the text in support of your discussion.

30 '*Othello* is a play in which innocent characters are condemned to suffer as much as guilty ones, and in which no happy ending is possible.' Write a response to this observation, making appropriate reference to the text.

31 'Desdemona falls in love with Othello's autobiography rather than with him.' Discuss this idea, with reference to the text.

32 'Iago is desperately anxious to believe the worst about human nature and to drag everyone down to his own level.' Write a response to this statement, with appropriate reference to the text.

33 'What Iago does is to exploit the virtues as well as the weaknesses of Othello, Desdemona and Cassio, weaknesses both of character and situation.' Give your views on this statement, supporting these views by reference to the text.

34 'In *Othello*, we observe the operations of jealousy in several different characters – in the comic dupe, Roderigo, in Bianca, in Iago and in Othello himself.' Explore this idea, supporting your comments with evidence from the text.

35 '*Othello* dramatises the difficulty of discovering reality behind appearance.' Write a response to this statement. Support the points you make by reference to the text.

36 'Several of Shakespeare's tragic heroes are anxious not to leave a wounded name behind them, but Othello is unique in his concern from the first act to the last with his reputation.' Write a response to this statement, referring to the text in support of your comments.

37 Imagine you are Iago, recording your responses to the success of your plot as the action proceeds. Write a summary of these responses, basing this summary on the text of the play.

38 'We are liable to agree with Iago that Othello is "egregiously an ass" for believing his wife has played him false on the slender evidence provided. But credulous as Othello is, we do not ultimately regard him as stupid. We are prevented from doing so by the fact that Iago deceives Roderigo, Cassio and even Emilia, who knows him best.' Discuss this view of Othello, supporting your comments by reference to the text.

39 'There is one thing for which Othello must be condemned: he assumes that justice (as in Desdemona's case) demands revenge, and that revenge demands killing. The real enemy within Othello is his growing lust for revenge in response to Iago's poison, and it is Othello himself who first thinks in terms of killing: "I'll tear her all to pieces". With any other response, all of Iago's horrible mischief would have failed to bring about the tragedy.' Write your response to this interpretation of the play, supporting your views by reference to the text.

40 'Iago often lies, but he often gains his ends by actually telling the truth.' Discuss this idea, with reference to the text.

Sample essays

Suitable for Ordinary Level

1 (a) Why does Othello dismiss Cassio from his position as his lieutenant?

(b) In your opinion, does Cassio deserve to be dismissed?

(a) The scene in which the dismissal occurs opens with a brief interview between Othello and Cassio. This exchange is the origin of Cassio's dismissal. Othello gives him special instructions to see to it that the Venetian victory over the Turks is celebrated within proper limits, and that the participants are 'not to outsport discretion'. As Othello's deputy, Cassio is naturally expected to show a special sense of responsibility.

Othello has every reason to believe that Cassio, whom he recently promoted, will follow his instructions. However, when Othello retires from the scene, Iago gets to work to ensure that Cassio becomes drunk. With the help of Roderigo, Iago then engineers a riot involving the drunken Cassio, who fights Roderigo and, much more seriously, Montano, Governor of Cyprus. Montano is wounded when he tries to restrain Cassio.

A very angry Othello intervenes and stops the riot, threatening instant death to anybody tempted to resume the fighting:

He that stirs next, to carve for his own rage,
Holds his soul light, he dies upon his motion.

An increasingly furious Othello demands to know 'how this foul rout began'. Iago, who knows but pretends not to know, appears to make excuses for Cassio. These excuses have the effect of making Cassio seem the only guilty party. Othello, convinced that Iago is a thoroughly honest witness, then pronounces his verdict on Cassio:

I know, Iago,
Thy honesty and love doth mince this matter,
Making it light to Cassio. Cassio, I love thee,
But never more be officer of mine.

These are the circumstances in which Othello dismisses Cassio from his position as lieutenant. He is clearly motivated by a number of factors. First, he holds Cassio, as the senior officer on duty, responsible for allowing the riot to develop and thus endangering the security of the island and of the Venetian state, a most serious offence. Second, he had asked Cassio to be aware of the need for sober conduct on the night and is disappointed that Cassio failed to behave responsibly. Third, he is angry that the noise has disturbed Desdemona (and himself). Fourth, he has been strongly influenced by Iago's evidence, since his trust in Iago's honesty (so often emphasised in the play) is absolute.

(b) When considering whether Cassio deserves to be dismissed, a few reasonable points might be made for as well as against.

The arguments for dismissal include the fact that Cassio had been entrusted with a vital job on the night in question: to maintain the peace and security of Cyprus in a time of war. He fails to do this. Worse still, he becomes involved in a riot in which a senior government official is wounded. All this happens because he allows himself to get very drunk while on duty, which adds to the gravity of his offence. Cassio did not have to become drunk. While still sober, he acknowledged his 'very poor and unhappy brains for drinking'. Despite this, he let Iago ply him with alcohol. This would seem to justify Othello's action in dismissing Cassio.

There is also a compelling argument to be made against Cassio's dismissal. Othello takes the decision to dismiss him without having the benefit of a full and truthful account of the origin and course of the brawl. Iago ensures that Othello hears a misleading account. Othello does not know that Cassio has been the victim of a plot devised by Iago to discredit him in Othello's eyes or that getting Cassio drunk was an essential part of this plot. Not surprisingly, Iago does not reveal that he instructed Roderigo to provoke a quarrel with Cassio and then to 'go out and cry a mutiny' in order to inflame things further.

I would argue that if Othello had been aware of all the facts surrounding the brawl, he would have been obliged to take the severest action against Iago and his accomplice, Roderigo, and to reserve judgement on Cassio until he had time to investigate the incident and weigh the evidence calmly.

2 Does Brabantio deserve (a) sympathy; (b) blame; or (c) both of these for his behaviour and attitudes in the scenes in which he appears.

Brabantio appears in all three scenes of Act 1. It is clear from the presentation of Brabantio that he deserves both sympathy and blame.

The degree of sympathy he deserves depends largely on how one looks upon the circumstances of Desdemona's elopement with Othello, as well as on Brabantio's own perception of this event.

To take Brabantio's perception of the event first. As he hears an account of it from Roderigo, it comes as little surprise that Brabantio responds with shock and alarm. In the middle of the night, Desdemona has been conveyed in a hired gondola, without Brabantio's knowledge or consent, to a pre-arranged meeting with Othello, with the purpose of marrying him.

Desdemona's conduct has given Brabantio good reason to feel angry and alarmed, as well as betrayed. From his point of view, her elopement with Othello is a gross breach of his rights as a parent and as guardian of his daughter's reputation and honour. Also, it is bound to raise doubts about Desdemona's moral standing as well as Othello's. He has no doubt that what she has done is evil, and that he has every right to apprehend her and Othello. Nothing he knows about her character gives him reason to believe that she has stolen away after midnight of her own free will. He comes to the conclusion that she has been the victim of some magic spell that deprived her of her judgement. He regards Othello as a thief who has stolen his daughter. He is clearly suffering mental and emotional torture when he tracks Othello down. Given all these circumstances, it is difficult not to feel some sympathy for him.

There is another aspect to the elopement that adds to the shame Brabantio would be certain to feel no matter what kind of man Desdemona eloped with. This becomes clear when he confronts Othello with the charge of abusing Desdemona with 'drugs or minerals', and binding her 'in chains of magic'. If Othello had not used drugs and magic on her, Brabantio is sure that she would never have risked public ridicule and mockery by running away 'to the sooty bosom' of so terrifying a creature as Othello must have seemed to her. Brabantio cannot come to terms with the fact that his 'fair and happy' daughter shunned marriage with wealthy Venetians of her own social class and instead chose a foreigner,

who was also black, and who, in Brabantio's eyes, was so repulsive that Desdemona 'feared to look on' him.

When Brabantio puts his grievances before the Duke and the senate, he fails to win much sympathy and is told to accept the elopement and the marriage he so strongly deplores. Desdemona blandly talks of the duty and respect a good daughter owes to her father, but does not apologise to him for failing to do her duty and to show him respect when she married Othello without his knowledge and in so furtive a way. What Desdemona has done to her father is soon to have more terrible consequences for him than this. Gratiano later reveals that her action has led to Brabantio's premature death: 'Thy match was mortal to him and pure grief shore his old thread atwain.' Nobody sensitive to human suffering could withhold sympathy from Brabantio for what he has had to endure.

On the other hand, I believe that Brabantio must take some of the blame for what happens to him. The evidence for this largely comes from Othello's account of how he won Desdemona's affections. Othello recalls that Brabantio loved and admired him, and because of this invited him to his home to question him constantly about the story of his life and adventures. There is no reason to doubt Othello's account. If Othello believed that Desdemona's father loved and admired him, it seems only natural for him to think that Brabantio would look kindly on him as a son-in-law.

In this Othello was deceived, as we know from everything Brabantio says about him after the elopement. It is clear from this that Brabantio admired Othello for his military abilities, but that he was appalled by the idea that his daughter would marry a black man. Yet Brabantio invited Othello to his house and permitted him to have free access to Desdemona, thereby running the risk that the two might fall in love, as they did. It might thus be argued that Brabantio deserves blame for poor judgement.

A modern reader of the play, free of prejudice against mixed-race marriages, would be entitled to feel that Brabantio is to blame for his racial prejudice, a flaw that is not present in positive characters such as the Duke and Desdemona.

Suitable for Higher Level

1 'Shakespeare's play *Othello* demonstrates the weakness of human judgement.'
Discuss this statement, supporting your answer with suitable reference to the text.

In my opinion this statement cannot be properly addressed without considering the role and nature of Iago. Is it credible that one man, however clever he might be, would have the ability to deceive everybody he comes in contact with? Or to make others believe everything he tells them, because they never doubt that he is anything other than 'honest Iago'? Is it also credible that this same man could, on flimsy evidence, cause people to set aside their judgement and believe what seems improbable, since they have his word for it? Credible or not, this is what the play gives us. Moreover, the play does not suggest that the deceived characters are lacking in intelligence or ability. What it does suggest is that profoundly destructive evil, combined with a smooth, plausible manner – the two essential features of Iago's character – can undermine human judgement to a remarkable degree.

Not all the examples of weak human judgement relate to the destructive work of Iago. The first instance in the play in which a lapse of judgement is made evident involves Desdemona's father, Brabantio. This lapse is confirmed by Brabantio himself, who confesses his failure to realise in time that his daughter was capable of abandoning him without warning and eloping with a man he would never have permitted her to marry. Brabantio believes that Desdemona would not have suffered such a lapse of judgement unless she had been subjected by Othello to 'spells and medicines'. Brabantio has learned a hard lesson, indeed a fatal one, from his own lapse of judgement, as we are to discover at the close of the play, when Gratiano tells Othello that Brabantio died of 'pure grief' as a result of his daughter's marriage to Othello.

Early in the play Brabantio suggests that Othello, too, may have sacrificed his better judgement to his passion for Desdemona, and may also have to pay a price for this:

> Look to her, Moor, if thou hast eyes to see,
> She has deceived her father, and may thee.

Three inter-connected cases of defective human judgement are involved here. Brabantio has been deceived in his judgement of his daughter, Desdemona, and also of Othello, who will in turn come to an outrageously false judgement of both Desdemona and Cassio. Desdemona will find that her earlier judgement of Othello was misleading. To complicate the pattern of defective judgements, we may add Brabantio's suggestion that Desdemona may deceive Othello when in fact her loyalty to him is one of the key features of her character.

It is one of the ironies of the play that Iago, who values himself as a shrewd judge of human nature and of the weaknesses of the other characters, should himself suffer a severe lapse of judgement. This is in the case of his wife, Emilia. He takes it for granted that no matter how he behaves, Emilia will never oppose or betray him. In this respect his judgement proves fatally flawed. When Emilia, who has unwittingly helped him to destroy Desdemona by giving him her handkerchief, discovers the true depth and purpose of his evil schemes, she feels morally obliged to expose his villainy in public, at the cost of her own life. Iago's judgement goes astray here because he lacks the ability to consider that the sheer goodness of Desdemona might influence Emilia for the better.

Any consideration of the weakness of human judgement demonstrated in the play must focus on Othello. There is no doubt that Othello's judgement of Desdemona and Cassio is progressively distorted by the insinuations and items of fabricated 'evidence' and 'proofs' that they are lovers. The questions about Othello's judgement raised in the third and fourth Acts of the play are complex ones. They mostly relate to how and why Iago succeeds in impairing Othello's judgement and even his powers of reasoning. As the action proceeds, particularly through the key scene of the play, Act 3, Scene 3, Othello is losing his emotional balance, as Iago inflames his imagination with images of Desdemona and Cassio engaging in 'stolen hours of lust' and other episodes of betrayal. Othello is reduced to incoherence, and then to frenzy. His powers of reasoning cease to operate, as does his judgement.

The failure of judgement shows in Othello's inability to distinguish between Iago's insinuations, spurious arguments and revolting descriptions on the one hand, and concrete proof of any kind on the other. His weakened judgement means that it does not occur to him to check what Iago tells him or to demand unquestionable proofs from the accuser. The 'temptation scene' looks like a triumph for Iago's devilish ingenuity and mind control, but it also dramatises the tragic collapse of Othello's judgement.

There have been earlier examples of Othello's weakness of judgement. After the brawl scene, he allows himself to come to a rash, hasty judgement on Cassio's dereliction of duty, dismissing him on the spur of the moment without making further enquiry into the circumstances leading to the brawl engineered by Iago. He relies instead on the self-serving and false account given by Iago, which damns Cassio while pretending to excuse him. Othello's comment shows how poor his judgement of others can be:

> I know, Iago,
> Thy honesty and love doth mince this matter,
> Making it light to Cassio.

There is little need to emphasise the lack of judgement shown here. The man who loyally serves and loves Othello to the end is discarded, while the one bent on Othello's and Cassio's destruction is honoured, and later promoted.

Othello shows the same failure of judgement in his willingness to believe Iago's slanders on Desdemona, and even to encourage them. His unexamined faith in Iago as a loyal and trusted friend more worthy of his confidence than Desdemona or Cassio is the ultimate comment on his weak judgement.

Cassio is another character who takes Iago on trust as a friend, without any obvious reason. His simple faith in Iago is revealed in the following comment he makes about him: 'I never knew a Florentine more kind and honest.' This is a high tribute coming from Cassio the Florentine. He regards Iago as the equal of any of his own countrymen for kindness and honesty at a time when the man he so admires is preparing to walk him into a trap. This raises doubts about Cassio's judgement.

Cassio's poor judgement is especially evident in the brawl scene. He knows that he has 'very poor and unhappy brains for drinking'. Despite this, he allows himself to be persuaded by Iago to drink one cup, and then another, until he becomes drunk. This lapse of judgement enables Iago to convince Montano that Cassio is a habitual drunkard and therefore not to be depended upon.

Even Desdemona exhibits poor judgement when she persists in badgering Othello to meet with Cassio even though it is clear that Othello is not in the mood to entertain such pleas. I agree, therefore, that the behaviour of each of the principal characters in *Othello* supports the observation that the play demonstrates the weakness of human judgement.

2 'Othello begins his career in the play as the focus of attention and admiration on every side. As the action proceeds, he gradually loses this privileged position, until, by the end of the play, he is isolated from the other characters, and his status in his society has been suspended.'

Trace the process of Othello's isolation, referring to the text in support of the points you make.

I believe that the above quotation gives a fair summary of one of the central themes of the play: Othello's progress from centrality to isolation. When the play opens, Othello is indeed admired and valued on all sides. He enjoys a position of great privilege and is at the centre of active public life in the state of Venice. As its irreplaceable leader in war, he is Venice's most valued and sought-after citizen at this time. When the Turks threaten to invade Cyprus, a Venetian possession, the Duke of Venice immediately summons Othello to a conference to deal with the emergency. The Duke appoints him to lead the forces of Venice against the Turks. He also bestows public praise on him when Brabantio wants him punished for eloping with Desdemona, remarking that 'your son-in-law is far more fair than black'.

The statement that Othello is admired and valued on all sides at the beginning of the play needs to be qualified, since the first scene makes it clear that he is hated by Iago and despised by the jealous Roderigo as 'a lascivious Moor'. However, Iago has no intention of deserting Othello. Instead, he attaches himself firmly to him, and does not make himself part of the developing pattern of isolation.

Leaving Iago aside, it is Brabantio from whom Othello is first cut off. Desdemona's father cannot reconcile himself to her marriage with Othello, which breaks his heart and leads to his premature death.

A more significant instance of isolation is Othello's breach with Cassio, brought about by his hasty decision to sacrifice his personal feelings to his perceived duty to maintain discipline. His parting from Cassio is a formal one: 'Cassio, I love thee; but never more be officer of mine'. This parting marks the loss to him of the friendship, support and loyalty of a valued lieutenant, and the sinister acquisition of Iago as a close confidant. This acquisition has consequences that prove far worse than if he were isolated from Iago.

In an important sense Iago works to intensify the process of Othello's isolation, particularly once he fulfils his promise 'to abuse Othello's ear' with suggestions that Cassio is Desdemona's lover. The isolation in question here has a number of aspects. One of these is psychological

and involves disturbing Othello's mental and emotional balance, mainly by implanting jealous thoughts and feelings in his mind. The result is that Othello's rational nature is impaired and he becomes temporarily isolated from the human reality around him, specifically the benign reality concerning his totally loyal wife, Desdemona, and his loyal follower Cassio. His mind is steadily transformed by Iago into a receptacle for monstrous fantasies and total distortions of reality.

During the 'temptation scene' (Act 3, Scene 3), Othello makes a significant remark about what Iago is doing to him:

> By Heaven, he echoes me
> As if there were some monster in his thought
> Too hideous to be shown!

Iago's technique is to persist in filling Othello's mind with versions of this 'monster', further isolating him from reality. Moving to the conviction, implanted by Iago, that his wife and Cassio have betrayed him, horrible fantasy becomes his only reality:

> I had rather be a toad,
> And live upon the vapour of a dungeon,
> Than keep a corner in the thing I love
> For others' uses.

The process of Othello's isolation from reality and from others is completed when Iago and he kneel and vow to each other to engage in bloody deeds of vengeance on the innocent victims of Iago's slanders. Iago implies that Othello won't need anybody else when he dedicates himself to Othello's service: 'I am your own for ever.'

Also in Act 3, Scene 3, Emilia deserts Othello's cause, though not deliberately so, when she takes Desdemona's handkerchief and decides to give it to Iago. The result of this decision, which will compromise Desdemona and Cassio further in Othello's eyes, will be to intensify his emotional and physical isolation from Desdemona.

Events in Act 4, Scene 1, mark the final phase of this isolation. Iago contrives to make it appear to Othello that Cassio has grown tired of Desdemona, and that he now feels nothing but contempt for her advances, when in fact it is Bianca, not Desdemona, who is the object of Cassio's contempt. Othello accepts Iago's version: 'see how he prizes the foolish woman your wife! She gave it [the handkerchief] him [to Cassio] and hath given it his whore [to Bianca]'. This prompts Othello to kill Desdemona and to let Iago be Cassio's 'undertaker'.

In the presence of Lodovico, newly arrived from Venice with notice that Othello is to be relieved of his command in Cyprus, Othello's isolation from his society takes a decisive turn. First, as a consequence of Othello's removal from command, Cassio is appointed commander in his place. With Othello's status in his society suspended, Cassio's is enhanced and he will now enjoy the centrality that accompanies the privileged position Othello had up to then occupied. Desdemona's innocent expression of pleasure at Cassio's promotion and Othello's removal to Venice provokes Othello to strike her in public and call her 'devil'. The process of isolation is confirmed, almost in a formal way, when Othello banishes her from his presence: 'Out of my sight!'

Othello now strikes a pitiable pose. He is no longer a man to evoke the admiration of those around him, but one whose speech has become incoherent, fragmented and chaotic. The contrast between this 'new' Othello, pitied perhaps but not admired, and the real Othello, the focus of general admiration and respect, is almost complete. His change is registered in one of Lodovico's comments:

> Is this the noble Moor whom our full senate
> Call all in all sufficient? This the noble nature
> Whom passion could not shake?

If Othello is now a focus of attention it is for his isolation from reality and his unfitness to function as a normal human being. This is recognised by Lodovico when he asks: 'Are his wits safe? Is he not light of brain?'

Othello has also come to see himself as an isolated figure, to be publicly ridiculed rather than, as he once was, admired:

> A fixed figure for the time of scorn
> To point his slow and moving finger at.

Here 'the time of scorn' is the scornful, mocking world. When Othello makes that comment, he still does not know the truth about Desdemona, and thinks that he will be mocked because he is a betrayed husband. When he is told the truth he is under arrest for murder, surrounded by those who are ready to bring him to justice, and told by Gratiano that it will be futile for him to resist:

> If thou attempt it, it will cost thee dear.
> Thou hast no weapon, and perforce must suffer.

Othello has suffered a steep descent from the dominant position he once held, when he could impose his will on a group of Brabantio's followers bent on arresting him and when he could quell a riot with a simple command: 'Hold, for your lives!'

In the final moments of the play Othello, an isolated figure in his society, faces the prospect of close confinement in a Cypriot prison until the authorities decide on his fate. He chooses suicide instead. The speech at the end of which he kills himself with his own sword has a significant feature. He relates an incident from his early career when he killed a Turk who 'beat a Venetian and traduced the state'. With these words he does the same to himself. In his mind he has become the Turk, since by striking a Venetian (Desdemona, daughter of a senator), he has traduced or defamed the Venetian state and deserved the same punishment that the Turk received, except that the punishment is self-administered.